America

People and Places

Die Fernsehreihe *America – The Freedom to Be ...*, zu der dieses Buch erschienen ist, wurde von der OM Produktion GmbH, Köln im Auftrag des Westdeutschen Rundfunks (Redaktion: Peter Teckentrup) produziert.
Drehbücher: Rhonda L. Bowen; Kamera: Klaus Overhoff; Regie: Josef Turecek

Die Deutsche Bibliothek - CIP-Einheitsaufnahme

America [Medienkombination] : people and places / Robert Parr. - München : TR-Verl.-Union

Buch. Begleitbuch zur Fernsehreihe des WDR, America, the freedom to be ... - 2000

ISBN 3-8058-3131-5

Zu *America – People and Places* sind zwei Audiocassetten (Best.-Nr. 34381) erschienen: eine Mitlesecassette mit Ausschnitten aus den Originalinterviews der Sendungen und eine Übungscassette mit ausgewählten Übungen aus dem Buch. Die auf der **Übungscassette** wiedergegebenen Texte sind im Buch jeweils durch das **Symbol** ○○ gekennzeichnet.

Beratung (Begleitbuch): Joseph Butler, Jr. (USA) und Margaret Davis (Kanada)

2. unveränderte Auflage 2002

Videoprints: aus den Fernsehsendungen
Übersichtskarten USA und Kanada: Polyglott-Verlag, München
Umschlaggestaltung: Franziska Schob-Bergmeir, München
Gesamtherstellung: Druckerei Bremberger, München
ISBN 3-8058-3131-5

America

People and Places

Robert Parr

TR-Verlagsunion

Vorwort

America – People and Places stellt ausgewählte Staaten und Provinzen in den USA und Kanada vor. Das Buch begleitet die Fernsehsendungen *America – The Freedom to Be ...* und bietet Ihnen Gelegenheit, mehr über „Land und Leute" zu erfahren und gleichzeitig Ihre Englischkenntnisse auszubauen und zu festigen.

Als *Warming-up* gibt es in jeder *Unit* ein kleines Quiz, das auf spielerische Weise allerhand Wissenswertes über den jeweiligen „Schauplatz" vermittelt.

Der doppelseitige *Overview* liefert sodann einen Überblick über alle Personen, die in der Fernsehsendung interviewt werden. Hier kommen bereits wichtige Namen und Begriffe der *Unit* vor. Dadurch wird auch die Wortschatzarbeit in den anschließenden Texten entlastet.

Das „Herz" jeder *Unit* bilden die Teile A, B und C, in denen drei Personen aus dem *Overview* – in ausgewählten Ausschnitten der Originalinterviews – sich und ihre Arbeit näher vorstellen. Lassen Sie sich an dieser Stelle nicht von der Unvollkommenheit der gesprochenen Sprache irritieren! Sie werden sich schnell an die Unzulänglichkeiten des spontanen Sprechens gewöhnen. Der auf die Interviews folgende Abschnitt *Working with the text* greift Fragen zum Textverständnis, zum Wortschatz und zur Aussprache auf.

Jeder der A-, B- und C-Teile beinhaltet einen weiteren Übungsblock, die *Exercises*, die sich bewusst vom Text des vorangegangenen Interviews lösen. In diesem Abschnitt haben Sie die Möglichkeit, Ihre Kenntnisse in Grammatik und Wortschatz aufzufrischen. Darüber hinaus wird zusätzliches landeskundliches Hintergrundwissen vermittelt. Einige der Übungen sind „offen" formuliert und sollen Sie dazu ermuntern, selbst ein wenig zu recherchieren.

Ausgewählte Wörter und Wendungen aus den Texten (jeweils durch Kursivdruck hervorgehoben) sind mit ihren deutschen, kontextbezogenen Entsprechungen auf der letzten Seite der *Unit* gesondert aufgelistet. Da hier ganz bewusst nur eine Auswahl vorgenommen wurde, empfiehlt es sich, bei der Arbeit mit diesem Band stets ein Wörterbuch (sowohl einsprachig als auch zweisprachig) zur Hand zu haben.

Im Anhang schließlich finden Sie sämtliche Lösungen, ein alphabetisches Register aller Vokabeln aus den *Wordlists* sowie einen kurzen Überblick über die Geschichte der USA und Kanadas.

Ich wünsche Ihnen viel Spaß und viel Erfolg mit *America – People and Places*.

Robert Parr

Contents

Map of the USA 7

1 **Massachusetts** 9
1A Nathalie Disfloth 12
1B Linda A. Hill 16
1C Ellen Spear 21

2 **Pennsylvania** 27
2A Caley McBride 30
2B Mark Cooper 36
2C Ralph Youmans 40

3 **Illinois** 45
3A Bruce Nelson 48
3B Alberta Brown 52
3C Paul Johnson, Jr. 57

4 **Washington, DC** 63
4A The Vietnam's Veterans Memorial 66
4B Elisabeth Lohah Homar 70
4C John W. Mountcastle 75

5 **Kentucky** 79
5A Josephine Abercrombie 82
5B Wesley Wittwer and Charles Northcutt 86
5C Michael Delk 90

6 **South Carolina** 95
6A James E. Talley 98
6B Robert M. Hitt and Roland H. Windham, Jr. 103
6C Alduous Williams 106

7 **Georgia** 111
7A Jonathan Mann and Raissa Vassileva 114
7B Major Vida Longmire 118
7C Pastor Joseph L. Roberts, Jr. 122

8 **Florida** ... 127
8A William Schwartz ... 130
8B Pablo Canton ... 134
8C Tom and Barbara Dwyer ... 139

Map of Canada ... 143

9 **Quebec** ... 145
9A Priscille LeBlanc ... 148
9B André Maesscheart ... 152
9C Betty Eitner ... 158

10 **Ontario** ... 163
10A Christine Trauttmansdorff ... 166
10B Ali Rahnema ... 170
10C Brenda K. Hobbs ... 175

11 **Alberta** ... 181
11A Ron Casey ... 184
11B G. Brooke Carter ... 189
11C Dr. Bruce Naylor ... 192

12 **British Columbia** ... 197
12A Peter Mitchell ... 200
12B John F. Timms ... 205
12C Firoz Rasul ... 210

13 **Nova Scotia** ... 215
13A Wayne Melanson ... 218
13B Alan Syliboy ... 222
13C Ralf Getson ... 226

A brief history of the USA ... 232

A brief history of Canada ... 234

Key to the exercises ... 236

Wordlist ... 262

USA
0 200 miles
0 200 km
CANADA
USA
MEXICO
PACIFIC OCEAN
ATLANTIC OCEAN
GULF OF MEXICO
ROCKY MOUNTAINS
Cascade Range
Baja California
British Columbia
Alberta
Saskatchewan
Ontario
Quebec
New Brunswick
Calgary
Lethbridge
Regina
Winnipeg
Thunder Bay
Geraldton
Timmins
Sault Ste. Marie
Sudbury
Ottawa
Montreal
Québec City
Sherbrooke
Saint-John
Toronto
London
Lake Superior
Lake Michigan
Lake Huron
Lake Erie
Lake Ontario
Great Salt Lake
Missouri R.
Mississippi R.
Ohio R.
Colorado R.
Rio Grande
Washington
Oregon
California
Idaho
Nevada
Utah
Montana
Wyoming
Colorado
Arizona
New Mexico
North Dakota
South Dakota
Nebraska
Kansas
Oklahoma
Texas
Minnesota
Iowa
Missouri
Arkansas
Louisiana
Wisconsin
Illinois
Michigan
Indiana
Ohio
Kentucky
Tennessee
Mississippi
Alabama
Georgia
Florida
South Carolina
North Carolina
Virginia
West Virginia
Pennsylvania
New York
Vt.
N.H.
Maine
Mass.
Conn.
R.I.
New Jersey
Del.
Md.
Seattle
Spokane
Astoria
Portland
Eugene
Eureka
Klamath Falls
Sacramento
San Francisco
Big Sur
Fresno
Bakersfield
Los Angeles
San Diego
Reno
Winnemucca
Boise
Pocatello
Salt Lake City
Las Vegas
Yuma
Phoenix
Tucson
Great Falls
Billings
Miles City
Casper
Cheyenne
Scottsbluff
Denver
Pueblo
Albuquerque
Roswell
El Paso
Ciudad Juárez
Hermosillo
Ciudad Obregón
Chihuahua
Los Mochis
La Paz
Culiacán
Torreón
Monterrey
Reynosa
Bismarck
Fargo
Rapid City
Sioux Falls
Omaha
Kansas City
Wichita
Tulsa
Oklahoma City
Amarillo
Lubbock
Wichita Falls
Fort Worth
Dallas
Arlington
Austin
San Antonio
Corpus Christi
Houston
Beaumont
Duluth
Minneapolis
Eau Claire
Milwaukee
Cedar Rapids
Des Moines
Chicago
Springfield
St. Louis
Memphis
Little Rock
Jackson
Baton Rouge
New Orleans
Mobile
Montgomery
Birmingham
Nashville
Knoxville
Louisville
Lexington
Cincinnati
Indianapolis
Grand Rapids
Detroit
Toledo
Cleveland
Columbus
Charleston
Pittsburgh
Erie
Buffalo
Syracuse
Atlanta
Macon
Savannah
Charleston
Columbia
Charlotte
Durham
Wilmington
Richmond
Norfolk
Washington
Philadelphia
New York
Providence
Boston
Portland
Jacksonville
Orlando
St. Petersburg
Miami
Key West
Bahama Islands
CUBA

Massachusetts

What do you know about Massachusetts? Try this quiz and find out.
(The answers are at the bottom of the page.)

1. **How many people live in Massachusetts?**
   a) 600,000 b) 6 million c) 60 million

2. **What is the postal abbreviation for Massachusetts?**
   a) MA b) MS c) MT

3. **What is 'Cape Cod'?**
   a) a type of food
   b) clothes that sailors wear
   c) a place to take a holiday

4. **Which of these is a famous university in Massachusetts?**
   a) Harvard b) Stanford c) Yale

5. **Which is the state flower of Massachusetts?**
   a) magnolia b) mayflower c) violet

6. **When did the Pilgrims, who went to North America in search of religious freedom, settle in Massachusetts?**
   a) 1420 b) 1520 c) 1620

7. **Which famous American family comes from Massachusetts?**
   a) The Clintons b) The Kennedys c) The Nixons

Answers: 1. b), 2. a), 3. c), 4. a), 5. b), 6. c), 7. b)

Overview

Nathalie Disfloth is an art director at 'The Boston Globe', one of the main newspapers in the Boston area. One of her jobs is to design the *cover page* for the calendar section of the paper. The calendar section is an entertainment section, not a news section, so the covers are often very different from the rest of the paper. Nathalie talks in detail about two covers and how she designed them on the computer: one cover is for a story about astronomy and the other is about Cape Cod, a part of Massachusetts where many people take their vacations.

Linda A. Hill is a professor at the Harvard Business School. She works in the area of Organizational Behavior with special responsibility for the *leadership course* in the *MBA program*. Linda is involved in a number of projects. Recently she has been trying to globalize the School's curriculum so that students can learn to work in any part of the world. This has meant spending time in *emerging market settings* such as China, South Africa and Latin America. Another project she has been working on is the use of technology in the classroom. As Linda herself explains, one of the most interesting aspects of this work was using the interactive quality of modern technologies to turn a book on management into a multimedia product.

Ian Mac Neil works at Ariad Pharmaceuticals, a bio-tech company in Cambridge, Massachusetts. Ariad is involved in three areas of research. First, they work on *rational drug design*. This means trying to understand the biology of a *disease* and *designing drugs* to cure it. This is done by identifying a protein and taking a three-dimensional picture of it. By looking at this picture Ariad can design a small molecule that will *fit into* a *groove* on the side of the protein and *inhibit* its function. Second, Ariad has a genomic center (genomics = study of chromosomes and genes), where new *targets* for drug development, such as drugs for osteoporosis, are identified. A third aspect of Ariad's work is the gene therapy group, where new ways of *regulating* therapy are developed. Ian gives an example with diabetes. Normally, Ian explains, people with diabetes inject themselves with insulin. To treat someone with diabetes using gene therapy, however, cells are taken from the patient's body, a gene for insulin is added, and then the cells are put back into the body. In this way the cells make the insulin and the patient does not have to inject it anymore. The problem is that the cells will make insulin all the time. There is no way to regulate it. Ariad has found a way of regulating the insulin so it copies what would happen in a normal person.

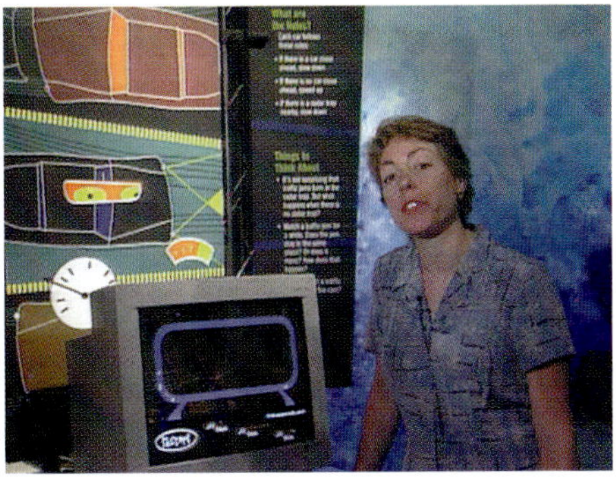

Ellen Spear is the Director of the Computer Museum in Boston. Ellen talks first about the oldest computer in the historical collection, the *Whirlwind computer*, which *dates back* to the 1950s. Another computer in the exhibition goes back to the early 1970s. Although it was an enormous machine by today's standard it only has the power of a *palmtop computer*. Ellen then goes to another part of the exhibition to talk about the latest developments in computer technology. The *virtual* fish tank is the world's largest virtual aquarium. Using high technology and advanced programming languages it helps visitors to the museum to understand things that happen in the natural world.

Find out more about ...

Nathalie Disfloth in **1A** (pages 12 – 15)
Linda A. Hill in **1B** (pages 16 – 20)
Ellen Spear in **1C** (pages 21 – 25)

1A Nathalie Disfloth

Nathalie Disfloth, an art director at 'The Boston Globe', designs the cover page for the calendar section of the newspaper. Nathalie explains how, using artistic creativity and state-of-the-art computing, she designed a *recent* cover about Cape Cod.

'There's a section of Massachusetts called the Cape and it's shaped a little bit like an arm so when people say 'I'm going to Orleans' or 'I'm going to Provincetown', they point to places on their arm to say where they're going. So when we were planning our *annual issue* for Cape Cod, where many people go to take their vacations, we thought it would be funny to take things out of the story and have it written on somebody's arm. But in fact nobody would have been able to read it if we had actually written it on the arm so this was all done with what's called photo illustration, and I can show you how I put this together.

This might take a minute to open up because it's a very large file but I did the type in one program and then I looked for little images of fish or suns or whatever I wanted to put on the arm to make it look like a tattoo, and I scanned those and then put them altogether on the arm, and you'll be able to see that in just a minute. The *type* looks like handwriting but it was actually done … there's a font, a typeface, that looks like handwriting, so I didn't actually have to write all this. I just used a typeface that looked like handwriting and then put it on curves, and then brought that into this program.'

Nathalie points to places on Cape Cod

Working with the text

I. Which is the correct ending to the sentence? Mark it.

1. 'The Boston Globe' is …
   a) a newspaper. b) a part of Massachusetts. c) a computer program.
2. The Cape is a part of …
   a) 'The Boston Globe'. b) Boston. c) Massachusetts.
3. To do her job Nathalie Disfloth must know a lot about …
   a) handwriting. b) fishing. c) computing.

II. Answer these questions. Use your own words as far as possible.

1. What cover did Nathalie do for the issue about Cape Cod?
2. What did the cover show exactly?
3. What did Nathalie have to do on the computer to create the cover?

III. What do the underlined words refer to in the text?

1. … and it's shaped a little bit like an arm (line 4)
2. … in fact nobody would have been able to read it (line 10)
3. This might take a minute to open up (line 13)
4. … and I scanned those and then put them … (line 16)

IV. Say these words and expressions out loud.

1. creativity
2. state-of-the-art computing
3. images
4. tattoo

V. Explain the meaning of the underlined words.

1. 'a cover of a magazine' (line 1)
2. 'an annual issue' (line 7)
3. 'we thought it would be funny to take things out of the story' (line 8)

VI. More questions. Use complete answers.

1. Why couldn't Nathalie use real handwriting on the arm?
2. What is 'photo illustration' exactly?
3. Why does it take Nathalie a minute to open the file?

VII. What do you think? Give reasons for your answer.

1. Does Nathalie enjoy her work?
2. Could you imagine doing a job like Nathalie's?

Exercises

I. In which part of a newspaper will you find the following information? Choose from the box.

business section ◆ cartoons ◆ advertisements ◆ foreign news ◆ editorial ◆ home news ◆ horoscope ◆ letters to the editor ◆ obituary ◆ sports pages

1. the share prices of big companies
2. the football results and analysis of the games
3. what readers think about certain subjects
4. what the newspaper thinks about certain subjects
5. what's happening in other countries
6. whether it's going to be a successful day for you or not
7. a short text describing a new kind of shoe polish and where you can buy it
8. what's happening in your country
9. a text written soon after a person's death describing their life
10. a small funny drawing often making fun of a topical item of news

II. Which sentence is good English? Tick it.

1. No news are good news.
2. No news is good news.
3. No items of news is a good item of news.

III. These sentences describe situations in the past. Use the correct form of the verb in brackets to complete them.

1. If she … (be) a bit more careful she … (not, have) the accident.
2. They … (lend) their daughter some money if she … (be) more sensible.
3. If the train … (not, be) late, he … (probably, get to) work on time.
4. If they … (tell) us they were coming, we … (certainly, wait) for them.
5. We … (drive over) and … (visit) you if we … (have) the time.
6. I … (help) you if you … (ask) me. Really!
7. Nobody … (be able) to read the poster if we … (do) it by hand.
8. She … (go) on vacation if she … (be able) to afford it.

IV. Is the 'd in these sentences the short form for 'had' or the short form for 'would'? Put a mark in the appropriate box.

	had	would
1. You'd better come and see what's happened.		
2. If we'd had the time, we would have phoned in.		
3. I'd like to book a flight to Boston.		
4. She'd have called you by now! Believe me!		

V. Make two lists: one with the names of five US newspapers and one with the names of five US periodicals. Use the names of the publications in the box below.

CHICAGO TRIBUNE ◆ EBONY ◆ NEW YORK TIMES ◆ READER'S DIGEST ◆ SPORTS ILLUSTRATED ◆ TIME ◆ USA TODAY ◆ VANITY FAIR ◆ WALL STREET JOURNAL ◆ WASHINGTON POST

VI. Complete this text about the power of the press. The first two letters of the missing words are given.

Newspapers have had an enormous in… on American society. In 1971, for example, the New York Times began publishing the Pentagon Papers. When the government tried to pr… their publication, the US Supreme Court upheld the ri… of the newspaper to print the material. The Pentagon Papers gave Americans a look behind the sc… at government policies that led to the US role in the Vietnam War.

Perhaps the best ex… of the power of the press, however, came about in 1974 when President Nixon re… after revelations about the Watergate scandal involving his ad… . These had first been brought to public at… by the Washington Post. The Watergate Af… also led to a renewal of investigative reporting by many newspapers throughout the co… .

VII. What was the Watergate Affair? Try and find out some information about it.

1B Linda A. Hill

Linda Hill is a professor at the Harvard Business School. Linda has responsibility for a number of areas at the School including the use of technology in the classroom. Linda talks about what happened when she got involved in a project to turn a book on management that she had written into a multimedia product.

'I had to meet with *graphic artists*, I had to meet with *script writers*, just a whole *slew* of people that I had never had to come into contact with before because the production of a multimedia product is actually quite a complex team effort. And so we *embarked on* the task of seeing if we could take a book and turn it into a multimedia product. And the advantages of that would be, one, that the individual could use it either at his desk or her desk. We could also sell it to the corporate markets so if the manager wasn't able to get to a training program or go to a school, they could do it from their home. They could also do it in a way that fit their schedules. If they liked to study at night, they could study at night. If they liked to study early in the morning, they could study early in the morning. So it was a very flexible product that people could use in the way they wanted to use it, that fit their lifestyle. So for me it has been really an adventure to try *to figure out* how you take ideas and *take* full *advantage of* the interactive quality of the technology to provide people with an entertaining but educational experience that will expose them to some of the complexities of leading and managing.

What I particularly liked about it was that we were able to take cases that we had developed about real situations. We hired actors to act out the various roles, and we could have people really watch, in real time, using full action video, a situation that had happened so they could get a feel for not simply … they could get a feel for the emotions that people were experiencing and what it really is like in the workplace. We could also give them a feel for the different kinds of people that are in the workplace; people from different backgrounds – we made sure to have *case protagonists* that were women, men, from the US, from the Far East and various countries in Europe – so we were able to actually show people what went on.'

Working with the text

I. *Are these statements true or false? If they are false, correct them.*

1. Linda Hill works at Harvard Business School.
2. She is a computer expert.
3. She has written a book about multimedia technology.
4. She enjoyed being an actress in her multimedia project.

A view of Boston

II. Answer these questions. Use your own words as far as possible.

1. What made Linda Hill's project so complex?
2. What are some of the advantages of working with a multimedia product rather than with a textbook or a conventional training program?
3. What was particularly exciting about the project for Linda Hill herself?
4. Why were actors needed for the project? Were they important?

III. Replace the underlined words or expressions with words or expressions with the same (or similar) meaning.

1. … I had to meet with a whole <u>slew</u> of people … (line 6)
2. … we <u>embarked on</u> the task of seeing if we could take a book … (line 8)
3. … it has really been an adventure to try to <u>figure out</u> how … (line 17)
4. … we made sure to have <u>case protagonists</u> that were women, men … (line 28)

IV. Link a verb in the left-hand column (1-8) to an expression in the right-hand column (a-h).

1. to embark on	a. responsibility for sth.
2. to get a feel for	b. actors for a film
3. to hire	c. a lot of people
4. to study	d. a task
5. to have	e. to the corporate market
6. to take	f. the emotions
7. to meet with	g. advantage of a situation
8. to sell sth.	h. at night

V. Continue these sentences. Use your own words as far as possible.

1. If you sell something to the ‘corporate market’ (line 11) you …
2. If an experience is ‘entertaining but educational’ (lines 18-19) it is …
3. If you ‘hire’ (line 22) actors it means …
4. If you ‘get a feel for’ (line 25) people’s emotions then …

VI. Say these words and expressions out loud.

1. Harvard Business School
2. technology
3. multimedia project
4. schedule
5. protagonist
6. women

VII. Put these words into the correct category according to their stress pattern.

advantage ◆ management ◆ media ◆ adventure ◆ quality ◆emotion ◆ idea ◆ video

▢▫▫	▫▢▫

VIII. What about you?

1. How do you like to learn? By yourself, in a group or with a teacher? Are you the sort of person who works better in the morning or at night? Write a short text in English about your preferred style of learning (50–60 words).
2. What’s your schedule? Write a short text in English about the sort of things you do on an average day. Write between 80 and 100 words.

Exercises

I. Use the words in the box to complete the sentences.

although ◆ as soon as ◆ because ◆ but ◆ so ◆ when

1. … the Dean talked to me about the project, I said I was curious to find out more.
2. I had to meet with a lot of people … the product was really a team effort.

3. … I had understood the advantages of multimedia learning, I agreed to do the project.
4. The course is very flexible … you can use it where and when you want.
5. … we filmed the cases in the States, we used actors from all over the world.
6. It was a lot of hard work … I enjoyed it.

II. *Join the half-sentences 1-5 to half-sentences a-e. Complete them by using the past perfect simple or continuous form.*

1. The book was not in the library	because	a. it … (snow) all afternoon.
2. It was difficult to get home		b. they (already, go) home.
3. We weren't able to meet them		c. someone … (steal) it.
4. We missed the train		d. I … (never, be) on TV before.
5. I felt a bit worried		e. we … (oversleep).

III. *Complete these sentences. You need a preposition and the -ing form of the verb.*

1. What are the advantages … (use) multimedia products?
2. They have a reputation … (not pay) their bills punctually.
3. He insists … (wait) until you come back.
4. Who has written a new book … (become) a successful manager?
5. We look forward … (meet) you next week.
6. Apart … (learn) English what else do you do in your free time?

IV. *Complete this text about the Kennedys, the best-known family from Massachusetts. Use the correct form of the words in brackets.*

Joseph and Rose Kennedy … (have) nine … (child), four boys and five girls. Joseph Kennedy, Sr. … (expect, sons, prepare) for public life. Even at an early age they … (encourage) to read the New York Times. At the dinner table small talk … (never, allow). John F. Kennedy is the … (famous) of the Kennedys. He … (become) US president when he was only 43. His presidency … (not, last) long, however. While … (ride) through Dallas in an open car in November 1963 he … (shoot) and … (kill). Robert Kennedy … (also, enter) politics becoming his brother's closest … (advise). In 1968, he, too, … (assassinate). When Joseph Kennedy, Sr. died in 1969, Edward … (read) a speech about his father which … (write) by Robert in 1967. 'Whether it was running a race, catching a football or competing in school – we were to try. And we were to try … (hard) than anyone else. "After you … (do) your best," he … (use, say), "the hell with it!"'

The Kennedy family in 1934

V. Put these five paragraphs (a-e) into the correct order (1-5) to make up a newspaper article about John F. Kennedy, Jr. When you've finished, write down a suitable heading for the article.

a. *Last night luggage and aircraft headrests were found on Philbin Beach, 17 miles west of the island's airport, including a suitcase with a label said to bear the name of Lauren Bessette, Mr Kennedy's sister-in-law.*

b. *The possibility that tragedy had once again struck the ill-fated Kennedy family shocked America, and television schedules were interrupted to provide continual coverage of the search.*

c. *It was not clear whether Mr Kennedy, 38, was piloting the plane or if his flight instructor was at the controls. But coastguard officials confirmed that Carolyn Bessette, 33, his wife of three years, and her sister Lauren were also on board.*

d. *John F. Kennedy, Jr., his wife and her sister were last night missing, feared killed, on their way to a family wedding after their small aircraft was believed to have crashed into the sea off Long Island, New York.*

e. *Mr Kennedy was flying to Martha's Vineyard for the wedding of his cousin, Rory, but his plane failed to arrive. Coastguard officials said the radar trace of their aircraft had disappeared when the plane was about 12 miles away from Martha's Vineyard.*

1C Ellen Spear

Ellen Spear, the Director of the Computer Museum in Boston, talks about a part of the exhibition which shows the *cutting edge* in computer technology.

'This is the virtual fish tank. It's the world's largest virtual aquarium and there are over a hundred virtual fish in these virtual waters. And it helps us through high technology and through advanced programming languages to understand some things that happen in the natural world.

Through computer technology we've learned that a lot of the things that we observe in nature are not because a leader, such as a lead fish in a school, decided which direction the school would go, but it's the result of a lot of individual decisions by fish; or a lot of individual decisions by drivers what causes a *traffic jam*; or the stock market, which is the result of individual decisions of investors. All of these things are governed by something called *complexity theory* and that's what our virtual fish tank explains.

The way that we do it is through actually building a fish and determining what its actual behavior will be, by what rules we chose its physical appearance is determined. So, to build a fish we can first decide whether or not he's hungry. If he's starving, his mouth will get larger and his teeth will get larger. And if he's full, his mouth will get smaller. If he's a calm fish, his eyes will be small and he'll be very relaxed and if he's a terrified fish, his eyes will grow larger. We can decide what he's interested in. If he's a friendly fish, he'll come up and greet us. If he's a shy fish, he'll tend to move away. We can determine whether he enjoys bubbles in the water or is annoyed by them and we can decide whether he likes bright objects or dislikes bright objects. And then we can decide where in the tank he would like to swim. If he likes to swim on the bottom or if he likes to swim above the *ocean floor*. Then we can put a *tag* on our fish so we'll remember who he is, and then we can release him into the tank and see what happens.'

Working with the text

I. Complete these sentences using the information in the text.

1. The virtual aquarium can be seen … .
2. The purpose of the aquarium is to show … .
3. People can make use of the technology themselves to … .
4. The example with virtual fish in an aquarium can help people to understand why other everyday things happen such as … .

II. Complete these sentences by using one word from the text.

1. To make a fish's mouth bigger you have to decide how … he is.
2. A small mouth means a fish is … .
3. A relaxed fish will have … eyes.
4. The eyes of a … fish will grow larger.
5. A … fish will greet us.
6. A shy fish will … away from us.

III. Answer these questions. Use complete sentences.

1. Which aspects of the virtual fish's behavior can be determined by the visitors?
2. What is a tag and what is it used for?

IV. Say these words and expressions out loud.

1. exhibition
2. the natural world
3. physical appearance
4. to determine
5. to release
6. calm

V. Put these verbs into the correct category according to their stress pattern.

decide ◆ determine ◆ develop ◆ enjoy ◆ entertain ◆ explain ◆ govern ◆ happen ◆ interact ◆ remember ◆ study ◆ understand

□■	■□	□■□	□□■

VI. Explain the underlined expressions. Use your own words as far as possible.

1. the <u>cutting edge</u> in computer technology (line 2)
2. <u>virtual</u> fish (line 3)
3. a <u>traffic jam</u> (lines 18-19)
4. the ocean <u>floor</u> (line 36)

Exercises

I. Write down the opposites of the underlined words.

1. huge eyes
2. to remember a number
3. the result of the traffic jam
4. a bright sky
5. the bottom of the sea
6. a theoretical problem

II. What about these opposites?

1. a sweet wine
2. fresh bread
3. well-done steak
4. tender meat
5. a mild curry
6. a soft drink

III. What are groups of animals or fish called in English? Link the numbers (1-8) to the letters (a-h).

1. a brood of	a. sheep
2. a colony of	b. bees
3. a flock of	c. ants
4. a gaggle of	d. fish
5. a pride of	e. monkeys
6. a school of	f. lions
7. a swarm of	g. hens
8. a troop of	h. geese

IV. There are words that are spelt the same way and said the same way but have different meanings. Give two meanings of the word ...

1. 'jam'.
2. 'study'.
3. 'fine'.
4. 'bright'.

If you don't know the answer, look up the words in a good dictionary!

V. There are words that are said in the same way but are spelt differently and have different meanings. Explain the difference in meaning between the words ...

1. 'weather' and 'whether'.
2. 'court' and 'caught'.
3. 'there' and 'their'.
4. 'it's' and 'its'.

VI. Whose statue?

The end of the film about Massachusetts shows a statue. Whose statue is it? Why is it in Boston?

VII. At the beginning of the 17th century settlers came from England to America and landed near what is today Provincetown, Massachusetts. What happened to these people? Read this text and decide which heading goes where in the text.

- Disagreements with England
- The birth of the United States
- In search of a new beginning
- War breaks out

•

In September 1620 a small group of English men and women left the port of Plymouth in England and sailed for America. They called themselves Pilgrims and wanted freedom to worship God in their own way. For sixty-five days the Pilgrims' ship, the Mayflower, battled through the waves of the Atlantic Ocean. At last, land was sighted. The Pilgrims rowed ashore, set up camp and called their home 'New England'. Not all the Europeans who sailed to New England with their families and belongings wanted religious freedom. Some were escaping from trouble at home. Others came in the hope of finding a better life or land of their own.

•

By the early eighteenth century these European settlers had formed 13 colonies. The colonists were independent-minded people and not afraid of working hard. Many of them objected to being controlled by the government in London. In the 1760s the English Parliament needed more money to pay for its wars. The King, George III, insisted on the colonists paying higher taxes on goods which were imported from Britain – especially tea. The colonists, however, refused. 'We have no representatives in Parliament,' they said, 'so why should we pay more tax?'

•

The argument between the colonists and England came to a head in 1773. A group of colonists, disguised as Indians, went onto British ships in Boston harbor and threw 342 cases of tea into the sea. 'I hope that King George likes salt in his tea,' one of them said. The 'Boston Tea Party', as it was later to be called, soon escalated into war. In 1774 British warships took up position outside Boston harbor. The colonists, led by George Washington, started to gather weapons and ammunition. The American War of Independence had begun.

•

In the meantime a group of colonial leaders had been meeting in Philadelphia. On July 4, 1776 they issued the Declaration of Independence. The Declaration said that the colonies were 'free and independent states' and, for the first time, it named them the 'United States of America'. The signing of the Declaration took place in Independence Hall. One of the first people to sign was John Hancock. He picked up the pen and wrote his name in large letters. 'Large enough,' he said 'for King George to read without glasses'.

The Pilgrims arrive in New England

Overview

cover page	Deckblatt, Titelblatt
leadership course	Kurs für Führungskräfte
MBA (program)	*Master of Business Administration*
to emerge	auftauchen
market setting	Standort
rational drug design	*die Entwicklung von Medikamenten auf der Basis der Biologie einer Krankheit*
disease	Krankheit
to design drugs	Medikamente herstellen, entwickeln
to fit into sth	in etw. hineinpassen
groove	Rille, Furche
to inhibit	hemmen
target	Ziel(bereich)
to regulate	regulieren, einstellen (*bei Krankheiten*)
Whirlwind computer	*Markenname*
to date back to	zurückgehen auf
palmtop computer	*ein Computer, den man in der Hand tragen kann* (*palm* = Handfläche)
virtual	virtuell

1A Nathalie Disfloth

recent	vor kurzem erschienen
annual issue	Jahresausgabe
type	Schriftart

1B Linda A. Hill

graphic artist	Grafiker(in)
script writer	Drehbuchautor(in)
slew	Haufen
to embark on	etw. anfangen / beginnen
to figure out	herausfinden
to take advantage of	Vorteil aus … ziehen
case protagonist	Hauptfiguren

1C Ellen Spear

cutting edge	neuester Stand
traffic jam	(Verkehrs)Stau
complexity theory	Komplexitätstheorie
ocean floor	Meeresboden
tag	Schildchen, Etikett

Pennsylvania

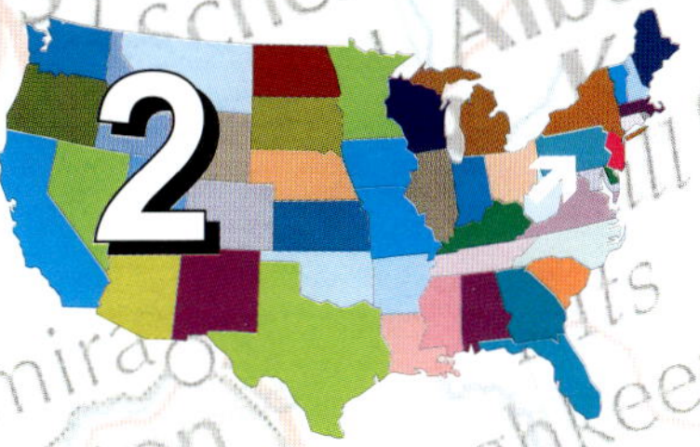

What do you know about Pennsylvania? Try this quiz and find out.
(The answers are at the bottom of the page.)

1. **What's Pennsylvania's state nickname?**
   a) The First State b) The Keystone State c) The Ocean State

2. **Which is the capital of Pennsylvania?**
   a) Harrisburg b) Philadelphia c) Pittsburgh

3. **What is the population of Pennsylvania?**
   a) 2 milllion b) 8 million c) 12 million

4. **What is the state flower of Pennsylvania?**
   a) golden poppy b) mountain laurel c) purple lilac

5. **Which important declaration was signed in Philadelphia in 1776?**
   a) The Declaration of Independence
   b) The Declaration of Liberty
   c) The Declaration of Peace

6. **Which is the most popular tourist attraction in Philadelphia?**
   a) JFK Plaza b) The Museum of Art c) The Liberty Bell

7. **What special status did Philadelphia have between 1790 and 1800?**
   a) It was the US capital.
   b) It had the country's only airport.
   c) It was the arrival point for European immigrants.

Answers: 1. b), 2. a), 3. c), 4. b), 5. a), 6. c), 7. a)

Overview

Caley McBride, 17, is a *senior* at Wellsboro High School, Pennsylvania. Outside school Caley is involved in a lot of activities. She plays *softball* in the summer and skis in the winter. Caley enjoys taking part in the Wellsboro Laurel Festival Parade. In fact this year she will be in the parade twice: first in the high school band and second on the softball *float*.

As Executive Director of the *Chamber of Commerce* in the Wellsboro area **Mary Worthington** is also involved in the preparations for the annual Laurel Festival. Mary knows how important tourism is for Pennsylvania as a whole but also for Tioga County and Wellsboro. The Laurel Festival, which started in 1938, takes place in June and lasts one week. The various comments from visitors show how popular the event has become for people from all over the state.

A lot of voluntary work goes on in Wellsboro. **John Erich**, for example, is a *volunteer medical technician* with the Volunteer Wellsboro Ambulance Association. In his regular job he works in environmental protection.

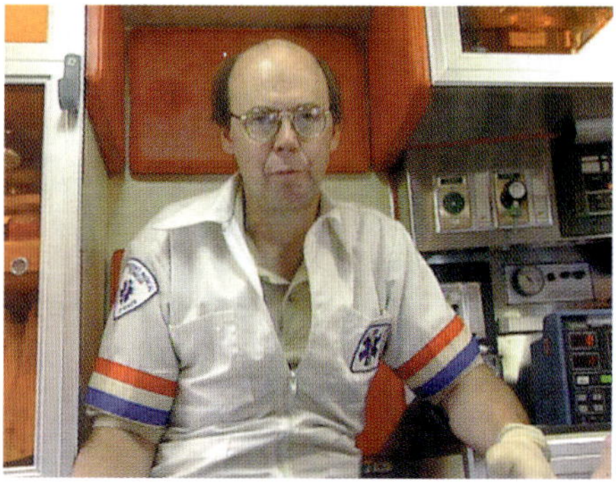

Mark Cooper is a volunteer *Fire Chief* in Wellsboro. When he's not *fighting fires* he runs a small store out of town.

Chaplain David Shultz, Chaplain at the Soldiers & Sailors Memorial Hospital in Wellsboro, talks about the people who do voluntary work at the hospital. Many of these people are retired. They have worked all their lives and get enormous satisfaction from giving something back to the community.

Peggy Osgood works at the information desk of the Soldiers & Sailors Memorial Hospital. She's very proud of the hospital and pleased to help patients who need advice or assistance.

Cathy Eldridge is the volunteer coordinator for the home help and *hospice* program. When hospice patients or home help patients need assistance, they can call Cathy and she will find a volunteer to come in and look after them.

Ralph Youmans is the *Warden* at Tioga County Prison. He's responsible for about 70 *inmates* and 40 officers. Ralph believes it is important that inmates have a chance to study and gain qualifications while in prison. Ralph contacted Mansfield State University and they agreed to help inmates with their education.

Find out more about ...

Caley McBride in	**2A**	(pages 30 – 35)
Mark Cooper in	**2B**	(pages 36 – 39)
Ralph Youmans in	**2C**	(pages 40 – 43)

2A Caley McBride

Caley McBride, a senior at Wellsboro High School, talks about some of the activities she is going to be involved in during the next school year.

'I play softball in the spring and in summer, but this summer we don't have a softball team because of *lack of interest* and not enough girls *signed up* to play. So tomorrow I'm leaving for softball camp at Penn State University, and I'll be spending five days there, practising and training for next year.

And in the fall I don't really do anything. I'*m in band* but I'm not going to do it next year. I'm just going to support the football team and watch my brother play. And I might play tennis but I'm not sure yet.

And then in the winter I ski. I'm a *certified ski instructor* at Denton Hill, and this is going to be my fourth year working there. In my second year I took a two-day training course to be professionally certified and that was … it was two days long and it was an intense *work-out*, and they just checked you on all your skills and your teaching skills and your skiing skills. And I passed that so I have this little pin now, and I'm a professional.

Then in the spring it's softball season and I *played varsity* this year and *JV* the past two years, and usually I play on two teams. We have the high-school team, and then the regular, it's like a little late season, and I play for that. And last year we *won districts*.'

Working with the text

I. Are these statements true or false? If they are false, correct them.

1. Caley is a university student.
2. Her favorite sports are softball and tennis.
3. Caley plays a musical instrument.
4. She is a qualified sports teacher.

II. Further questions. Answer them.

1. How can you see that Caley takes softball very seriously?
2. How do you know that Caley has probably been skiing since she was a child?

III. Which is the correct ending to the sentence? Mark it.

1. The word 'senior' (line 1) means …
   a) someone who has younger brothers or sisters.
   b) someone in their last year of high school.
   c) someone who is over 18 years old.
2. The expression 'I'm in band' (line 7) means …
   a) I play in a heavy metal band.
   b) I'm a member of the school marching band.
   c) I make CDs.
3. The word 'football ' (line 8) means …
   a) soccer. b) American football. c) baseball.
4. The expression 'I played varsity this year' (line 16) means …
   a) I played in the top school team.
   b) I played in a school team.
   c) I played in a university team.
5. The abbreviation 'JV' (line 16) means …
   a) jogging vigorously.
   b) junior varsity.
   c) jazz venues.

IV. What's the opposite? Find the words in the text.

1. sister
2. yesterday
3. to fail (a test)
4. to lose (a game)
5. too many (people)
6. in the next (two years)

V. Explain the underlined expressions. Use your own words as far as possible.

1. Not enough girls <u>signed up</u> to play … (line 4)
2. It was <u>an intense work-out</u> … (line 13)
3. We have the high-school team, and then <u>the regular</u> … (line 18)
4. And last year we won <u>districts</u> … (line 19)

VI. And what about you?

1. Did you take sports as seriously as Caley does when you were at school?
2. Which sports do you do? Do you have a summer sport and a winter sport?

The Laurel Festival Parade, Wellsboro

Exercises

I. The present continuous is often used to talk about future events. Decide if these sentences describe a present event or a future event. Put a cross in the appropriate column.

1. Are we going out tonight?
2. How are you feeling?
3. They're catching the first plane.
4. I'm waiting for a call from my parents.
5. We're leaving in five minutes. OK?
6. Ssh! I'm thinking.

present	future

II. Which questions must you ask to get the information which is missing?

1. I'm leaving for softball camp on .?. . It's at Penn State University.
2. They're staying at the .?. Hotel in Philadelphia. Have you heard of it?
3. We're having a holiday with .?. and .?. . Do you know them?
4. .?. is organizing a party at Christmas. Are you going as well?
5. She's arriving at ..? . Can you pick her up at the station?
6. We're driving to .?. at the weekend. Why not come with us?

III. What do the underlined expressions mean? Explain them.

1. 'My younger daughter is in second grade.'
2. 'He's going to college next year.'
3. 'She's a junior at Malcolm X High School.'
4. 'I got straight A's on my report card.'

IV. Which sport and which championship is it? Link the numbers (1-5) to the letters (a-e).

1. baseball	a. World Cup
2. golf	b. Davis Cup
3. American football	c. Ryder Cup
4. soccer	d. Super Bowl
5. tennis	e. World Series

V. What do you think?

If an American talks about 'football' what does he mean? Is he talking about the same sport as a British person?

VI. What would an American say? Underline the correct word in the brackets.

1. It's a quarter [before - of - to] six.

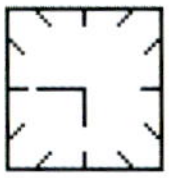

2. It's a quarter [after - past - to] ten.

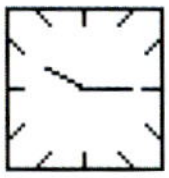

VII. Read these two statements. What do they say about Americans and American schools?

'I'm very proud of you. You always sound good. I've had people already tell me: "Boy, your band always sounds good!" Let's put the "look good" into it now. Keep the spacing good. Alrighty, please go change. I would like you to be out where you would be, out by the tennis courts, by quarter of two.'

Band leader, Wellsboro High School

'I'm very honored to be representing my school. This is kind of the cherry on top of the cake or whatever. I ... my school has done so well this year with athletics and music and now this, so I am very honored to represent my school. So thank you very much.'

Jessica Hall, Miss Laurel Queen

VIII. Softball, the sport Caley plays, is based on baseball. Everyone in the United States grows up with baseball. It's a national sport. But what are the rules of the game? A fan from Philadelphia explains. Read the interview and look at the illustration.

- Is it right that baseball is the most popular sport in America?
- Yes, it's a simple game, which everybody can play. All you need is a bat, a ball and a glove.

- It's a game for nine players, isn't it?
- That's right. There's a batting team and a fielding team. Each team has nine players.

- And the idea is to score points, I suppose?
- Yes, the aim of the game is to 'round the bases' once and score a run. The team with the most runs at the end of the game is the winner.

- What are bases exactly?
- Well, the field is divided into two parts: the outfield and the infield. The infield is a square, or 'diamond' as it's called, with a base at each corner: 1st base, 2nd base, 3rd base and 'home plate'. The distance between the bases is about 30 meters. To 'round the bases' means to run around these four bases.

- So there are nine players from the fielding team and a maximum of four players from the batting team on the field at any one time?
- That's right. The fielding team takes the field with 3 outfielders and 6 infielders. One of them is the pitcher who throws the ball. Another is the catcher who stands at home plate. The pitcher throws the ball to the catcher while a man from the batting team tries to hit the ball.

- So the pitcher and the catcher are important people, then?
- Yes, very. The pitcher tries to throw the ball in such a way that the batter either can't hit it or hits it badly. The batter tries to hit the ball either as far as he can or where there are no fielders.

- What happens when the batter hits the ball?
- If he hits the ball, the batter runs and tries to reach the furthest base he can before the ball is thrown back. If he reaches the base he wants to run to before the ball does, he is 'safe'. If the ball is there before he is, he is 'out'. When there are three 'outs', the teams change sides. This is done nine times a game.

- How many chances do I have as a batter to hit the ball?
- Good question. If you miss three good pitches in a row, you're out. Then the next batter comes in. We say the next batter is 'up'.

- But a batter can be out in other ways?

- Yes. If a fielder catches a ball before it hits the ground, the batter is out. Or, if a fielder who is holding the ball touches a batter as he is running, the batter is also out.

- When does the baseball season start?
- It starts in early spring and goes through to October.

- And are there professional baseball players?
- Of course. There are two leagues with 28 teams and one big competition every year.

- Is that the World Series?
- Yes, that's right.

- And what about the names of the teams?
- Well, there's the St. Louis Cardinals, the Boston Red Sox or the Chicago Cubs.

- And your favorite?
- The Philadelphia Phillies, of course!

- Thanks for answering my questions.
- You're welcome. Any time.

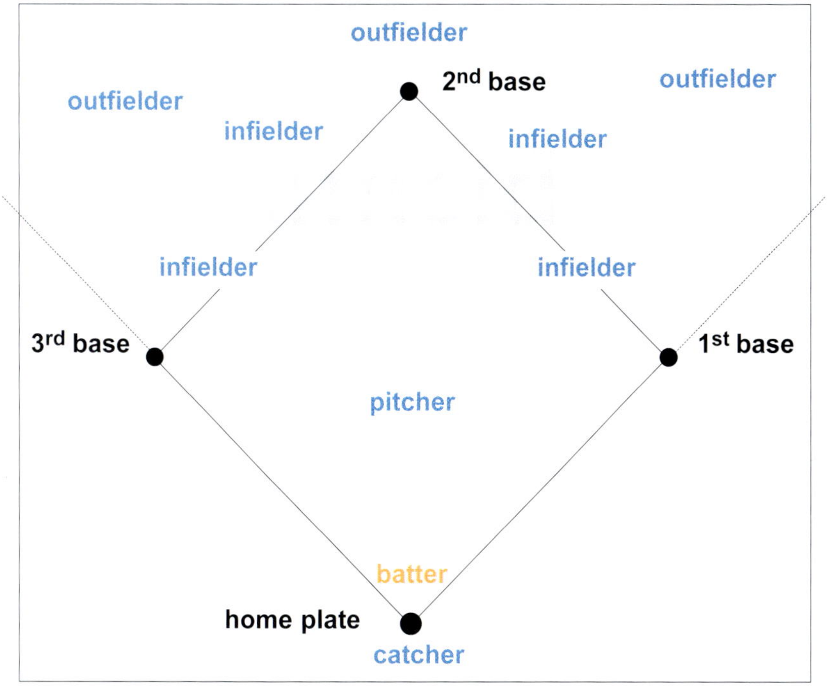

Note: The blue players are the fielding team. The yellow player is a batter.

2B Mark Cooper

Mark Cooper is the volunteer Fire Chief at Department One in Wellsboro. What does his work involve?

'What we do mainly is rescue in fire. We have approximately 400 fire calls a year and approximately 40 volunteers at this station that are active. We do anything from snow rescue with snow mobiles to … we do rescue from fires, we fight fire and anything we're asked to do, we do. We've been known to do cat rescues. Anything that the community needs, we try to do ourselves.'

How is the work financed?

'We've raised most of our own money through a *carnival* once a year and the other *funding* that we get is from the state for the equipment. We have approximately seven *front-line trucks* – that's all manned by volunteers. We have different shifts of volunteers because they have to work, so at certain times we have a good *turnout* and at certain times not such a good turnout.'

Finally Mark talks about the long tradition in volunteer fire organizations in Pennsylvania.

'We have members here who've had their sons in here and their grandsons, and they've all been volunteers. I, personally, have a son-in-law who is in the department. In the neighboring department I have an uncle and four cousins and a nephew. During the day when we're not fighting fires everybody has their own job or their own life. I, personally, run a small store out of town, three miles out of town, and I have three grandchildren, two children and a wife, and almost everyone here has another life besides this, but when the alarm *goes off*, that's the time when they usually give up that part of their life and *devote* it to this part.'

Working with the text

I. Answer these questions. Use complete sentences.

1. Does Mark Cooper work full-time as a fireman?
2. Is the work of fire organizations financed wholly by the state?
3. Are volunteer fire organizations new to Pennsylvania?
4. Has Mark got relatives in the fire service?

II. What do you think?

1. How many calls on average per week does the Department One fire station have? Is it a lot?
2. How seriously do the volunteer firemen in Wellsboro take their work?
3. What time of the week do you think Department One has a good turnout?
4. Is there a chance that one day Wellsboro will not have enough volunteers for its fire service?

III. Match the verb (1-6) to the correct expression (a-f) in the right-hand column.

1. to raise	a. funding from the state
2. to fight	b. part of your life
3. to run	c. fires
4. to get	d. money to buy equipment
5. to give up	e. a truck
6. to man	f. a small store

IV. Explain these expressions. Use your own words.

1. 'to do cat rescues' (lines 6-7)
2. 'to have a good turnout' (line 13)
3. 'a neighboring department' (line 18)
4. 'when the alarm goes off' (line 22)

V. Say these words and expressions out loud.

1. volunteer 2. approximately 3. son-in-law 4. to devote

Exercises

I. Complete the sentences.

1. If Tom is Jack's grandfather then Jack must be his … .
2. If Jessica is Mark's sister then Mark must be her … .
3. If Mary-Jo is Luke's aunt then Luke must be her … .
4. If Sally is Ralph's mum then Ralph must be her … .
5. If Joseph is Annette's father-in-law then Annette must be his … .
6. If Charles is Josephine's uncle then Josephine must be his … .

II. What's the difference between …

1. 'a friend' and a 'boyfriend'?
2. a 'friend of mine' and a 'friend of ours'?
3. a 'father' and a 'stepfather'?
4. a 'daughter' and a 'daughter-in-law'?

III. John Erich, a volunteer medical technician with the Volunteer Wellsboro Ambulance Association, describes what happened when he helped a young lady who fell on the sidewalk. Put his story (a-f) into the correct order (1-6).

a. *We applied a splint to her leg and have taken her blood pressure, getting her past medical history, such as things like: is she allergic to any medications, is she taking any medications, her last meal, things like that to determine if there might be any problems with her.*

b. *I happened to be in Wellsboro when this young lady tripped on the sidewalk and broke her ankle.*

c. *When we're done here with this ambulance call I will then return to my regular job.*

d. *Then we'll be taking her to the hospital.*

e. *Since I was available at that time, I, with some other people from our department, made this ambulance call and picked her up in front of the local theatre.*

f. *We'll give our report to the doctors and the nurses at the hospital so that they can take proper care of her.*

IV. On July 4, 1776 the Declaration of Independence was signed at Independence Hall in Philadelphia. What was the Declaration of Independence exactly? Complete the text by using the correct form of the words in brackets.

The signing of the Declaration of Independence

The Declaration of Independence proclaimed the … (separate) of the thirteen American … (colony) from Britain. It … (write) on one single page and it … (take) Thomas Jefferson two weeks … (complete).

V. The Declaration of Independence. Are you happy with the German translation? What would you change, if anything?

'We hold these truths to be self-evident: that all men are created equal, that they are endowed by their Creator with certain unalienable rights, that among these are Life, Liberty and the Pursuit of Happiness.'

'Folgende Tatsachen erachten wir als selbstverständlich: dass alle Männer gleich geschaffen sind; dass sie von ihrem Schöpfer mit gewissen unveräußerlichen Rechten ausgestattet sind, dass dazu Leben, Freundschaft und das Streben nach Geld gehören.'

2C Ralph Youmans

Ralph Youmans talks about his responsibilities as Warden at Tioga County Prison in north-central Pennsylvania.

> 'When we first moved here to this vicinity, I invited Mansfield State University to provide some *GED programs* for our inmates. They *obliged* that *request* and we do receive some *grants* to provide the inmates with some education. I believe that we have a responsibility of care, *custody* and control of inmates. And one of those responsibilities is to try to correct the inmate and to steer them in the right direction, and, of course, an education is one way of doing that.'

An inmate at Tioga County Prison is talking to his math teacher.

Teacher: How many times a week would you like to have me come over and help you?

Inmate: Well, that would all depend on your *schedule*. I have a lot of time here!

Teacher: You have a lot of time here! What is your goal? You go through this math. Why? Why do you want to continue to study? I think it's important for both of us to think about that.

Inmate: Well, by trade I'm a carpenter, and in the carpentry business math is real important.

Teacher: Yes.

Inmate: And not knowing math the way I should, I kind of *adopted* my own way of doing things and it doesn't always work and I kind of go through trial and error.

Teacher: Right.

Inmate: I want to get more study and learn math and help me get my GED so that when I'm doing carpentry in the future, I'll be able to do the job right the first time, so to speak, and I even … I have some interest of maybe going to college for some, a few more courses that has to do with either carpentry or business. Since I've started taking the GED with Mrs Kennedy, it just … it's like learning is fun.

Working with the text

I. Which is the correct ending to the sentence? Mark it.

1. The Warden at Tioga County Prison would like the inmates …
   a) to receive money for a proper education.
   b) to study and to gain more qualifications.
   c) to visit the local university.
2. The inmate in the dialogue wants to …
   a) become a carpenter. b) improve his math. c) play football.

II. What does the underlined word refer to?

1. '… an education is one way of doing <u>that</u> …' (line 9)
2. '… <u>that</u> would all depend on your schedule …' (line 13)
3. '… it's important for both of us to think about <u>that</u> …' (line 17)
4. '… and <u>it</u> doesn't always work …' (line 22)

III. Underline the correct word in the brackets.

1. An 'inmate' is somebody who is [at high school – your friend – in prison].
2. A 'carpenter' works with [metal – plastic – wood].
3. The letters 'GED' stand for General Educational [Drive – Development – Drug].'
4. With your 'GED' you can [leave prison – go to college – become a math teacher].
5. Doing things 'by trial and error' means doing them [often – correctly – cheaply].

IV. Explain the underlined expressions in your own words.

1. 'they <u>obliged that request</u>' (line 4)
2. 'that would all depend on <u>your schedule</u>' (line 13)
3. 'I <u>kind of adopted my own way of doing things</u>' (lines 21-22)
4. 'I want to <u>get more study</u>' (line 25)

V. Say these words and expressions out loud.

1. a warden
2. the vicinity
3. a request
4. the GED program

VI. What do you think? Use complete sentences in your answer.

1. During their conversation the inmate and the teacher laugh. Why?
2. Would you agree that math is important for carpentry?
3. Who do you think Mrs Kennedy is? Why is she so important for the inmate?
4. Is this inmate going to be successful in his learning?

Exercises

I. *What does the expression 'kind of' really mean? Read these examples and then choose the best answer from below.*

- I had a kind of feeling this might happen.
- I kind of go through trial and error when I'm doing math.
- He's a kind of teacher at a prison in Tioga County.
- I kind of like her.

You use the expression 'kind of' when you are …

a) not happy about something.
b) not certain about something.
c) not honest about something.

II. *Your English-speaking friend sees you reading a German text and wants to know what it's about. Tell him or her in four or five sentences. Don't translate word for word!*

Von dem Interesse und Spaß meiner Mutter an klassischer Musik wurde ich schon früh angesteckt. Ich hatte jedoch nie den Versuch unternommen, ein Instrument zu spielen. Mein Bruder verspürte eines Tages den Drang, Geige zu lernen. Er bekam eine Violine und ging zum Unterricht, aber nicht lange. Ihn haben die Rolling Stones schließlich mehr fasziniert, und die hatten nur ein Stück mit Geige ('As tears go by'). Die Geige lag nun herum, und ich wurde in ihren Bann gezogen. Nachdem ich ungefähr ein Jahr lang autodidaktisch gespielt hatte, ging ich mit etwa 17 Jahren zum Geigenunterricht. Es hat mir enorm Spaß gemacht. Für eine Weile galt mein ganzes Interesse diesem Instrument. Fast jeden Tag nach der Schule habe ich über ein Jahr lang fünf Stunden gespielt, wie besessen. Dabei habe ich keineswegs nur nach Noten gespielt, sondern auch sehr viel improvisiert. Ich trat unserem Schulorchester bei, das sogar zu einigen öffentlichen und offiziellen Anlässen spielte. Durch diese Aufgabe bekam ich noch mehr Distanz zur Schule und wurde ständig … besser – erstaunlich, nicht? In diesem Jahr war ich nach Noten sogar Klassenbester. Das hat mich aus dem Grund sehr gefreut, weil es für mich der Beweis war, daß es auch anders geht als mit Selbstdisziplin und Fleiß, nämlich mit Freude und Begeisterung. Ich hatte etwas begriffen, oder besser, ich hatte es erfahren: Mit Freude und Spaß lernt man zehnmal schneller und besser.'

Gerd Binnig (Nobelpreisträger für Physik, 1986): "Aus dem Nichts – über die Kreativität von Natur und Mensch"

III. *Amy is in her first year at college. She has written to her friend, Mary-Jo. Replace the underlined words with the correct words from the box.*

BS ◆ co-ed ◆ cute ◆ the dormitory ◆ freshmen ◆ graduate school ◆ hunk ◆ junior ◆ his master's thesis ◆ NCAA ◆ no kidding ◆ off-campus ◆ went out for

Hi Mary-Jo!

Life on campus is great! The school does so much for *first-year students*. There's always something going on in *university accommodation* - which is *male and female* by the way. Hey! You know what? I met this great guy, Greg! He's a *third-year student* from Harrisburg. He's so *good-looking*. If the relationship works out we might move in together *in non-university housing* next year.

Greg is studying for a *first degree* in Psychology. Then he wants to go to *an institution where you go after you have your first degree*, just like me. He's already got a topic for *the long paper he will have to write there*.

Greg is a real *attractive, muscular man*. Believe me! *It's not a joke*. And you know what? He *tried to get a place on* the football team and had no trouble making it. Did you know the team was voted one of the top twenty in the *college sports association* last year? Not bad, is it?

That's all for now. Greg's coming around any minute now. Bye!

Amy

Overview

senior	*vergleichbar mit Schüler der Oberstufe*
softball	*eine Form des Baseballspiels*
float	Parade-Wagen in einem Umzug
Chamber of Commerce	Handelskammer
volunteer medical technician	freiwilliger (Hilfs)Sanitäter
fire chief	Feuerwehrhauptmann
fighting fires	Feuer bekämpfen
hospice	Pflegeheim, Hospiz
warden	Gefängnisdirektor
inmate	Häftling, Insasse

2A Caley McBride

lack of interest	mangelndes Interesse
to sign up	sich einschreiben, sich eintragen
to be in band	im Schulorchester spielen
certified ski instructor	staatlich geprüfter Skilehrer
work-out	Training
to play varsity	*in der ersten Mannschaft spielen*
JV (junior varsity)	*zweite Mannschaft*
to win districts	die Bezirksmeisterschaften gewinnen

2B Marc Cooper

carnival	*im Sinne von Straßenfest*
funding	finanzielle Unterstützung
front-line truck	Feuerwehrwagen
turnout	Teilnahme, Beteiligung
to go off	*hier:* losgehen
to devote	sich widmen

2C Ralph Youmans

GED (program)	*General Educational Development*
to oblige	entgegenkommen
request	Anfrage
grant	Zuschuss
custody	Obhut, Verwahrung
schedule	Zeitplan
to adopt	sich zu Eigen machen, sich aneignen

Illinois

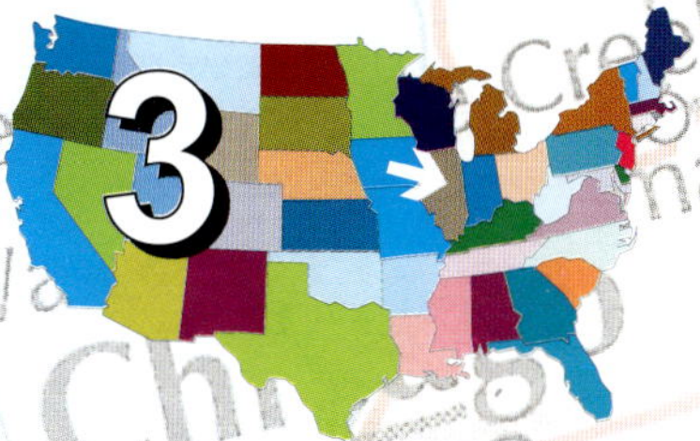

What do you know about Illinois? Try this quiz and find out.
(The answers are at the bottom of the page.)

1. Which of the Great Lakes lies at the north-east tip of Illinois?
a) Lake Erie b) Lake Michigan c) Lake Superior

2. How many people live in Chicago?
a) about 30,000 b) about 300,000 c) about 3,000,000

3. Chicago has a nickname. What is it?
a) The Oak City b) The Snow City c) The Windy City

4. Chicago boomed in the 19th century. Why?
a) The first telephone company opened there.
b) Railroads were built there connecting the east to the west.
c) Gold was discovered there.

5. Which is the tallest building in the USA?
a) The Empire State Building
b) The Sears Tower
c) The World Trade Center

6. Which famous American president is buried in Illinois?
a) Abraham Lincoln b) Richard Nixon c) Theodore Roosevelt

7. What is the name of the most important airport in Illinois?
a) JFK b) O'Hare c) Stapleton

Answers: 1. b), 2. c), 3. c), 4. b), 5. b), 6. a), 7. b)

Overview

Frank Bernardo has been working as a *train operator* in Chicago for twenty-seven years. He *works Monday through Friday*, from seven o'clock until two o'clock. We see Frank in his train on a summer's day. Although it is hot outside, the trains are cool inside and Frank knows that most people are enjoying their ride from and to downtown Chicago. Frank obviously likes his job and gets pleasure from dealing with the problems that arise on the line.

Bruce Nelson also works for the CTA (= Chicago Transit Authority). He's a transportation manager and one of his main functions is to coordinate special movements. He's responsible for chartered trains and for the *rerouting* of trains for *maintenance* or *construction work*. Bruce is aware that the CTA is not without its faults and sees it as one of his tasks to improve the system and make it more user-friendly.

Alberta Brown is a student at Malcolm X College in Chicago. At the moment she is taking her GED (General Educational Development) class. Afterwards she would like to do a course to become a *medical assistant*. In the past Alberta has been in low-paid employment. Now she is determined to get more education and a qualified job in a hospital.

Therese Turnipseed, Dean at Trueman College in Chicago, talks about the students on the GED program and the teaching methods used at her college. Students are encouraged to do independent work, group work, and to take part in discussions. The Dean wants her students to get a well-rounded education so they will be able to compete with students who have gone through high school. Indeed statistics show, says Ms Turnipseed, that the students who get the GED and go to college do as well – or better – than the students who have their high school diplomas.

Al Gehrke works as a *building engineer* at the Sears Tower in Chicago. His job is to run the window-washing machines. There are 16,500 windows in the Sears Tower and the windows have to be washed all year round. Al talks in detail about his work. The washing of the windows takes place in four cycles so that means the Sears Tower gets washed four times a year from top to bottom. The window-washing machine is positioned on the 90th floor and takes approximately one hour to go down to the *mezzanine* and back. The machine has *spray nozzles*, brushes, *squeegees* and a water return system so that the water can be reused. The washing machine can also be replaced by a work basket so that carpenters or other tradesmen can carry out their work from the outside.

Paul Johnson, Jr. works at the Chicago *Board of Trade*, the largest *exchange* in the world where there is an *open outcry*. Paul works for a Dutch firm. His job involves talking to people all around the world and telling them what is happening around him in the various *pits* on the floor. Paul explains why the people working at the Exchange wear brightly-colored jackets and what some of their gestures mean.

Find out more about ...

Bruce Nelson in **3A** (pages 48 – 51)

Alberta Brown in **3B** (pages 52 – 56)

Paul Johnson, Jr. in **3C** (pages 57 – 61)

3A Bruce Nelson

Bruce talks about the Chicago Transit Authority.

‘The CTA has been in existence since 1947 but parts of our system were built by private companies as far back as 1892. Right now we have seven rail lines and we serve about 450,000 passengers each weekday. The train we’re on was built in 1992, but the track we’re on dates from about 1907. One of the challenges we have in this company is making the best for our passengers having an old part of the system, an older antique part, and a new modern *train set* like we have here.

I’m a transportation manager for the CTA and one of my main functions is to coordinate special movements. That includes moving productions, it includes chartered or rented trains and it includes the rerouting of trains that sometimes has to occur for maintenance or construction work. Most people in Chicago like the CTA system. It’s not without its faults or its problems, but that’s one of our jobs, is to make the system better and more user-friendly.’

Working with the text

I. Are these statements true or false according to the text? If they are false, correct them.

1. The CTA is over 100 years old.
2. The CTA trains are 100 years old, too.
3. Bruce Nelson is a train operator.
4. Bruce thinks that the CTA does a good job – but it could do better.

II. Find a word or expression in the text which means …

1. people who travel on trains or busses.
2. the lines which trains run along.
3. to pay money to use a plane or a train for a special purpose.
4. to keep something (such as a machine) in good working order.

III. Replace the underlined words with words of the same or similar meaning.

1. … parts of our system were built by different companies as far back as 1892 … (line 3)
2. Right now we have about seven rail lines … (line 3)
3. … one of my main functions is to coordinate special movements. (line 9)
4. … it includes the rerouting of trains that sometimes has to occur … (line 12)

IV. Explain these expressions. Use your own words.

1. 'we serve about 450,000 passengers each weekday' (line 4)
2. 'the track we're on dates from about 1907' (line 5)
3. 'that includes moving productions' (line 10)
4. 'the rerouting of the trains' (line 11)

V. Say these dates out loud.

1. 1907	3. 1774
2. 1892	4. 2002

VI. Say these words out loud.

1. antique
2. company
3. rerouting
4. fault

Exercises

I. Past simple or present perfect? Complete the sentences.

1. She … (never, be) to America but she'd like to one day.
2. He … (live) in Springfield before he moved to Chicago.
3. They … (not, have) a holiday last year. They couldn't afford it.
4. Hi! It's me. I … (take) your gloves. Is that OK?
5. You … (be) in hospital at the weekend! Why was that?
6. He … (buy) the tickets but I don't know how much they cost.
7. We … (not, go) out at all last week. We were both ill.
8. She … (see) the film *Philadelphia* three times.

II. Is it 'been' or 'gone'? Put one word in each sentence.

1. John's not here. He's … to work.
2. My brother has … to Chicago three times.
3. The office is empty. Everyone has … home.
4. Welcome back! Where have you … ?
5. Is Sally there, please? – No, I'm sorry. She's … away for a few days.
6. Your hair looks different. Have you … to the hairdresser?

III. Complete the questions. Use the present perfect continuous form of the verb. Then choose the best answer from the box below.

Watching TV. ◆ I don't know. I've just heard it. ◆ For over an hour! ◆ My pen pal in Boston. ◆ Good question. Let's ask them! ◆ I don't know. You tell me!

1. How long … (they/wait) for us? Not long, I hope! …
2. Why … (your girlfriend/talk) to my boyfriend so secretively? …
3. What … (he/do) all day? I haven't seen him since breakfast! …
4. Who … (you/write) to all morning? Somebody important? …
5. Why … (you/worry) about it so long? It wasn't worth it. …
6. How long … (it/make) this funny noise? …

IV. Say these numbers out loud.

1. 135	4. 17.5
2. 33.3	5. fl
3. 438,677	6. 35,287,956

V. Put these prepositions into Frank Bernardo's text.

besides ◆ by ◆ for ◆ in ◆ on ◆ through ◆ till

'I'm Frank Bernardo. I've been working on this same line … the last twenty-seven years, and I work Monday … Friday, seven o'clock … two o'clock, and I have different things that I do … run the train. Everybody has to have different qualifications. You do operating a train, working switching … the yard, and many different things, so it's not the same old thing every day. You do different things and it makes the day go … faster and it makes for enjoyment … the job.'

VI. Which job would you prefer to do – Bruce Nelson's or Frank Bernardo's? Why? Write a short text (50–60 words) explaining your preference.

VII. The USA is a large country with more than one time zone. Look at the map of the continental USA and answer the questions below.

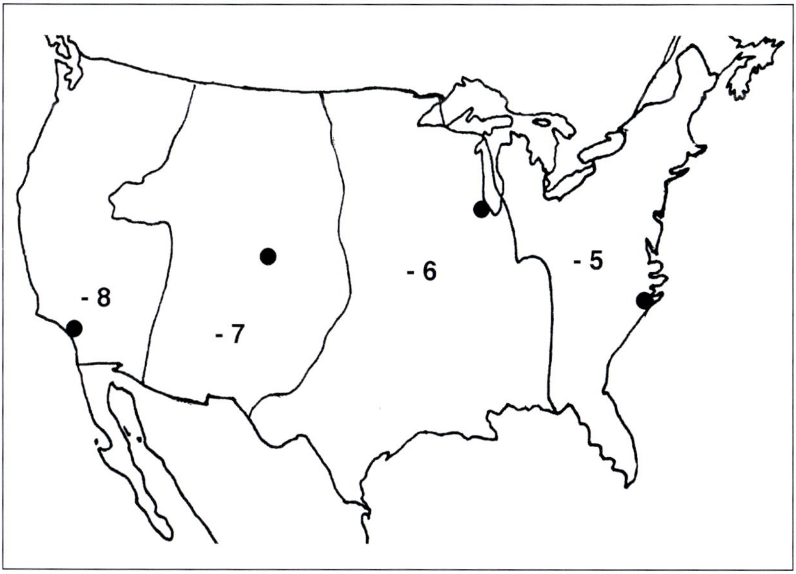

Note: Clock times are shown behind Greenwich Mean Time.

1. If it's 2 o'clock in New York, what time is it in Chicago?
2. If it's 11 o'clock in Los Angeles, what time is it in Denver?
3. Between November and April the abbreviations for the time are EST, CST, MST and PST. The 'S' stands for 'Standard'. Between April and November the abbreviations for the time are EDT, CDT, MDT and PDT. What does the 'D' stand for?
4. Which US states are missing from this map?

Downtown Chicago

3B Alberta Brown

Alberta talks about her career plans:

'After many rejections and many low-paid jobs I discovered the only way to success is a higher education. And Malcolm X opened the doors for me by letting me get my GED and with that my desire just grows bigger. It's like eating a good meal. More, more, more. The more you get, the more you want. And I'm at that stage now so I don't intend to stop. I'm fifty-seven, so I want to go until I have to stop. So right now I don't feel the need to have to stop. I'm going to continue and am going to get as much as I can.

And after I get my *associate degree* in medicine, then I plan on working in the hospital and then applying my love and care toward other people because so many people showed me love by my coming here and getting my GED. My teacher was an excellent person. The input she put in me showed me that people do care and they do love, and with her knowledge she gave me a mind to want to increase my knowledge. So now I can *pass* it *on*. It's like planting a seed and with this, with the help that I got, I can give other people help and it's just a continuing, continuing thing to do. I get, they get, and then they give, and I think this is the best part of life: when you receive you give, and not try to keep it all for yourself, just let it go on. This is what education is about.'

Working with the text

I. Which is the correct ending to the sentence? Mark it.

1. Alberta Brown would like …
   a) to become a teacher. b) to get a job in a bank. c) to work in a hospital.
2. In the past Alberta didn't have a good job because …
   a) she stayed at home to look after her children.
   b) she preferred simple, low-paid work.
   c) she did not have enough qualifications.
3. It's obvious that Alberta …
   a) wants to learn as much as she can.
   b) is bored with college.
   c) just wants to do her courses as quickly as possible.

II. Answer these questions. Use your own words as far as possible.

1. How important is education for Alberta?
2. What sort of influence has Alberta's teacher had on Alberta?
3. What would Alberta like to do with the knowledge she has acquired at college?

III. What does Alberta mean? Explain the underlined expressions using your own words.

1. 'Malcolm X opened the doors for me … ' (line 3)
2. 'The more you get, the more you want.' (line 5)
3. '… she gave me a mind to want to increase my knowledge … ' (line 13)
4. 'It's like planting a seed … ' (lines 14-15)

IV. Link the verbs on the left (1-7) with the correct words on the right (a-g).

1. to get	a. studying
2. to work	b. your knowledge
3. to stop	c. an associate degree in medicine
4. to increase	d. a seed
5. to plant	e. five subjects for the GED test
6. to drop out of	f. as a nurse in a hospital
7. to take	g. high school

V. What do you think? Write two or three sentences for each answer.

1. Do you agree with Alberta that you can only get a good job if you have good qualifications?
2. Are you surprised that Alberta wants to work in one of the 'caring professions'?

VI. Outside Malcom X College you can see the words 'Empowerment through Education'. What does this mean?

Exercises

I. Join up the beginnings and ends of the sentences.

1. When I was small …
2. After high school I went to college …
3. I work as a train operator …
4. I dropped out of school …
5. I really want to get the GED certificate …
6. When I finish college …

a. for my own benefit.
b. to study Medicine.
c. I'm going to apply for a job.
d. I always wanted to become a nurse.
e. for the CTA.
f. when I was 15.

II. What's the difference? Explain.

- What do you do?
- What are you doing?

III. Explain these expressions. Give examples if you wish.

1. to apply for a job
2. to work freelance
3. to be on maternity leave
4. to work shifts
5. to be promoted
6. to have flexitime
7. to take early retirement
8. to be made redundant

IV. Which job is the odd one out? Can you say why?

1. train operator – secretary – nurse
2. carpenter – attorney – plumber
3. clown – hairdresser – actress
4. driving instructor – teacher – farmer

V. Choose one of the questions and write a short text in English (between 80 and 100 words).

1. Describe your present job. Say what you like about it. What career plans do you have?
2. Which job would you like to have? What sort of qualifications do you need to get it? Do you think that one day you will be doing it?

VI. Who was Malcolm X? Put these sentences (a-j) into the correct order. Start with sentence g.

a. *By the late 1950s he had become the Black Muslims' most effective speaker.*

b. *He became interested in a religious group called the Black Muslims.*

c. *He changed his name to Malcolm X.*

d. *He had a difficult childhood.*

e. *In 1946 he was sent to prison for burglary.*

f. *Malcolm had to earn money instead of going to school.*

g. *Malcolm Little was born in 1925.*

h. *This was to show that it was not his name but that it came from white slaveholders.*

i. *When he was 6 his father was murdered.*

j. *While in prison he taught himself to read.*

VII. Complete this story from 'The Autobiography of Malcolm X'. Use the correct form of the words in brackets.

One afternoon when Wilfred, Hilda, Philbert and I … (come) home from school, my mother and father … (argue). My father … (take) one of the rabbits we raised and … (order, my mother, cook) it. We … (raise) rabbits but we … (sell) them to whites. My mother … (cry). She started … (skin) the rabbit before … (cook) it. But my father … (be) so angry he … (leave) the house and started … (walk) up the road. My mother was upset but she finished … (cook) the food.

Our father … (not, come) home by our bedtime. Our mother … (hug) us in our beds. We felt … (strange) because she … (never, behave) liked that before. I remember … (wake) in the night. My mother … (scream). We children knew without … (have to, ask) anything that something terrible … (happen) to our father. In the morning we … (tell) that he … (kill) by some whites. I … (be) six at the time.

VIII. Find out more!

What do the Black Muslims believe in?
What happened to Malcolm X in 1965?

IX. Read this text. Link the underlined states to the numbers in the map. Where exactly is Chicago?

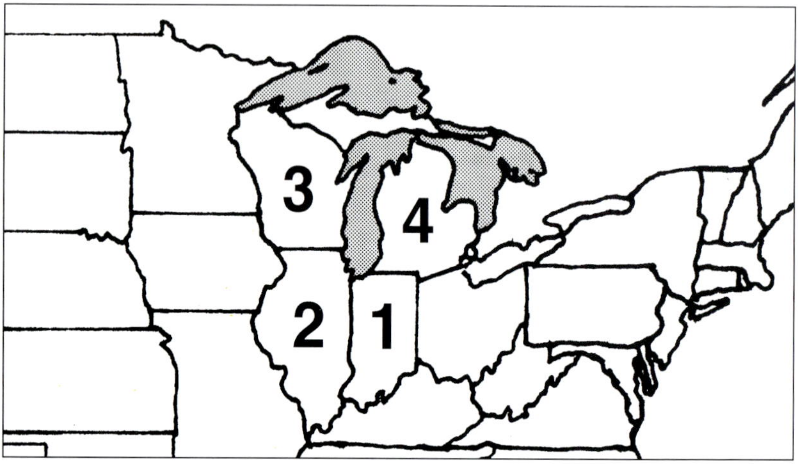

Lake Michigan is the third largest of the Great Lakes and the only one lying completely within the United States. It is bordered by Michigan on the north and east, Indiana on the south and Illinois and Wisconsin on the west. The lake itself is 494 km long and up to 190 km wide with a maximum depth of 282 m.

X. Complete the text about the Empire State Building in New York by adding the seven words which are missing. Six of them are in the box below.

engine ◆ heart ◆ breathtaking ◆ comic book ◆ telescopes ◆ suburbs

The Empire State Building is in the … of Manhattan. It's a huge construction, although not as tall as the World Trade Center or the Sears Tower in Chicago.

There are some interesting stories about the Empire State Building. Once, for example, an airplane crashed against the walls of the building and one … went straight through it and out the other side. Seven floors above a boy was reading a … and did not notice a thing.

Every year about a million people visit the building's Observatory. The view is … . With one of the … you can spot ships forty … out to sea. One visitor put it like this: 'Up there it's like the sun and stars are … of New York.'

3C Paul Johnson, Jr.

Paul talks about the Chicago Board of Trade (CBOT).

'What you see behind me is the largest exchange in the world where we have open outcry, which allows for *price discovery* so that people that *trade* US *treasuries* – or that have *mortgages*, shall we say, in the United States – can keep *mortgage rates* down, *interest rates* down, for the United States government, and people can transfer the risk of borrowing and lending money.'

What's Paul's job at the Exchange?

'What I do personally is I *serve businesses* through a firm, a Dutch firm actually – ING, the International Nederland Group – and we have a *trading desk* on the floor behind me here, and what I physically do during the day is I'll talk to people all around the world, whether they be in Germany or in London or in New York, Chicago, or in Asia, and my customers are different banks, different *funds* that are trading with the *commodities*, if you will, or the interest rate *futures* that you see behind me. And we'll talk to these people about what's happening in different markets around the world because what happens in Germany before I get here is very important, and then what happens around this during the day is very important. So I'll talk to people and discuss those things with them.'

What happens on the Exchange floor?

'Now what I see around me are various pits. And you'll see that the *bond* pit, which is the most active *contract* traded in the world you have, which is thirty-year bonds. There you have, over in the far corner, you have two-year and five-year *notes*, you have ten-year notes, and then you have options on all these contracts. You have bond options, ten-year options, five-year options and so on. And in the far corner we have the Dow Jones Industrial Average, which is a name that you should all know around the world. We trade with the thirty Dow Jones *stocks*, but it's *a basket*. So if it goes up or down, we are trading all thirty stocks at once.'

Working with the text

I. Which sentence in the text shows you that …

1. the CBOT is a marketplace?
2. the CBOT is part of a global market?
3. there's a significant time difference between Germany and Chicago?
4. trading in bonds is a popular method of investing money.

II. Join up the beginnings and ends of the sentences.

1. A 'commodity' is	a. another way of saying 'US government bonds'.
2. A 'pit' is	b. a portion of the value of the money, equipment and buildings of a company, ie. its capital.
3. A 'mortgage' is	c. a certificate from a government saying that it has been lent money and will pay it back with interest.
4. A 'bond' is	d. a large opening at the CBOT where people work.
5. 'US treasuries' are	e. an agreement to buy or sell a commodity some time in the future at a specified price.
6. An 'option' is	f. a loan from the bank to buy a house.
7. A 'stock' is	g. the right to buy or sell something at a certain price and within a certain time.
8. A 'future' is	h. a product which is bought and sold between countries.

III. Underline the correct word or expression in the brackets.

1. The aim of the futures market is to manage the [risk – tasks – stress] involved in trading commodities.
2. Futures are agreements to buy or sell a commodity some time in the future. The quality and quantity of the commodity is standardized. Only [the location – the price – the color] is not.
3. Traders use [hand signals – skate boards – mobile phones] so that they can process information quickly and 'translate' that information into a fair price for others in the market.
4. Trading in futures is like [a party – a nightmare – a game] where buyers move the market so that sellers are willing to sell, and where sellers move the market so buyers are willing to buy.

IV. Explain in your own words the underlined expressions.

1. … we have open outcry, which allows for price discovery … (line 8)
2. What I do personally is I serve businesses through a firm … (line 20)
3. … the bond pit, which is the most active contract traded in the world … (line 32)
4. We trade with the thirty Dow Jones stocks, but it's a basket … (line 38)

V. Say these words and expressions out loud.

1. mortgage
2. interest rate
3. commodity
4. the Dow Jones

VI. What do you think? Answer the questions in complete sentences.

1. Why are the pits at the CBOT octagonal in shape?
2. Why do some traders have the palms of their hands facing towards them when they trade and others have the palms of their hands facing outward? What do these two positions signify?
3. Why does a loud bell sound twice a day at the CBOT? What does it mean?
4. Why do the jackets that the traders wear have bright colors? And why are they lightweight and loose-fitting?

Exercises

I. Make one sentence out of two. (Use an adjective with a hyphen).

1. He completed the run in 45 minutes. (It was 10 kilometers long.)
2. They've got a mortgage on their house. (It runs for 30 years.)
3. We had a short flight to Chicago. (It lasted 2 hours).
4. She gave us a new bill. (It is worth 20 dollars.)
5. I read a book in a weekend. (It has 350 pages in it.)
6. They've just built a new golf course in our village. (It has 18 holes.)
7. Let's have a break, shall we? (For five minutes.)
8. The Osage tribe is located in eastern Oklahoma. (It has 15,000 members.)
9. The tribe has a huge reservation. (It's about 1.6 million acres.)
10. We had a superb meal. (There were five courses.)

II. Write these sums of money as numbers.

1. ninety cents
2. sixty-three dollars thirty-six
3. a hundred and fifty-one dollars
4. six thousand eight hundred and seventy-five dollars

III. Which words form a common pair?

1. supply and
2. goods and
3. stocks and
4. bulls and
5. assets and
6. profit and

a. bears
b. liabilities
c. demand
d. shares
e. loss
f. services

IV. Choose the most suitable word from exercise III to complete the sentences below.

1. A … is a speculator who buys shares hoping they will rise in value so he or she can sell them at a profit.
2. A company's … are, for example, the machines and buildings it owns.
3. If the … for a product is suddenly very high, the price will increase.
4. A company's … is the difference between the money it has spent and the money it has earned.

V. Read out these sentences making sure you say the numbers, weights and measures correctly.

1. The government spent over $400,000,000,000 on defense last year.
2. Does he really weigh 150 lbs?
3. Add 2 tsp of red peppers.
4. At halftime Chicago is ahead of Detroit 21-0.
5. You're not 5' 9", are you? You look much taller!
6. We're recording over 100° F in downtown Chicago.

VI. Test yourself! What do these words and expressions mean?

1. The Fed
2. A checking account
3. Wall Street
4. business card
5. blue chip
6. the greenback

VII. Read this text about Al Capone, a famous gangster from Chicago. There are three sentences in it which don't belong there. Can you find them?

Al Capone (1899-1947) was an Italian-American gangster of the Prohibition era. He was also known as 'Scarface' because of a knife cut on his cheek. He was born Alfonso Capone in Naples and raised in Brooklyn, New York. He didn't want to go to bed when his mother told him to. He left school at an early age and spent nearly ten years with gangs in Brooklyn.

In the 1920s Capone took over a Chicago organization dealing in illegal liquor, gambling and prostitution. He usually cycled to work. In the following years he eliminated his competitors in a series of gang wars. The most spectacular of these was the Saint Valentine's Day massacre of 1929. He became a national hero and was invited to the White House for lunch. This won Capone control of Chicago's underworld.

In 1931 Al Capone was convicted of income tax evasion and sentenced to 11 years in prison. He was released on parole (= *auf Bewährung*) in 1939 but was crippled (= *verkrüppelt*) by syphilis and spent the rest of his life in his mansion at Miami Beach, Florida.

VIII. What was the Prohibition era? Try and find out some information about it.

IX. Read this text about a famous US businessman. What sort of man was he?

Billionaire who made the Mars Bar dies aged 95

Forrest Mars, the reclusive billionaire who built one of the largest businesses in the world as head of the Mars chocolate empire, has died aged 95 in Miami, Florida.

Mr Mars started his company in England in 1932, where he successfully launched the Mars Bar, then made entirely by hand in a single-room factory and costing two pence. Today Mars companies employ 30,000 people worldwide, and is the fifth biggest food business in the world with sales of £8.75 billion a year.

The business began in 1922 with Frank C. Mars's small firm in Tacoma, Washington. However, it was his son Forrest who was responsible for the success of its best-known brands and its global expansion. Today Mars products are sold in more than 150 countries.

Mr Mars moved to Europe after a bitter rift with his father over how they should manage the business in America. However, out of gratitude, Frank C. Mars gave his son $50,000 and the foreign rights to one of his chocolates which he marketed as Mars in Britain. He returned to America in 1939.

In a book published earlier this year, Joel Glenn Brenner, a Washington Post reporter, portrayed Mr Mars as ill-tempered and a business monster. At a marketing meeting he once ordered his son John, then 29, to kneel and pray for the company and left him on the floor for nearly an hour. His sons, Forrest Jr. and John, are now co-presidents of the privately owned company.

X. Do you remember the end of the film? Who's singing? And what's the title of the song?

Overview

train operator	Zugführer
to work Monday through Friday	von Montag bis Freitag arbeiten
rerouting	Umleitung
maintenance	Wartung
construction work	Bauarbeiten
medical assistant	medizinische Hilfskraft
building engineer	Bauingenieur
mezzanine	niedriges Zwischengeschoss (zw. EG u. 1. Stock)
spray nozzle	Spritzdüse
squeegee	Gummiwischer
Board of Trade	Warentermin-Börse
exchange	Börse
open outcry	(Parketthandel auf) Zuruf
pit	Box

3A Bruce Nelson

train set	*gemeint ist hier:* der komplette Zug

3B Alberta Brown

associate degree	*Abschluss nach zweijährigem College-Studium*
to pass sth on	etw. weiter geben

3C Paul Johnson, Jr.

price discovery	Kursbestimmung
to trade	handeln mit
treasury	Schatzanweisung
mortgage	Hypothek
mortgage rates	Hypothekenzinsen
interest rate	Zinssatz
to serve businesses	Handel treiben mit anderen Firmen
trading desk	Schalter
fund	Fonds
commodity	Ware
future	Termingeschäft
bond	Obligation
contract	Terminvertrag
note	Schuldverschreibung
stock	Aktie, Wertpapier
a basket	ein Aktienkorb

Washington, DC 4

What do you know about Washington, DC? Try this quiz and find out.
(The answers are at the bottom of the page.)

1. **What do the letters 'DC' in 'Washington, DC' stand for?**
   a) Department Capital b) District of Columbia c) District County

2. **Washington, DC is the US capital and …**
   a) has special status within the US.
   b) lies in the state of Maryland.
   c) is situated in the state of Virginia.

3. **The 'Capitol' is …**
   a) another word for 'capital'.
   b) the building which houses the US Senate and House of Representatives.
   c) the part of Washington, DC where all the tourist attractions are.

4. **Why did George Washington, the first US president, not live in the White House?**
   a) He didn't like the color white.
   b) He preferred to live in Philadelphia.
   c) The White House had not been built yet.

5. **Where in Washington, DC can you see the Declaration of Independence (1776)?**
   a) in the White House b) in the Capitol c) in the National Archives

6. **When was the American Civil War?**
   a) 1773-1776 b) 1861-1865 c) 1914-1918

7. **There's a V-shaped wall in Washington, DC with 58,000 names on it. These are the names of people …**
   a) who died or went missing in the American War of Independence.
   b) who died or went missing in the American Civil War.
   c) who died or went missing in the Vietnam War.

Answers: 1. b), 2. a), 3. b), 4. c), 5. c), 6. b), 7. c)

Overview

Eleanor Holmes Norton is the *congresswoman* for Washington, DC. As such she is well informed about the city she represents. When Washington, DC was chosen as the nation's capital, she explains, nobody thought about what its legal status within the United States would be if thousands of people moved there and made it their home. Even today, 200 years after the nation was founded, the status of the residents of the District of Columbia is not clear. Congresswoman Holmes Norton spends a lot of her time trying to increase the power of the residents in the District of Columbia. She is also concerned that she herself, as the congresswoman, does not have full voting rights in Congress.

Kevin Leahy is a park service ranger for the National Park Service in Washington, DC. Kevin talks about the Vietnam's Veterans Memorial, a wall containing the 58,214 names of the dead and missing in the Vietnam War. Kevin explains why people come to the wall. Some want to pay their respects to the men who gave their lives fighting in the war. Others want to try and heal the wounds they might have. Kevin's views are confirmed by the comments of the visitors to the Memorial.

Elisabeth Lohah Homar, member of the Osage *tribe* in Oklahoma, is Director of the Office of the American Indian Trust in the United States *Department of the Interior*. One of Elisabeth's job is to make the public more aware of what Indian tribes are, of their history and of their culture. Elisabeth would like tribal governments to make sure that their communities can achieve their fullest potential and still be a part of a tribal community with enough opportunities so that in the future American Indians will still be who they are today.

Brigadier General **John W. Mountcastle**, the army's Chief of Military History, is at Manassas, a battlefield park near Washington, DC. John talks about the American Civil War and why he thinks it was a turning point in US history.

Superintendent **Robert K. Sutton** says that two major battles in the Civil War were fought at Manassas and that one of most famous American generals of all time, Stonewall Jackson, received his nickname on the battlefield at Manassas. Walking around the battlefield site, he explains, you can get a good idea of what the battleground looked like in 1861.

Find out more about …

Visitors to the Vietnam's Veterans Memorial in	**4A**	(pages 66 – 69)
Elisabeth Lohah Homar in	**4B**	(pages 70 – 74)
John W. Mountcastle in	**4C**	(pages 75 – 77)

4A The Vietnam's Veterans Memorial

Find out how Americans today feel about the Vietnam War.

Visitor A: 'Well, I have to admit first of all that I don't know, personally, any of the people whose names are on the wall, but I am *awestruck* and a little *overwhelmed* when I look at the number of names there because it reminds me that each name stands for a husband or a son or a father who lost their lives, who never came home and that somebody, somewhere, has lost someone very dear and important to them and probably still *grieves* even now.'

Visitor B: 'Well, I've been here a number of times and I've come here a number of times for the strict reason that, as an officer in the United States Army, I want to make sure that we all remember that we don't want to repeat this mistake again, so I come here, and I bring my children, and I bring my family, and I bring my relatives to try to understand that 58,000 *service members* died and we want to make sure that we don't make the same mistake ever again.'

Visitor C: 'Walking through here was a very sad experience for me because I was old enough to know the protests were happening, didn't exactly know why, learned it as I got older, but it is a sad thing that so many people died for nothing. That's probably the saddest thing and I cried all the way through this and I didn't know one person on that wall but it's just the whole thing that happened to this country, and thank God we got through it and hopefully it will never happen again.'

Visitors read the names of the service members

Working with the text

I. Answer these questions.

1. Which of the visitors have seen the wall before?
2. Which of the visitors seem to get most upset when they see the wall?
3. Which of the visitors have a similar opinion about the war?
4. Which of the visitors actually fought in the Vietnam War?

II. Find a word in the text which means …

1. suddenly filled with surprise and respect.
2. to feel sad after somebody has died.
3. the people in your family.
4. to do something again and again.

III. Explain the meaning of the underlined words.

1. … or a father who lost their lives, who never came <u>home</u> … (line 6)
2. … I've come here a number of times for the <u>strict</u> reason that … (line 9)
3. … to try to understand that 58,000 <u>service members</u> died … (line 12)
4. … it's just a sad thing that so many people <u>died for nothing</u> … (lines 16-17)

IV. What do you think? Give answers.

1. How genuine are the feelings of the people interviewed in front of the Vietnam's Veterans Memorial?
2. Is there anything like the Vietnam's Veterans Memorial in your country?

Exercises

I. Is it 'make' or 'do'? Use the correct verb in the correct form to complete the sentences.

1. Yesterday they … a lot of progress with their work.
2. We've been … business with them for over 30 years.
3. Has somebody … a complaint?
4. Could you … me a favor, please?
5. Oh no! I've … a silly mistake!
6. Can you … without your computer for a day while it's being repaired?

II. Say these nouns and verbs out loud. What happens to the stress?

1. a protest	–	to protest	4. a conflict	–	to conflict
2. an increase	–	to increase	5. an export	–	to export
3. a record	–	to record	6. a decrease	–	to decrease

III. Read this text about the Vietnam War (1959-1975). Three sentences in it do not make sense. Can you find them?

From the 1880s until World War II, France had governed Vietnam as part of French Indochina. After the war, however, Vietnam struggled for independence from France.

In 1954 Vietnam was divided into North and South Vietnam. President Nixon announced that he had a secret plan to end the war. North Vietnam came under the control of the Vietnamese Communists. The South was controlled by the Vietnamese who had collaborated with France.

The United States became involved in Vietnam because it believed that if the whole country fell under a Communist government, Communism would spread throughout Southeast Asia and beyond. The average age of a US soldier in Vietnam was 19. This belief was known as the 'domino theory'.

In 1965 the United States sent in troops to Vietnam to prevent the South Vietnamese government from collapsing. Two days later two students were killed in Mississippi. In the end, however, the United States failed to achieve its goal. In 1975 Vietnam was reunified under Communist control and in 1976 it officially became the Socialist Republic of Vietnam.

During the war approximately 3 to 4 million Vietnamese on both sides were killed in addition to another 1.5 to 2 million people who were drawn into the war. More than 58,000 Americans lost their lives.

IV. Match three sights of Washington, DC (a-f) to the pictures (1-3).

a. *The Washington Monument is a large white obelisk. Around its base are 50 American flags, representing the fifty states of America. George Washington was America's first president.*

b. *There must be very few people who don't know this building. The White House was built between 1792 and 1800 and is the official residence of the US president. The first president who lived in the White House was John Adams.*

c. *The Capitol is the seat of the US parliament. It is usually called Congress. One wing of the building is for the Senate, whose 100 members are called senators. The other wing is for the House of Representatives, whose 435 members are congressmen and congresswomen.*

d. *Another tourist attraction in Washington is the Jefferson Memorial. It contains a large statue of Thomas Jefferson, who Americans see as one of the fathers of the United States.*

e. *Inside the Lincoln Memorial is the statue of Abraham Lincoln. Lincoln was US president during the American Civil War (1861 to 1865).*

f. *Near the Lincoln Memorial on the other side of the Potomac in Virginia is Arlington National Cemetery. Here you can see the Tomb of the Unknown Soldier and the grave of John F. Kennedy.*

1.

2.

3.

4B Elisabeth Lohah Homar

Elisabeth Lohah Homar is the Director of the Office of the American Indian Trust in the United States Department of the Interior. Which tribe is she a member of?

'I'm a member of the Osage tribe, as I said, which is about a 15,000-member tribe located in north-eastern Oklahoma. The Osage tribe has a reservation of about 1.6 million acres of *rolling* prairie lands. The *primary economy* of the tribe is *oil* and *gas development*. Recently a *preserve*, a prairie park preserve, was established in the middle of the reservation and we again have buffalo *roaming* the Osage prairie lands so we're pretty happy about that.'

What does Elisabeth's job involve?

'Few people truly understand the legal status of American Indian tribes within the *constitutional framework* of the United States of America. So one of the things that I do here at the Office of the American Indian Trust is to provide this kind of background so people can more easily understand how all of these concepts work together. So one of the questions that people often have is: so what are Indian tribes? There are cultural groups, there are ethnic groupings of people, there are linguistic groupings of people. There are various kinds of cultures and religious beliefs. But importantly, you add to that, character of those things – the fact that they are *political entities*. Now, what does that mean? Well, it's very simple. It means that tribes are governments. They have governmental authority and they have governmental responsibilities. They also have managerial responsibilities over their lands and natural resources. So taken together, what this means is that within the constitution framework of the United States we have a federal government, we have state government and we have tribal governments and all three are interdependant on one another but none are the same. They are separate entities.'

Working with the text

I. Are these statements true or false according to the text? Correct the false statements.

1. Elisabeth Lohah Homar works in eastern Oklahoma.
2. She is a member of the Osage tribe.
3. Elisabeth's job involves fighting for more land for American Indians.
4. American Indians have few rights and few responsibilities.

II. What do the underlined words refer to in the text?

1. … we're pretty happy about <u>that</u>. (line 8)
2. <u>They</u> have governmental authority … (line 19)
3. … <u>we</u> have a federal government … (line 23)
4. <u>They</u> are separate entities. (line 25)

III. Replace the underlined words or expressions but keep the same meaning.

1. The <u>primary</u> economy of the tribe is oil and gas development.
2. <u>Recently</u> a preserve was established in the middle of the reservation …
3. They also have <u>managerial responsibilities over their lands</u> …
4. So <u>taken together</u>, what this means is within the constitution …

IV. Define the following expressions. Use your own words as far as possible.

1. a preserve (line 6)
2. a buffalo (line 7)
3. a natural resource (line 21)
4. a federal government (line 23)

V. Look at the text and complete the grid.

	noun	adjective		noun	adjective
1.	constitution		5.	law	
2.	culture		6.	politics	
3.	government		7.	religion	
4.	language		8.	tribe	

VI. What does Elisabeth say about people's attitudes to American Indians? Read the text and find out.

'Tribal people want to live in tribal communities but they don't believe being Indian necessarily means that you have to be poor or somehow have a lower standard of living than the rest of the people in the world. Tribal governments are working very hard to try to change these kinds of attitudes and to make members of their community feel proud to be from their communities.'

Exercises

I. Which word or expression in the brackets is correct?

Large numbers of European [explorers/settlers] arrived in America in the [16th and 17th/18th and 19th] centuries. They came in search of a new [home/house]. Travelling in [canoes/wagons] packed with everything they needed these 'new' Americans moved [eastward/westward]. The Indians' land seemed [vacant/crowded] to them. There were no fences, no buildings and no towns. They felt they had [every/no] right to be there.

The [American/British] government saw the future of the Indians [differently/similarly]. 'If the Indian tribes do not become civilized, they will decline and become extinct,' wrote President Monroe in the [1930s/1830s]. Soon the US government started to pressure the Indians to [give up/keep] their traditional way of life. The Indians fought many battles with the US [Cavalry/Air Force] but in the end they were not able to survive in the wilderness. As the [animals and crops/shopping malls and casinos] they needed disappeared, they were [forced/asked] to live on special reservations.

II. There is something wrong with this text! Can you put the words in brackets into their correct position?

The Indians hunted (skins). It gave them everything they needed to live. They ate its (bones) and used its (meat) to make (buffalo). With its (clothes) they were able to make (tools). They carved its (fur) to make knives and other (tents).

III. What's the difference, if any, between ...

1. the 'capital' and the 'Capitol'?
2. the 'white house' and the 'White House'?
3. 'Native Americans' and 'American Indians'?
4. 'state government' and 'federal government'?
5. 'Washington, DC' and 'Washington State'?
6. the 'USA' and the 'United States'?

IV. Read this story about Elisabeth's grandfather. What does this story say about the teachers at the school he attended?

'My great-grandfather's name was Olohowallah. When my grandfather went to boarding school, they asked him his name and he said his name was Niwallah. And the people at the boarding school didn't understand that. They said: "No. Your real name? Your American name?" And he said: "Well, my real name is Niwallah." They said. "No. You have to have a real name. What's your father's name?" So he said: "Well, my father's name is Olohowallah." And they said: "OK. Your name is going to be Lohah," – because that's what the person heard.'

V. How many people came to America? Read the text and choose the correct figures – a, b or c?

a) 330,000 • 1.5 million
b) 1.5 million • 33 million
c) 15 million • 33 million

Between 1492 and 1820 … million people came to North America and between 1820 to 1920 another … million immigrants arrived in the United States.

VI. Complete the text. Use the words from the box below and find out the answer to the question in the last paragraph.

border ◆ Afro-Americans ◆ life ◆ Asian-Americans ◆ ancestors ◆ Hispanics ◆ reservations ◆ Native Americans ◆ Thailand ◆ will ◆ slaves

About 270 million people live in the USA today. They are from many different backgrounds.

About 2 million US citizens are … . Their forefathers inhabited North America before the Europeans arrived. Today many of them live on special … . The 3.5 million … who have settled in the US are from countries such as China, Japan and … . Another large ethnic group which has been emigrating to the States quite recently are the … . Many of them have made their way across the … from Mexico and a large number originate from Cuba. … , who number 29 million, are the only Americans who came to the United States against their … . They were brought as … between the seventeenth and nineteenth centuries. Over 200 million people in America are white. These are the people whose … left Europe to start a new … in the New World.

The US population is not distributed evenly across the 50 states. However, it's not difficult to work out which US states are the most populous: they're California (31 million), New York (18 million), Texas (18 million), Florida (14 million) and Pennsylvania (12 million). But which state has the smallest population? Is it Alaska, Vermont or Wyoming?

1600 Pennsylvania Avenue, Washington, DC

VII. Read this text and choose the answer to the question below.

Until Texas became part of the United States it had the honor of being the largest US state. There's a story about Texas representatives who were trying to block Alaska's statehood because they didn't want Texas to be the second-largest state. The man fighting for Alaska stood up and said: 'Hey! If they don't shut up, we'll divide Alaska in two and Texas will have to be satisfied with being number three!'

When did Alaska become a state of the United States?

a) 1875 b) 1923 c) 1959

VIII. Read about the White House.

The White House is the official residence of the US president and is situated at 1600 Pennsylvania Avenue in Washington, DC. Known through its history as the President's Palace, the President's House and the Executive Mansion, the building has always been popularly known as the White House although this designation did not became official until 1901 when Theodore Roosevelt had the name engraved on his stationery. Over the years the White House has been extended and renovated but it has still kept its classically simple character.

4C John W. Mountcastle

Brigadier General John W. Mountcastle is standing at Manassas, one of the battlefield parks in the United States. What does the army's Chief of Military History say about the American Civil War?

'I think one of the things that many Americans are proud of is that their ancestors, from wherever they may have come from, joined together in their new country to defend those ideals in which they had developed very strong feelings. We know that because of the huge number of German immigrants who came to this country in the years, the twenty years, before the American Civil War, that we had, not just regiments, but whole divisions where German was the language spoken around the campfire and the bands that played the regiments into action would have been perfectly at home in Potsdam.

'We also know that many Americans today see our Civil War as a defining point in our history where two separate economic systems, one increasingly industrial, in the north-east, and in the south-east an agricultural system that was largely supported through the use of other human beings, Africans brought to this country in slavery, was maintained as an agricultural system. And these two systems conflicted intellectually and emotionally. And this is one of the major reasons that we had this Civil War. It was, yes, about economics, yes, it was about politics, too, but the issue of slavery was *key* and *critical* to this war.'

Working with the text

I. Which is the correct ending to the sentence? Mark it.

1. The first part of John's text is about …
   a) the battles that were fought in the Civil War.
   b) the people who fought in the Civil War.
   c) the music that was played in the Civil War.
2. The second part of John's text is about …
   a) the aims of the Civil War.
   b) the cause of the Civil War.
   c) the result of the Civil War.

II. Answer the questions.

1. What does John W. Mountcastle say about the feelings people on both sides had in the Civil War?
2. What, in John's view, was the main cause of the Civil War?

III. *Which word or expression from the text is it?*

1. a standard of perfection
2. a large military group
3. owning people and making them work for you
4. a man, woman or child

IV. *Explain the meaning of these words and phrases.*

1. military history (lines 2-3)
2. ancestors (lines 4-5)
3. an immigrant (line 7)
4. an issue (line 19)

V. *What do you think? Answer these questions.*

1. Why did so many European people leave their home and emigrate to America in the middle of the 19th century?
2. Why do you think Americans are proud of their ancestors who fought in the Civil War?

Exercises

I. *Complete the text. Use the words in the box.*

alphabet ◆ chance ◆ documents ◆ farmer ◆ farmowner ◆ father ◆ friends ◆ lodge ◆ region ◆ slavery

When Abraham Lincoln was fifteen years old, he hardly knew the … and could not write at all. His first home had been a hunter's … in Kentucky, but one day his … sold it and moved to a lonely … in Indiana where Lincoln began to earn money as a … .

As soon as he could read, Lincoln wanted to learn more and more. He read a lot: not only children's books but also complicated … like the US Constitution. One day in New Orleans he saw the horrors of … for the first time. A black girl was being sold to a … right before his eyes. Lincoln said to his …: 'If I ever get a … to hit this, I'll hit it hard.'

II. *What's the odd word out? Can you say why?*

1. cotton – Confederacy – South – Abraham Lincoln
2. Vietnam – Washington, DC – July 4 – Memorial
3. wagon – buffalo – skin – reservation
4. National Archives – Liberty Bell – White House – Capitol

III. Write down the opposite. The first letter has been given.

1. ancestors	⟷	d…	4. (to) defend	⟷	a…
2. immigrant	⟷	e…	5. major	⟷	m…
3. huge	⟷	t…	6. industrial	⟷	a…

IV. Put the sentences (a-h) into the correct order (1-8) to make up a text about the background to the Civil War. Start with sentence a.

a. *In 1861, just before the Civil War started, serious economic and ideological differences – in particular the question of slavery – divided the nation.*

b. *During the Civil War the North and South had very different aims.*

c. *As a result, eleven of the southern states withdrew from the Union and formed the Confederate States of America.*

d. *Fifteen southern states, whose economies depended on agriculture, permitted the ownership of slaves.*

e. *Nineteen states, including the industrialized northern states, prohibited slavery.*

f. *The South, on the other hand, wanted independence and only had to defend itself.*

g. *The North wanted to restore the Union, which meant it had to force the Confederate States to give up their hopes to found a new nation.*

h. *These differences also divided the country geographically.*

V. Read what Superintendent Robert Sutton says about the number of US citizens who died in the Civil War. Do you remember how many people died in the Vietnam War?

'The Civil War was a major event in American history. It's something that Americans have always been fascinated with. Some have been troubled with it because of the amount of life that was lost in this war. There were about 640,000 Americans that were killed, who died in the Civil War, and almost every war that the Americans have fought, besides the Civil War, would equal the number of deaths in the Civil War.'

VI. Do you remember the end of the film? What are the people celebrating?

Overview

congresswoman	Kongressabgeordnete
tribe	Stamm
Department of the Interior	*Ministerium mit Zuständigkeit für Bergwerke, Naturschutzgebiete, „Indian Affairs" u.a.*

4A The Vietnam's Veterans Memorial

awestruck	vor Ehrfurcht ergriffen
overwhelmed	überwältigt
to grieve	trauern
service member	Militärangehöriger

4B Elisabeth Lohah Homar

rolling	hügelig
primary economy	Hauptwirtschaftsfaktor
(oil/gas) development	Erschließung (von Erdöl- / Erdgasquellen)
preserve	Naturschutzgebiet
to roam	wandern, ziehen
constitutional framework	grundlegende verfassungsmäßige Struktur
political entity	politische Einheit

4C John W. Mountcastle

key	Schlüssel-, wichtigste(r,s)
critical	entscheidend

Kentucky

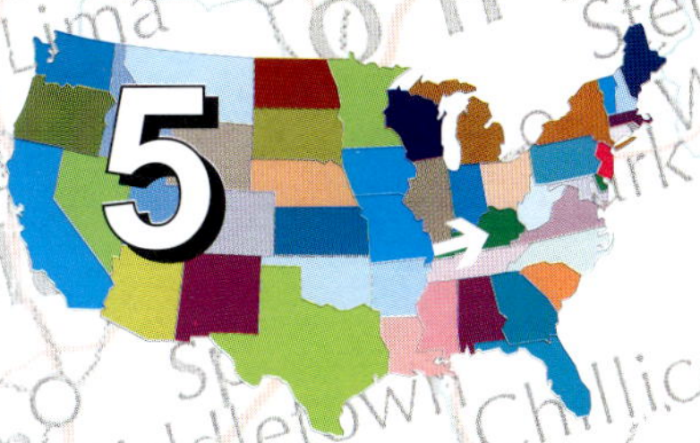

What do you know about Kentucky? Try this quiz and find out.
(The answers are at the bottom of the page.)

1. **What's the state nickname for Kentucky?**
   a) the Bluegrass State b) the Pine Tree State c) the Sunflower State

2. **What is the racial/ethnic population distribution in Kentucky?**
   a) 92% black – 7% Hispanic – 1% white
   b) 92% white – 7% black – 1% Hispanic
   c) 92% Hispanic – 7% white – 1% black

3. **What is the 'Kentucky Derby'?**
   a) a horse race b) a football stadium c) a basketball competition

4. **Kentucky is famous for its Mammoth Cave National Park. How long are the underground passages in Mammoth Cave?**
   a) about 3 miles b) about 30 miles c) about 300 miles

5. **What is the Ku Klux Klan?**
   a) an organization, founded in 1866, whose aim is to terrorize black people
   b) an organization, founded in 1945, whose aim is to work for peace
   c) an organization, founded in 1971, whose aim is to protect the environment

6. **Which of the following is the main crop in Kentucky?**
   a) corn b) melons c) tobacco

7. **Which of the following is a famous Kentuckian?**
   a) Michael Jackson b) Elvis Presley c) Muhammad Ali

Answers: 1. a), 2. b), 3. a), 4. c), 5. a), 6. c), 7. c)

Overview

Josephine Abercrombie owns Pinnock Farm in Versailles, Kentucky. Josephine *raises horses*. She looks after them, *breaks* them and prepares them for the *race track*. Josephine thinks Kentucky is the perfect place for raising horses. There's a *limestone base* under the soil and this is the best environment for what horses like best – bluegrass.

Before he trained to become an auto mechanic **Burdette Kretzer** worked in the coal mines in Van Lear. Burdi talks about the people he worked with and the different countries they came from. He also mentions the Ku Klux Klan and the influence they have on the people who live in the part of Kentucky he comes from.

Wesley Wittwer, who comes from Paris in Kentucky, would like to make a living from farming. However, the situation for farmers in the US is not easy so at the moment Wesley is working in a factory where he can rely on a regular income.

Charles Northcutt also works in a factory. When he's not at work he enjoys *raising tobacco* at home and *giving concealed weapons classes*.

Tom Edwards leads groups of people in 4-H (head, heart, hands and health), an organization for young people which helps them to become capable and *caring* citizens. We see Tom working with a group of people studying environmental issues. What he wants them to do is to go out into the woods, study a specific area and come back with suggestions for ways of protecting it for one particular bird, the *mourning dove*.

Edwin Orange, President of Kentucky 4-H, is a member of the National 4-H Technology Corps and he is particularly interested in using Internet relay chat to communicate with others around the United States. Recently, for example, Edwin worked with a group of 4-Hers to help develop a T-shirt design. Using Internet relay chat they were able to design a T-shirt, post that design to a web page, then email a distributor of T-shirts that designed the T-shirt and printed it, and then they distributed the T-shirt among themselves at the National 4-H Conference.

Michael Delk is pastor at the Episcopal Church of the Good *Shepherd* in Lexington. Michael talks about the history of the church, the *wood carvings* and the *stained glass windows*. Later we see him in a bible class working with some of his *parishioners*.

Find out more about …

Josephine Abercrombie in	**5A**	(pages 82 – 85)
Wesley Wittwer and Charles Northcutt in	**5B**	(pages 86 – 89)
Michael Delk in	**5C**	(pages 90 – 93)

5A Josephine Abercrombie

Josephine Abercrombie raises horses on Pinnock Farm in Versailles, Kentucky.

Interviewer: Can you give us some details about the farm?

Josephine: Well, for instance, we have *stallions* here. We *breed mares*. We have six stallions, and we've *raced* one of them ourselves, and the others that stand here are horses that are owned by ourselves and by other people. And so we breed mares. That's one thing we do. We have our own mares, we have *a band of* about 28 or 9 *brood mares*. We breed those mares, we raise the babies, we break them, as you see here, these are the ones we're breaking here on the track right now, and we get them ready to go to the race track, and we race all of the young horses that we breed.

Interviewer: So, how many horses do you have here at the moment?

Josephine: Here on the farm? I'd say about a hundred, including the young, the babies, the horses in training, the yearlings and so forth.

Interviewer: And why do you think horses and Kentucky are such a wonderful thing? Why did you become involved with this?

Josephine: Well, in the first place, Kentucky is the place to be if you're going to raise horses because of the bluegrass. There is apparently a limestone base under all this wonderful soil, and that is the best sort of atmosphere to raise bluegrass, and that is what horses *thrive on*. So that is one of the reasons that Kentucky is so special for horses. And the reason that I'm here is because way back in the forties I used to *show horses*, and I came here with my father, and we loved it, decided to buy a farm, and we did that. So I've been here ever since.

Working with the text

I. Mark the correct ending to the sentence using the information in the text.

1. Josephine Abercrombie …
   a) has just arrived in Kentucky.
   b) has been in Kentucky for a few years.
   c) has lived in Kentucky for over fifty years.
2. Josephine Abercrombie …
   a) has a riding school. b) looks after horses. c) is a sheep farmer.
3. Josephine Abercrombie probably …
   a) has more younger horses than older horses on her farm.
   b) has more older horses than younger horses on her farm.
   c) has just old horses on her farm.

II. More questions on the text. Answer them.

1. What does Josephine do with horses besides breeding and raising them?
2. Why is Kentucky so special for horses?
3. How can you see that Josephine has spent all her life working with horses?

III. Which word in the text means …

1. a male horse?
2. a female horse?
3. a female horse which is at the right age to have a foal?
4. the part of the earth that flowers and plants grow in?
5. a type of white rock?
6. the years between 1940 and 1950?

IV. Which definition is the best? Mark it.

1. If you 'breed mares' you …
   a) buy female horses.
   b) keep female horses in order to produce foals.
   c) race female horses.
2. If you 'show horses' you …
   a) show them to the public.
   b) show them to your family and friends.
   c) show them to other horses.
3. If you 'break horses' you …
   a) put them in isolation.
   b) sell them.
   c) train them to be ridden.

4. If you 'raise horses' you …
   a) take care of them.
   b) transport them.
   c) race them.

V. Replace the underlined expressions with words of the same (or similar) meaning. Don't change any other words in the sentence.

1. '… and we get them ready to go to the race track … .' (lines 10-11)
2. 'Well, in the first place, Kentucky is the place to be … .' (line 17)
3. 'There is apparently a limestone base under all this wonderful soil … .' (line 19)
4. … and that is the best sort of atmosphere to raise bluegrass … (line 20)

VI. What do you think?

1. Do you remember the interview with Josephine. What sort of impression does she have on you? Does she seem happy with her work?

Exercises

I. Use an -ing participle to join the two sentences together.

1. He hurt his arm. He fell off a horse.
2. She ran upstairs. She was holding a letter.
3. They got home late. They felt exhausted.
4. We often spend the evening at home. We listen to country music.
5. I stayed in the US for six months. I worked on a farm.
6. She looked at the camera. She tried not to laugh.

II. Use a participle construction to shorten the relative clause.

1. Did you see that little horse which jumped over that huge fence?
2. He'd like to have a job which can offer a regular income.
3. The man sat on the park bench. He was talking to himself.
4. Do you know about the problems which are facing farmers in Kentucky?
5. They stayed in Paris, Kentucky where they were visiting their daughter-in-law.
6. Who is that friendly old woman who lives in the same road as you?

III. Lengthen these sentences by using a full relative clause.

1. Many people living in Kentucky love horses.
2. Passengers not holding a US passport should fill in this form.

3. Did you see that dog barking at those poor children?
4. Drivers using Interstate 80 can expect delays at the Route 202 interchange in Wings.
5. We had a lovely apartment overlooking the lake.
6. Students wanting to use the library must first register with the librarian.

IV. Complete the grid. Use the words in the box.

cub ◆ drake ◆ gander ◆ kid ◆ mare ◆ ram

	animal	**male**	**female**	**young**
1.	horse	stallion		foal
2.	duck		duck	duckling
3.	lion	lion	lioness	
4.	sheep		ewe	lamb
5.	goat	billy-goat	nanny-goat	
6.	goose		goose	gosling

V. What does the verb 'get' mean in these sentences?

1. Can you get some peanut butter from the store?
2. Did you get that email I sent you yesterday?
3. It's getting cold, isn't it? Let's go in.
4. Shall I get you something to drink?
5. We got to the airport after the plane had left.
6. He likes telling jokes but I never get them!

VI. Use these words in complete sentences to show their meaning.

principal –	principle	stationary –	stationery
desert –	dessert	brake –	break
fair –	fare	it's –	its

VII. The city of Louisville, Kentucky was named after Louis XVI of France but what about Frankfort? Read the text to find how it got its name.

Frankfort was settled in 1786. The site had first been known as Frank's Ford in honor of Stephen Frank, a frontiersman who was killed in 1780 during a fight with Native Americans at a ford in the river. The present version of the name was adopted in 1786, but Frank's Ford was in popular use until about 1830. Frankfort was chosen as state capital in 1792 when Kentucky was admitted to the Union.

5B Wesley Wittwer and Charles Northcutt

Read about Wesley Wittwer.

'I'm from Paris, Kentucky. I was originally born in Lexington, Kentucky. I moved to Bourbon County when I was three years old. I was born and raised on a farm. There's nothing that I would enjoy any more than to be able to continue farming and to make a living farming. Due to the economics of the United States as far as agriculture goes, it's really made it tough on the farmer in America. So, because of that fact, I decided that I was going to have to do something different than my forefathers, and tried to get a job in a factory where I could have a good solid salary plus insurance and be able to work and continue farming as well on the side. It is like I almost have to have a full-time job to pay for my part-time job at home farming.'

Who is Charles Northcutt? What does he do?

'I'm a *maintenance supervisor* at Rexroth Pneumatics. When I'm not working here at Rexroth, I'm involved in raising tobacco at home. I raise around 6,000 lbs of tobacco. When I'm not doing that, I'm also involved in dealing with concealed weapons classes for people that want to carry a concealed weapon. I was also involved at that time as a police officer part-time. I gave that up after I started to work here at Rexroth about eight years ago.'

Working with the text

I. Which part of the text shows you ...

1. that Wesley would like to be a farmer?
2. that Wesley's father and grandfather were farmers?
3. that Wesley still enjoys farming?

II. Answer these questions about Wesley.

1. Why does Wesley think it's difficult being a farmer in the US?
2. What, for Wesley, is the attraction of working in a factory?

III. True or false? Correct the statements that are false.

1. Charles is a tobacco farmer.
2. Charles also works as a part-time police officer.
3. Charles teaches people how to conceal weapons.

IV. What do you think? Answer the questions.

1. What is Charles's job exactly?
2. Why do people in the US carry concealed weapons?

V. What do the underlined words refer to in the text?

1. 'So, because of <u>that fact</u>, I decided that I was going … .' (line 7)
2. 'When I'm not doing <u>that</u>, I'm also involved in … .' (line 15)

VI. Which word in the text means …

1. the money you earn every month for the job you do?
2. a unit of weight which is a little less than half a kilo?
3. the people in your family who lived before you?
4. 'to hide' or 'to keep something from being seen'?

VII. Say these words out loud.

1. tough
2. forefathers
3. pneumatics
4. concealed weapons

VIII. Look at this sign in the place where Wesley and Charles work. What do these statements mean exactly? What effect do you think this sign has on the people working in the factory?

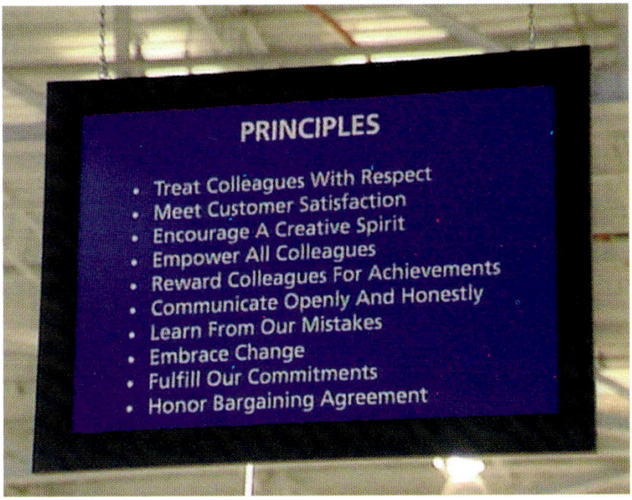

Exercises

I. Shorten the relative clauses by using a participle construction.

1. Orders which are placed before 2 pm will be processed on the same day.
2. The computers which are sold in this shop are all made in China.
3. Which job which was offered to you did you accept in the end?
4. The people who were injured in the accident have been interviewed by the police.
5. The shop windows which were destroyed in last week's riots have been repaired.
6. Has anybody recorded the program about gun laws which was shown on CNN last night?

II. Lengthen these sentences by using a full relative clause.

1. Born in Chicago, he was raised in Washington, DC.
2. Educated in Louisville, Kentucky, he spoke with a distinct American accent.
3. Warned about the problems facing farmers he decided to apply for a job in a factory.
4. Before being offered the job he had to fill out lots of forms.
5. Pleased with the regular salary he stayed with the company for over ten years.
6. Offered the chance to return to farming full-time, he immediately agreed.

III. Practice your pronunciation. Say these words out loud.

1. psychology	4. psalm
2. pneumonia	5. pseudo
3. physics	6. physiotherapy

IV. Which word or expression in each pair is American English? Mark it.

1. corporation	–	company
2. a pay rise	–	a pay raise
3. labor unions	–	trade unions
4. president	–	managing director
5. shareholder	–	stockholder

V. Explain the difference between ...

1. an 'employee' and an 'employer'.
2. a 'part-time job' and a 'full-time job'.
3. to be paid on a 'piecework basis' and to be paid 'on commission'.
4. a 'capital-intensive' industry and a 'labor-intensive' industry.
5. a 'white-collar' worker and a 'blue-collar' worker.
6. 'flexitime' and 'overtime'.

VI. Muhammad Ali is the world's most famous Kentuckian. Put the eight paragraphs (a-h) into the correct order (1-8) to tell his story.

a. *After returning from the Olympics Clay turned professional. He became more vocal about his successes and he was given the nickname 'Louisville Lip'.*

b. *Ali was fond of boasting. He once said: 'I'm so fast, when I turn out the light at night I'm in bed before the room goes dark'. Today, however, he is a mere shadow of the past, hardly able to walk or talk and displaying many of the symptoms of Parkinson's disease.*

c. *Eventually Ali was allowed to return to the ring. Between 1970 and 1980 he had a string of spectacular fights watched by millions of fans all around the world.*

d. *By the age of 18 Clay had won 108 amateur fights, including a gold medal as the light heavyweight champion at the 1960 Olympic Games in Rome.*

e. *In 1964, still only 22, Clay became heavyweight champion. He became a Muslim, changed his name to Muhammad Ali and went on to defend his title five more times until 1967.*

f. *At the height of his fame, Ali was one of the most famous athletes in the world, and even after his retirement he was recognizable wherever he went.*

g. *In the middle of the Vietnam War Ali refused to join the United States Army saying that he was a black Muslim minister and a conscientious objector. He was convicted of draft evasion* (Wehrdienstverweigerung) *and his heavyweight title was declared vacant* (für unbesetzt erklären, hier im Sinne von aberkennen).

h. *Muhammad Ali was born in Louisville, Kentucky. His original name was Cassius Marcellus Clay, Jr. He began boxing at the age of 12 after his bicycle was stolen and a police officer suggested that the young Clay should learn how to box.*

5C Michael Delk

Pastor Michael Delk talks about the Episcopal Church of the Good Shepherd in Lexington.

'We started out in 1887 as a mission of Christ Church Cathedral, the first Episcopal Church in Kentucky down on Broadway Street in a small house. We then moved a little bit closer to our current location, but were burned out in 1918 on New Year's Day. That's when we purchased this land here on East Main Street. Then we built up some plans for a church that we would like to have under the *enterprising command* of a very *involved* priest, the Reverend Thomas Settle, an Englishman.

About the same time he came to town the Kentucky General Assembly, our legislature, was considering *outlawing* parimutuel horserace betting, a *staple of* the Kentucky *economy*. Needless to say, many people in Lexington were very concerned. So the Reverend Settle, concerned about the future of many of his parishioners, made some comments at dinner parties that eventually landed him on the floor of the General Assembly, where he argued against the legislation that would have outlawed the betting. And that *bill* was *defeated by one vote*.

Now horse people from across the country and around the world were very grateful because Reverend Settle had really saved their *livelihood* and so they asked him "What can we do for you?" They said: "We know. We'll buy you one of Henry Ford's finest new cars. You'll be able to go around in style to visit your people. And he said: "No, thanks. I'm a horse man. I don't really want a car." "Well," they said. "Well, how about, you know, a nice house to live in?" And he said: "I've already got a very nice house to live in – thank you very much – and moving is such a pain." They said: "Well, Reverend. We're so grateful for all that you have done for us but what can we do for you?" Then he said: "Well, I've got these plans for a church. I'd like you to help me build it." And so in 1923 men and women, Jew, Christian and Muslim, from all across the country and all over the world donated nearly 300,000 dollars, which in the 1920s was an awful lot of money – it would be worth millions of dollars today – to build this *parish*, and now we have what you see before us.'

Working with the text

I. Put these sentences into the correct order to reconstruct Michael Delk's story about the Episcopal Church in Lexington. Start with sentence d.

a. *Building began in 1924 and the church was finished in 1926.*

b. *Everybody agreed.*

c. *In the meantime Reverend Settle helped to stop a bill banning betting.*

d. *The Church bought some land on East Main Street.*

e. *Reverend Settle asked the people to help him build a church.*

f. *People were pleased with Reverend Settle's intervention.*

g. *They donated a lot of money.*

h. *They wanted to do him a favor.*

II. Answer the questions.

1. What did Reverend Settle argue against in the General Assembly?
2. Why were his parishioners so grateful?
3. How did the parishioners help Reverend Settle?
4. Should today's parishioners of the Episcopal Church in Lexington be grateful to Reverend Settle? If so, why?

III. Choose the correct ending to the sentence.

1. The word 'reverend' (line 8) is …
   a) a name. b) a title. c) a rank.
2. If you outlaw something (line 11), you …
   a) say something is legal.
   b) say something is illegal.
   c) say something is out of control.
3. A 'staple of the economy' (lines 11-12) is …
   a) an unstable part of the economy.
   b) an illegal element of the economy.
   c) an important section of the economy.
4. A 'bill' (line 16) is …
   a) a plan for a new law. b) some money. c) a silly idea.

IV. What do the underlined words mean? Replace them with a synonym or a word with a similar meaning.

1. We then moved a little bit closer to our <u>current</u> location … (line 5)
2. That's when we <u>purchased</u> this land here … (line 6)
3. … moving is such a <u>pain</u> … (line 25)
4. … and all over the world <u>donated</u> nearly 300,000 dollars … (line 29)

V. Say these words out loud.

1. to purchase
2. legislation
3. to outlaw
4. livelihood
5. parishioner
6. to donate

Exercises

I. Complete the sentences. Use the words in the box.

although ◆ despite ◆ even though ◆ eventually ◆ nevertheless ◆ so ◆ unless

1. You won't get in … you have a ticket.
2. The old system of queueing wasn't perfect but … it was preferable to the new one.
3. There was a long delay before the train … moved.
4. I'm a bit late … I'm going to take a cab.
5. We had a great holiday … the terrible weather.
6. They lost the game … they had played really well.
7. I like her … she can be very annoying sometimes.

II. Write down two things that ….

1. … you can save.
2. … you can make.
3. … you can do.
4. … you can raise.
5. … you can study.
6. … you can lose.

III. How would you describe them? Join the adjective (1-6) to its noun (a-f).

1. a delicious → d. meal
2. a handsome
3. a brilliant
4. glorious
5. devastating
6. an hilarious

a. weather
b. idea
c. news
d. meal
e. joke
f. man

IV. Which verb is missing? Choose the appropriate one from the box and put it in its correct form.

cater ◆ donate ◆ leave ◆ present ◆ provide ◆ supply

1. It gives me great pleasure to be able to … you with this painting.
2. Who … your business with the computer hardware?
3. His grandmother … over $10,000 to the old people's home.
4. This windmill … the whole village with electricity.
5. The company restaurant … for 2,000 people every day.
6. When I'm older I'm going to … all my books to the local hospital.

V. There's something wrong with this grid. The third column ('reasons') is mixed up. Can you put things in their proper places?

	Day	**Date**	**Reason**
1.	Martin Luther King Day	3rd Monday in January	marks the anniversary of the day when America is thought to have been discovered (1492)
2.	Presidents' Day	3rd Monday in February	honors all those who died in US wars
3.	Memorial Day	last Monday in May	celebrates American colonies' independence from Britain (1776)
4.	Independence Day	July 4	celebrates the birth of the civil-rights leader (1929)
5.	Columbus Day	2nd Monday in October	honors the veterans of US wars
6.	Veterans Day	11 November	celebrates the first Thanksgiving Day by the Pilgrims (1621)
7.	Thanksgiving	4th Thursday in November	celebrates the births of George Washington and Abraham Lincoln

Overview

to raise horses	Pferde züchten
to break a horse	ein Pferd zureiten
race track	Rennbahn
limestone base	Kalksteinuntergrund
to raise tobacco	Tabak anpflanzen
to give concealed weapons classes	Kurse für den Umgang mit nicht sichtbaren Waffen geben
caring	sozial denkend, engagiert
mourning dove	Trauertaube (*amerikanische Verwandte unserer Turteltaube*)
shepherd	Hirte
wood carvings	Holzschnitzereien
stained glass window	Buntglasfenster
parishioner	Gemeindemitglied

5A Josephine Abercrombie

stallion	Hengst
to breed	züchten
mare	Stute
to race a horse	ein Pferd bei einem Rennen starten lassen
a band of	Schar
brood mare	Zuchtstute
to thrive on	prächtig gedeihen durch, mit
to show horses	Pferde bei Veranstaltungen vorführen

5B Wesley Wittwer and Charles Northcutt

maintenance supervisor	Wartungskontrolleur

5C Michael Delk

enterprising	engagiert
command	Führung, Leitung
involved	engagiert
to outlaw	für ungesetzlich erklären
staple of economy	wichtigste wirtschaftliche Einnahmequelle
bill	Gesetzesvorlage
to defeat by one vote	mit einer Stimme Unterschied ablehnen
livelihood	Lebensunterhalt
parish	Gemeinde

South Carolina

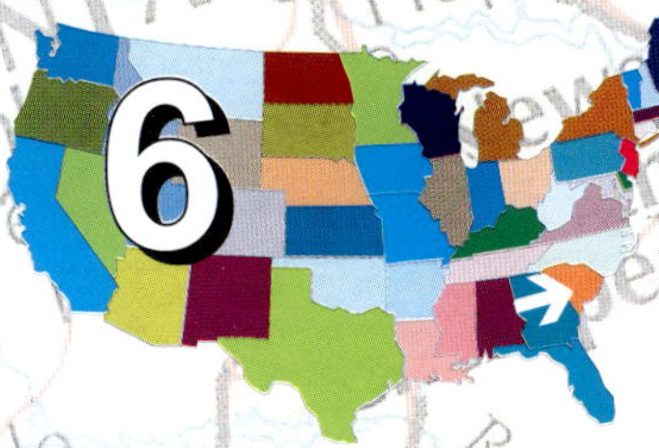

What do you know about South Carolina? Try this quiz and find out.
(The answers are at the bottom of the page.)

1. **Which ocean does South Carolina border?**
   a) the Atlantic Ocean b) the Indian Ocean c) the Pacific Ocean

2. **What is the climate in South Carolina like?**
   a) dry b) humid sub-tropical c) wet

3. **What is the racial/ethnic population distribution in South Carolina?**
   a) 69% Hispanic – 30% white – 1% black
   b) 69% white – 30% black – 1% Hispanic
   c) 69% black – 30% Hispanic – 1% white

4. **What is the main industrial activity in South Carolina?**
   a) aircraft b) electronics c) textiles

5. **Which European car manufacturer has part of its production in South Carolina?**
   a) BMW b) Fiat c) Renault

6. **Why is there a national monument at Fort Sumter in South Carolina?**
   a) It marks the site of the first battle of the American Civil War.
   b) It marks the site of the first Apollo mission to the moon.
   c) It marks the site where the first Olympics in the USA were held.

7. **What is a 'southern belle'?**
   a) a type of whiskey made in Georgia
   b) a beautiful woman from the US South
   c) a new kind of telephone

Answers: 1. a), 2. b), 3. b), 4. c), 5. a), 6. a), 7. b)

Overview

James E. Talley is the Mayor of Spartanburg. Spartanburg has a population of 46,000 including an increasing number of people from outside the US who have come to South Carolina to work for international companies. There is no doubt in the Mayor's mind how much his city has gained from having such a *diversified* community.

Ulrich Granz moved from Germany to South Carolina in May 1995. It has been a challenge for him to live and work abroad. Ulrich thinks the US is an exciting country and now, several years on, he's learned quite a lot more about the people, the language and the way of life in the States.

Robert M. Hitt works for BMW at their plant in Spartanburg. He talks to **Roland H. Windham, Jr.**, a government official, about the next stage of the company's expansion program. Robert is concerned about the *problems* the company may *encounter* with the interstate highway. If there was a crash on one of the exits outside the plant, for example, this would have a severe effect on production. Another important issue for BMW is the *deregulation* of the electric industry. BMW would like to know how much the state of South Carolina can help them to generate power as efficiently as possible.

Alduous Williams is a *process engineer* responsible for industrializing new products at the BMW *plant* in Greenville, South Carolina. Alduous enjoys working for a German company. He has found the German people helpful and cooperative. Alduous has been to Germany on many occasions and is taking German classes. Even his next door neighbor is German.

John Kincaid, Jr. is Director of Business Development in South Carolina for Duke Power Company. John talks about the history of the Duke Power Company. It started in 1904 building hydro-electric plants to generate electricity for the textile industry. In the meantime Duke Power has formed numerous partnerships with the communities where it operates. It has also been fortunate in areas like Spartanburg and Greenville where *community leadership* has made efforts to establish contacts internationally. Today Duke Power is the largest energy company in the United States. It is proud of the *surveys* which show it to be the No. 1 *utility* in the US from a customer satisfaction standpoint.

Find out more about ...

James E. Talley in 6A (pages 98 – 102)

Robert M. Hitt and Roland H. Windham, Jr. in 6B (pages 103 – 105)

Alduous Williams in 6C (pages 106 – 109)

6A James E. Talley

James E. Talley, Mayor of Spartanburg, talks about the foreign companies that have been attracted to *upstate* South Carolina in recent years. The people who have arrived in Spartanburg have had a positive effect on life in the city. James Talley has seen a much more diversified community develop. Would the Mayor and his colleagues mind if more people from abroad made Spartanburg their home?

'Oh, it wouldn't bother us not one bit because the contributions that have been made by people that come from the outside – we say from the outside but we call them *home citizens* now, they are almost like they're home-grown – but the contributions that have been made to our community, especially to the upstate, it's been tremendous. It's been one that … we've *flourished*, we've enjoyed the relationship, the partnership, and being able to travel from one country to another to see their hometowns and see how they live. And we can take the "they" out of it and call it "we" because it is a "we-type community", where the people here now just really enjoy being here. We enjoy everybody being here.'

What is the Mayor's function within South Carolina?

'Well, I'm the State President of the Municipal Association of the State of South Carolina. And in that we continue to lobby the state government for different aspects that *affect* different cities, and it deals largely with the cities of the State of South Carolina. And what happens there we have two conferences a year and we have *board meetings* every quarter. And there we have an opportunity to *share best practices*. In those best practices we get an opportunity to talk about what's good in our community, and what's good in other communities. And we kind of borrow from each other. Being the largest – one of the largest – cities in the State of South Carolina, and probably, without a doubt, the largest, I guess the largest city with the multi …, I guess we call it the multicultural diversity that we have here, we are able to share that with most people in South Carolina as to the progress that we make, and the benefits that we gain from having such a diversified community.'

Spartanburg

Working with the text

I. Answer these questions on the first part of the text.

1. Why does Spartanburg have such a diversified community?
2. What sort of people have come to the city?
3. How does the Mayor of Spartanburg react to the people from 'outside'?

II. Continue these sentences using the information in the second part of the text. Use your own words as far as possible.

1. The task of the Municipal Association is … .
2. At regular meetings people in the Municipal Association can … .
3. At these meetings the Mayor of Spartanburg is able to … .

III. Which word from the text means …

1. part of a state away from the main cities, especially the northern part?
2. to persuade a politician to do (or not to do) something?
3. a group of people in control of a company or organization?
4. an advantage?

IV. Replace the underlined words with a word of the same (or similar) meaning.

1. … it wouldn't <u>bother</u> us not one bit … (line 7)
2. … but the contributions that have been made to our community, <u>especially</u> to the upstate … (line 10)

3. … it deals largely with the cities of the state of South Carolina … (line 20)
4. … and we have board meetings every quarter … (line 22)

V. *What do the underlined words refer to in the text?*

1. … to see their hometowns and see how they live (line 13)
2. … We enjoy everybody being here … (line 15)
3. And there we have an opportunity … (line 22)
4. … we are able to share that … (line 28)

VI. *Say these words out loud.*

1. foreign
2. company
3. mayor
4. citizen

VII. *How has Ulrich Granz, a German in South Carolina, been treated in South Carolina?*

'I guess it's really true if they are talking here in this house about the southern hospitality, and the people are really very friendly. And we were really welcome when we arrived here in the US.'

VIII. *Try to remember the section of the film where Ulrich Granz is talking. What did you notice about the way his name was written on his overall?*

Residential Spartanburg

Exercises

I. Underline the correct expression in the brackets.

1. The meeting has had to be [cancelled/postponed/reorganized] until April 25.
2. Where are the [details/minutes/notes] of the last meeting?
3. We always let people have [an agenda/the discussion points/the diary] of the meeting in advance.
4. If there's a problem that we want to look at in more detail we usually form [a commission/a committee/a company].
5. Decisions do not have to be reached [as a group/together/unanimously].
6. The last proposal we voted on was quite close: there were five in favor, three against and two [abstentions/don't knows/not sures].

II. Complete the text. Use the verbs in the box in their correct form.

appoint ◆ elect ◆ nominate ◆ second ◆ speak ◆ vote for

At a formal business meeting there is usually no need … a chairperson. The reason is simple. The person in charge … in advance. At less formal meetings, a chairperson … by one of the participants at the meeting and another person … the suggestion. If there are two candidates then the one most people … will chair the meeting. Of course many meetings today are quite informal. In such cases it's obvious who … first.

III. There's something wrong with this agenda. Put everything in the right order.

AGENDA

9.00 – 12.00
Room 1018a
April 25, 2002

Sales Meeting (Teams 01, 02 and 03)

1. Any other business
2. Sales figures 2001
3. Retirement of James Blackley
4. Apologies for absence
5. Targets for 2003
6. Minutes of the last meeting

IV. What about you? Write a short comment (40-50 words) in English.

What's your experience of meetings? Have you found them useful? Or have you found them unproductive?

V. Hours and minutes.

☺ Where do people spend hours but take minutes?

☹ No idea. Where?

☺ At a meeting!

VI. Read about a famous actress and model from South Carolina. Which 15 words are missing from the text? Take a guess!

Andie MacDowell was … in Gaffney, South Carolina in 1958. She was the youngest of four daughters. When she was six her … divorced and depression drove her mother to alcoholism. 'My mother … when I was 23 but I believe she is still involved in my life. It was a huge loss for me because we had become very close. I am convinced that all the great things that happened in my … have come to me through her angelic (*engelhaft*) intercession (*Fürsprache, Vermittlung*).'

Although she left her home … for New York more than two decades ago, Andie MacDowell's southern accent still adds a certain panache (*Schwung, Elan*) to her speech. However, it wasn't always like that. After a successful career as a model MacDowell landed her first major … in GREYSTOKE: THE LEGEND OF TARZAN, LORD OF THE APES (1984). Her accent turned out to be the most problematic … of her performance. Her 'southern drawl' (*„schleppende" südliche Aussprache*) was felt to be too difficult for cinema audiences and in the end her … had to be dubbed (*synchronisieren*) over by Glenn Close. 'For a while many people had the opportunity to ridicule me,' recalls MacDowell, 'but I was more … than ever. I couldn't give up because of that!'

Soon Andie MacDowell had established herself as a serious … . Her talent blossomed with GREEN CARD and GROUNDHOG DAY and she hit a career high opposite Hugh Grant in FOUR WEDDINGS AND A FUNERAL. In 1996 MacDowell appeared in MULTIPLICITY, proving beyond a doubt her … for comic timing and for simultaneously projecting (*zeigen, zur Geltung bringen*) both intelligence and sex appeal.

Andie MacDowell lives on a ranch a long way from the US film industry. 'My life in Montana is so … from my Hollywood life that it even feels odd for me to go from one life to the other.' She has a son and two … . 'I want to be a great mother but sometimes I feel … at it because I don't do it all the time. I never feel like I do it as well as I could if I had all the time in the … .'

6B Robert M. Hitt and Roland H. Windham, Jr.

Robert M. Hitt, *Community Relations Manager* at BMW, talks to Roland H. Windham, a *county administrator*, about BMW's expansion program at Spartanburg. First the two men discuss the problem of waste water. Then Robert turns to another issue – the exit on the interstate highway outside the plant.

Roland: Well, that's a very good point. From the very beginning BMW has let the county know that it is very dependent on just-in-time delivery. And with the current exit ramps that we have off the interstate with your *suppliers* coming in and bringing supplies for the just-in-time delivery to manufacture the product. We want to have to look at that situation because if there's a *wreck* or some other accident on the interstate now, that blocks that one exit ramp because, you know, it could have a *critical impact* on your production schedule. And we don't want to be the cause of you not being able to *meet* your *production guidelines*.

Robert: Well, I will have …, we've got a consultant that is looking at that traffic flow for us. We now think we've got a *window* of about an hour and a half before we would have production interruption if there was an accident on the roadway and we lost *access*. So that's a pretty thin window if you think in terms of the future of all these people being employed, who could *be idled* by something as small as a traffic accident. So, *alternate* access to the plant is going to really become key for us as we get into the next century, and I appreciate your willingness to help us with it. The other thing that we are focused on is the deregulation of the electric industry. And as we go to a potential of multiple suppliers and having maybe even an increase in the amount of power we generate on the site. And we may need some help from the county again particularly dealing with the issues of water in order to accomplish the generation of the steam and so forth we need for drying. Do you see any problems in *covering* that area?

Roland: No, I really don't. I think the deregulation issue that you mentioned is going to be one that causes a great deal of conversation here in the future in the way it's going to impact BMW, is going to be significant, ever which way it goes. So, as county government, we're here to assist you in whatever you think is going to be the most efficient way for you to achieve power, to generate power, in order for you to continue to do the great things that you've been doing for the county.

Working with the text

I. Which is the correct ending to the sentence? Mark it.

1. In his discussion with the county official Robert mentions …
   a) two issues. b) three issues. c) four issues.
2. Why is Robert so concerned about the interstate highway?
   a) He drives to work every morning.
   b) Parts for the cars are delivered by road.
   c) BMW want to use it as a test track.
3. The county government is …
   a) not very happy to help BMW.
   b) quite happy to help BMW.
   c) perfectly happy to help BMW.

II. Complete these sentences using the information in the text.

1. If there was a crash on the exit ramp …
2. If there was an interruption in delivery …
3. An ideal solution for BMW would be …

III. Answer these questions.

1. Why do BMW need so much electricity in their plant?
2. Why does the company need to generate steam?

IV. Replace the underlined words with a word of the same (or similar meaning).

1. … it could have a critical <u>impact</u> on your production schedule … (line 11)
2. … people being employed, who could be <u>idled</u> by something … (line 18)
3. … alternate access to the <u>plant</u> is going to really become <u>key</u> for us … (lines 19-20)

V. Explain the meaning of these sentences. Use your own words.

1. … it could have a critical impact on your production schedule … (lines 11-12)
2. We now think we've got a window of about an hour and a half before we would have production interruption … (lines 15-16)
3. … the deregulation issue that you mentioned is going to be one that causes a great deal of conversation here in the future … (lines 28-29)

VI. What do you think?

1. What is the advantage for BMW of having just-in-time delivery?
2. Why is the county official so helpful?

Exercises

I. Look at this exchange. What other words could the speakers have used?

A: Would you mind if I closed the door?

B: No, not at all.

II. Look at the underlined word in this exchange. What sort of verb form is it?

A: Would it be OK if I <u>rang</u> you after ten tonight?

B: That's fine.

III. Rewrite these sentences. Using a 'have + noun' construction instead of the underlined verb. (You will need to make other small changes to your sentences.)

1. The two men <u>chatted</u> about the company's expansion program.
2. They <u>discussed</u> just-in-time delivery.
3. They agreed to <u>look at</u> the transport situation very carefully.
4. They both know the exit ramp could <u>affect</u> production quite critically.
5. They need to <u>increase</u> the amount of power that is generated.
6. They also <u>thought</u> about what to do with the waste water produced at the plant.

IV. Rewrite these sentences using a passive construction of the underlined verb.

1. People <u>produce</u> the new cars in Spartanburg and Greenville.
2. Someone <u>is going to build</u> a new interstate exit near the plant.
3. They <u>have to generate</u> more electricity.
4. We <u>have invited</u> a party of new employees to visit our factories in Germany.
5. High production costs at home <u>are forcing</u> the company to move to the US.
6. The government <u>will renew</u> your work permit if you are in full employment.

V. 'PC' stands for political correctness – using language that will not offend a particular group of people. Which expression in the brackets is PC?

1. What is the role of the [chairman/chairperson]?
2. If he got six F's on his report card, he must be [dumb/an underachiever]!
3. What do you know about [the Native Americans/the Indians]?
4. She works as [a stewardess/a flight attendant] for Air Canada.
5. The firm [is getting rid of half of its workforce/has been forced to downsize].
6. It was [difficult/challenging] but I sort of enjoyed it.

6C Alduous Williams

Alduous Williams is a process engineer responsible for industrializing new products at BMW's plant in Greenville, South Carolina.

Interviewer: What was the motivation to come to a plant like BMW and start to work here?

Alduous: OK. Previous to this I worked for a French company that builds tires in the area. That didn't exactly *float my boat*. So I wanted to come to a product that ah … I'm a mechanical engineer, I wanted to work in a project, a product, that more fit my education and my personal goals. And BMW builds one of the best mechanical products that exist.

Interviewer: And how do you feel now about working hand in hand in America with German people here in the plant?

Alduous: Actually, I've really enjoyed it so far. I found the German people to be very *straightforward* and *forthcoming* with information, very free and open with information and willing to teach and help us grow as a plant.

Interviewer: I noticed before you said something in German. Have you spent time in Germany or have you learned German here or how did that come about?

Alduous: OK, I've probably been to Germany, I think, approximately eight times. I've travelled to Munich, Regensburg and Dingolfing. But I've also been taking lessons here. I want to grow as an individual.

Interviewer: OK. Excellent. And as far as cultural exchange is concerned, these people not only work here but they also live here and have their families here. Is there any *interaction* on that level?

Alduous: Actually, there is. It turns out my next door neighbor is German. But he doesn't work for BMW. He works for another company here locally. And we interact quite often. We work on our German together. Likewise we often have social functions where we all go out as a team inside the plant. Er … we had one a couple of weeks ago, we had a potluck, where we all brought dishes from our ethnic and/or national origins to share and experience that together.

The windshield is carefully positioned

Working with the text

I. *Answer the questions. Use complete sentences.*

1. Why did Alduous apply for a job with BMW?
2. What impression of German people does Alduous have?
3. How can we see that Alduous wants to improve his German?
4. What sort of contact does Alduous have with Germans outside his place of work?

II. *Mark the best ending for the sentence.*

1. If something 'floats your boat' (line 6) it means …
   a) you find it difficult. b) you find it silly. c) you find it interesting.
2. If somebody is 'straightforward' (line 14) they …
   a) use simple words.
   b) are open and honest.
   c) work quickly and efficiently.
3. If you 'interact' (line 29) with somebody, you …
   a) talk to them.
   b) perform on stage with them.
   c) go on business trips with them.

4. If you ‘have a potluck’ (line 32) with people, you …
   a) play board games with them.
   b) bring your own food to share with them.
   c) show photographs of your home country to them.

III. Replace the underlined words with words of the same (or similar) meaning.

1. … I wanted to work in a project, a product, that more fit my education … (line 8)
2. … I’ve probably been to Germany, I think, approximately eight times … (line 20)
3. It turns out my next door neighbor is German … (line 27)
4. … we had a potluck, where we all brought dishes from … (line 33)

IV. What do you think?

1. Why has Alduous been to Munich, Regensburg and Dingolfing and not to other places in Germany?
2. Could you imagine living and working in Greenville?

Exercises

I. Which of the expressions in the box do you use to say hello? Which do you use when you want to say goodbye?

Catch you later! ◆ Take care! ◆ Hi there! ◆ See you! ◆ How you doing? ◆ How’s it going? ◆ Long time, no see! ◆ So long!

‘hello’	**‘goodbye’**

II. What is an idiom?

An idiom is a fixed expression but its meaning is not usually clear from the individual words. The expression ‘to float your boat’, for example, has nothing to do with boats. If you are not sure what an idiom means or whether it can be used in a certain situation, don’t use it!

III. Here are some idioms (1-6). Link them to their explanations (a-f).

1. Let's get down to the nitty gritty.
2. I'm keeping a low profile.
3. It was a piece of cake.
4. He's over the moon.
5. I can't get a word in edgeways.
6. I'm going to have forty winks.

a. He's delighted.
b. I'm going to sleep for a short time.
c. There's no chance for me to say something.
d. Let's look at the details.
e. It was easy.
f. I'm making sure nobody notices me.

IV. Which idiom comes next? Choose one from exercise III.

1. I'm so tired. I think … .
2. The test? Oh, that! I finished it in five minutes. … !
3. We've talked about the problem in a general way. … .
4. Did you hear? He got the job! … !

V. Studying at college. Match the English (1-8) with their German equivalents (a-h).

1. Dentistry
2. Precision Engineering
3. Information Technology
4. Business Management
5. Economic History
6. Electrical Engineering
7. History of Art
8. Mechanical Engineering

a. Informatik
b. Betriebswirtschaft
c. Zahnmedizin
d. Maschinenbau
e. Kunstgeschichte
f. Feinwerktechnik
g. Wirtschaftsgeschichte
h. Elektrotechnik

VI. What does Alduous mean? What 'purchase' is he talking about? Find out!

'No. I'm from Natchitoches, Louisiana. The oldest settlement of Louisiana Purchase. I have been here about five years, previous of this I was in Cincinnati, Ohio. And I worked for GE Aircraft Engines.'

Overview

diversified	verschieden(artig)
to encounter a problem	auf ein Problem stoßen
deregulation	Wettbewerbsfreiheit
process engineer	Verfahrenstechniker
plant	Werk
community leadership	die Führungsspitze der Gemeindeverwaltung
survey	Untersuchung, Umfrage
utility	Versorgungsbetrieb

6A James E. Talley

upstate	im Norden des Bundesstaates
home citizen	Einheimischer
to flourish	blühen, gedeihen
to affect	sich auswirken auf
board meeting	*eine Art Vorstandssitzung oder Beiratssitzung*
to share best practices	Erfahrungen austauschen

6B Robert M. Hitt and Roland H. Windham, Jr.

community relations manager	*Referent mit Zuständigkeit für die Beziehungen zwischen dem Unternehmen und der Gemeinde*
county administrator	Bezirksverwalter
supplier	Zulieferer
wreck	Unfallwagen
critical impact	starke Beeinträchtigung
to meet production guidelines	den Produktionsvorgaben entsprechen
window	(Zeit-)Fenster
access	Zugang
to be idled	zur Untätigkeit gezwungen sein
alternate	alternativ
to cover	*im Sinne von: eine Lösung finden*

6C Alduous Williams

This doesn't float my boat.	Das reißt mich nicht vom Hocker.
straightforward	aufrichtig, ehrlich
forthcoming	mitteilsam
interaction	Austausch

Georgia

What do you know about Georgia? Try this quiz and find out.
(The answers are at the bottom of the page.)

1. **How long has Georgia been part of the United States?**
   a) since 1789 b) since 1844 c) since 1888

2. **Which is the capital of Georgia?**
   a) Austin b) Atlanta c) Albany

3. **What percentage of the population in Georgia are black?**
   a) 7% b) 27% c) 47%

4. **At the end of the Civil War the US constitution was changed. In what way?**
   a) Slavery was abolished.
   b) Women could vote.
   c) Alcohol was banned.

5. **Which famous book takes place against the background of the American Civil War?**
   a) The Old Man and the Sea
   b) The Color Purple
   c) Gone with the Wind

6. **What did Martin Luther King say in 1963?**
   a) 'Ask not what your country can do for you but what you can do for your country.'
   b) 'Free at last! Free at last! Thank God Almighty, we are free at last!'
   c) 'It's one small step for a man. It's one giant leap for mankind.'

7. **James Brown, Gladys Knight and Otis Redding are all from Georgia. What are they famous for?**
   a) their politics b) their music c) their poetry

Answers: 1. a), 2. b), 3. b), 4. a), 5. c), 6. b), 7. b)

Overview

Jonathan Mann and **Raissa Vassileva** both work for CNN International in Atlanta. Jonathan talks mainly about Atlanta, the future of the city and the people who live there. Raissa tells us more about herself – about how she came to the USA from Bulgaria and how, months after getting her *anchoring job* with CNN, she began to realize how much she needed to *adapt* in a country so far away from home.

Major Vida Longmire is a Military Police Officer in the United States Army. She works at Forces Command in Atlanta. At present she does administrative duties supporting the MP units within the United States. We see Major Longmire in various *everyday encounters* – talking to colleagues, borrowing a book from the library and working out in the gym.

Pastor Joseph L. Roberts, Jr. is pastor of a famous church – Ebenezer Baptist Church in Alabama. This is the church that Martin Luther King *pastored* with his father from 1960 to 1968. Pastor Roberts talks about Dr. King, his struggle against *segregation*, his policy of non-violence and his belief in educational opportunities.

Annette Winn-Miles is the *Aviation* Design and Construction Manager at Hartsfield International Airport, Atlanta. Annette's responsibilities include managing the construction projects at the airport. One of the projects she has been working on recently is designing new office space for the police department at the airport.

Robert Weinberger works at Stone Mountain Park. The park is a memorial to the southern states which fought in the American Civil War. The huge carvings on the mountain show Jefferson Davis, President of the Confederate States of America, General Robert E. Lee, one of the South's most beloved leaders, and General Stonewall Jackson. Robert is the Museum Director at the Park. The museum shows the history of the mountain and the carvings and what life in Georgia was like before the outbreak of the Civil War in 1861.

Find out more about …

Jonathan Mann and Raissa Vassileva in **7A** (page 114 – 117)

Major Vida Longmire in **7B** (page 118 – 121)

Pastor Joseph L. Roberts, Jr. in **7C** (page 122 – 125)

7A Jonathan Mann and Raissa Vassileva

Jonathan Mann and Raissa Vassileva work for CNN International in Atlanta. First Jonathan talks about life in Atlanta.

'Atlanta is a city that is rebuilding itself and that hasn't quite placed itself with its history. This is a part of the world that is probably most famous for slavery and for segregation, and that really only moved out of that a very recent … a recent time ago. Atlanta really hasn't decided how it feels about all of that. It doesn't have a clear conscience, and so this is a city that doesn't want to contemplate questions about the past. It wants to plan for the future. There's enormous amounts of construction, there's enormous amounts of growth, there's enormous amounts of change, there's enormous amounts of immigration, and we're examples of that. We work in a hi-tech company, on a hi-tech product that's global, and we don't really think about what's been here before us, and we don't really think much about the people who are around us, who are from here. Atlanta is a place where people are looking out more than they're looking in, and they're looking forward more than they're looking past.'

Raissa Vassileva goes on to describe how she got a job with CNN International.

'I was working for a show on CNN called "World Report". I was doing stories about Bulgaria in English for this show and CNN got to know my work through that. I came for a *professional program* at CNN and CNN *put me on the air* as an experiment to anchor the show. I went back to Bulgaria, Bulgarian TV made me an anchor and a year later I got a phone call from CNN and they said, "We're building this new international network, CNN International. Are you interested in *trying out for* an anchoring position?" I said, "Of course," and so I arrived here six-and-a-half years ago, and that's how I started working here.'

Working with the text

I. Look at Jonathan Mann's part of the text. Answer the questions.

1. In Jonathan's opinion Atlanta has been trying to deal with a problem. What problem is he talking about?
2. Does he think Atlanta has handled the problem well so far?
3. How do you know that Jonathan is not from Georgia?

II. Further questions on Jonathan Mann's part of the text. Answer them.

1. What does Jonathan mean when he says there is 'enormous amounts of construction' in Atlanta? (lines 8-9)
2. What does the expression 'hi-tech' mean? (line 11) Can you give some examples of a hi-tech industry?
3. Jonathan says that 'people are looking out more than they're looking in'. (lines 14-15) What do you understand by this expression?

III. What do the underlined words in the text refer to?

1. Atlanta really hasn't decided how it feels about all of <u>that</u>. (line 6)
2. … and we're examples of <u>that</u>. (line 11)
3. … we don't really think about what's been here before <u>us</u>. (line 12)
4. … <u>they</u>'re looking forward more than they're looking past. (line 15)

IV. Look at Raissa Vassileva's part of the text. Find the sentences which show that she …

1. … began working in English early in her career.
2. … has worked for more than one TV station.
3. … doesn't mind taking risks.
4. … has been successful at CNN International.

V. Complete these sentences. Use your own words.

1. To 'do stories' for a TV station means …
2. If you 'anchor a show' you …
3. To 'put somebody on the air' means …
4. If you 'try out' for a position then you …

VI. Say these words out loud.

1. slavery	3. hi-tech	5. anchor
2. immigration	4. conscience	6. Bulgaria

VII. What's the difference, if any, between the following?

1. 'conscience' and 'conscious'?
2. 'immigration' and 'emigration'?
3. 'enormous' and 'huge'?
4. 'program' and 'programme'?

VIII. What do you think? Discuss these questions.

1. What does 'segregation' mean in the context of the USA?
2. Jonathan Mann says: 'We don't really think much about the people who are around us, who are from here.' How do you feel about this statement?

Exercises

I. *Complete the sentences. Use the correct preposition and the gerund form of the verb in brackets.*

1. She was interested … (try) out for an anchoring position.
2. There are plenty of ways … (get) work in Atlanta.
3. He's proud … (work) for CNN International.
4. Many people in Georgia are afraid … (talk) too much about the past.
5. The city has succeeded … (rebuild) itself.
6. Thank you … (take) the time to speak to us.

II. *Say these acronyms and abbreviations out loud. What do they stand for? Choose the full form from the list (a-f).*

1. NBC	a. Federal Bureau of Investigation
2. WHO	b. North Atlantic Treaty Organization
3. NATO	c. Cable News Network
4. UN	d. National Broadcasting Company
5. FBI	e. World Health Organization
6. CNN	f. United Nations

III. *These words are all to do with the news on television. Link the right-hand column with the left-hand column to form six complete sentences.*

1. Breaking news	a. is news about political events happening around the world.
2. Current affairs	b. is a machine which shows the newsreader the words to read.
3. The headlines	c. is a person who presents a TV or radio broadcast.
4. A teleprompt	d. are the main news stories in a few short sentences.
5. A newsflash	e. is a dramatic story which is happening at the moment it's shown.
6. An anchorman	f. is a short piece of very important news.

IV. *Who says this? About whom? Do you agree?*

'I think she is an enormously brave person, an enormously clever one, I'll be very honest. It's easy for me, coming from Canada, which is a sister culture to that of the United States, but this is a woman who came from a country which is as different from this one as any one can be. She doesn't work in her native language.'

V. Complete this text about one of America's most influential television executives (of the late 20th century). Use the correct form of the words in brackets.

Robert Edward Turner … (educate) at Georgia Military Academy and Brown University. After his father committed suicide in 1963, Turner … (inherit) the family billboard-advertising business.

In 1970 Turner … (buy) a failing television station in Atlanta but by 1975 he … (transform) it into a 'superstation' by … (transmit) low-cost sports and entertainment programs via satellite to cable systems throughout the US. In the next two years Turner … (take) control of two sports teams: the Atlanta Braves (baseball) and the Atlanta Hawks (basketball).

In 1980 Turner … (launch) Cable News Network (CNN), the first 24-hour television news station. Its live coverage of fast-breaking news (*Eilmeldungen*) around the world helped it … (become) a highly respected news organization and it eventually … (achieve) a global viewership. In 1985 Turner purchased MGM/UA Entertainment Company, which owned the Metro-Goldwyn-Mayer (MGM) and United Artists (UA) film studios. Within months, however, Turner … (sell) most of the company, but not without … (retain) MGM's massive library of films, … (include) such classics as GONE WITH THE WIND and THE WIZARD OF OZ. Many of the movies … (show) on Turner Network Television (TNT), which … (launch) in 1988.

In 1996, in a deal … (value) at $7.6 billion, entertainment giant Time Warner … (acquire) Turner Broadcasting System (TBS), the parent company for all of Turner's businesses. The … (acquire) made Time Warner the world's largest media and entertainment company. Turner … (become) vice chairman of Time Warner's board of directors with special … (responsible) for the division … (contain) TBS businesses.

In 1997 Turner pledged (*versprechen, zusichern*) to make a $1 billion … (donate) to the United Nations (UN), one of the largest single charitable acts in history. He designated (*festlegen, bestimmen*) the money for UN … (humane) causes.

7B Major Vida Longmire

Major Vida Longmire is a military police officer in the United States Army. She works at Forces Command in Atlanta. At present she carries out administrative work to support the MP units within the United States.

After getting some information on *emissions testing* from her colleague Sergeant Bender, Major Vida Longmire goes to the library. First she returns some books. Then she asks about something which she would like to borrow.

Major Longmire: There was another book that I was really interested in also. I was wondering if you had the … a book called 'The Lawyers'.
Librarian: Oh yeah, but we have a waiting list for that so you have to fill out this little form and … there's a form right down there in the plastic holder.
Major Longmire: OK.
Librarian: If you want to fill that out. Or there's one right down there in that plastic holder.
Major Longmire: OK. And I just fill out this information and wait for the book to be returned?
Librarian: Yes, and I'll call you whenever it comes in for you.
Major Longmire: OK.

Finally, Major Longmire goes to the gym where she speaks to Maurice, an instructor.

Major Longmire: Oh, hi Maurice!
Instructor: How are you?
Major Longmire: Good. How are you?
Instructor: How is your program going today?
Major Longmire: Oh, it's working really well. I think that I have a *PT test* coming up this week and I think the program you designed for my *abs* and my upper body is going to work out really well. I think I'm going to *score* really *high*.
Instructor: That's good. All right.
Major Longmire: You've been working hard?
Instructor: I sure have.
Major Longmire: Good. Good.
Instructor: I do my best. You look *in shape*.
Major Longmire: Well, thank you.
Instructor: You look ready for this PT test.
Major Longmire: I've been *sticking with it*. I've been working out about four days a week, four to five days a week.
Instructor: All right.

Asking about a book

Working with the text

I. Mark the correct ending to the sentence.

1. Major Longmire …
   a) seems bored with her job.
   b) obviously enjoys her work.
   c) cannot speak about herself and her responsibilities.
2. Being in the military police means that Major Longmire …
   a) has many opportunities to do sports and other leisure activities.
   b) can't have a life outside her job.
   c) has to be with military people all day.
3. In this sequence Major Longmire seems to know …
   a) the librarian better than the instructor.
   b) the instructor better than the librarian.
   c) the instructor as well as the librarian.

II. Answer the questions. Use complete sentences.

1. Why does Major Longmire go to the library? What problem is there?
2. In her conversation with the instructor Major Longmire says she's going to 'score really high'. What does she mean?

III. *Locate these expressions in the text. Say what the speaker means.*

1. 'If you want to fill that out … '
2. 'I do my best … '
3. 'You look in shape … '
4. 'I've been sticking with it …'

IV. *Which part of the text does the underlined word refer to?*

1. You want to fill <u>that</u> out … (line 13)
2. I'll call you whenever <u>it</u> comes in for you … (line 17)
3. … <u>it</u>'s working really well … (line 25)
4. <u>You</u> look in shape … (line 33)

V. *Say these words out loud.*

1. colleague
2. sergeant
3. library
4. gym

VI. *What do you think? Give some reasons for your answers.*

1. From the way they talk to each other do you think Major Longmire knows Maurice very well?
2. Is looking good and being fit important for a lot of people in the US?

Exercises

I. *Rewrite these sentences. Start with 'This is … ' and end the sentences with a preposition.*

Example: I'm interested in this book. This is the book I'm interested in.

1. I'm interested in this film.
2. She spoke to this man.
3. We were waiting for this fax.
4. They looked at this picture.
5. She trained with this team.
6. You said hello to this woman.

II. *Make these questions sound more polite. Start with 'I was wondering … '.*

1. Do you have the book 'Gone with the Wind'?
2. Can I get some information on emissions testing here?
3. Do you sell newspapers?
4. When does the library close on Saturday?
5. Do you need some help?
6. How does this running machine work?

III. Put in the correct form of 'borrow' or 'lend'.

1. Would you mind … me your notebook for a day?
2. I was wondering if I could … your car next week?
3. Do you know why I don't … people my books? I never get them back!
4. Hey! Who … my umbrella without asking? Was it you?

IV. Complete the mini-dialogues. Add 'will' and choose a verb from the box.

borrow ◆ help ◆ lend ◆ open ◆ see ◆ wait ◆ watch

1. It's hot in here.	– OK. I … a window.
2. Where's my English book.	– Here you are. I … you mine.
3. Bye! Have a nice time!	– Bye. I … you later!
4. This exercise is quite difficult, isn't it?	– Don't worry. I … you.

V. Present perfect simple or present perfect continuous? Complete the sentences using the correct form of the verb in brackets.

1. He … (write) three letters today.
2. He … (write) letters all morning.
3. I'm losing my voice because I … (talk) all afternoon.
4. They're coming to the meeting. I … (tell) them when it is.
5. I … (never, cycle) down a mountain. Have you?
6. I need to sit down. I … (cycle) all day.
7. He … (repair) his motorbike and now it works properly.
8. He … (repair) his motorbike so I don't know if he can visit us later.

VI. Cross out the wrong word in each pair of brackets.

1. We walked up and up and [perhaps/eventually] we came to the top.
2. Do you know the chemical [formula/form] for carbon monoxide?
3. You [mustn't/don't have to] walk over the railway lines! It's dangerous!
4. Can I borrow your [handy/mobile] to make a quick call?

7C Pastor Joseph L. Roberts, Jr.

Joseph L. Roberts, Jr. has been pastor of Ebenezer Baptist Church in Alabama since 1975. Why is his church so famous?

'Of course, a number of people know that this was the church that Martin Luther King pastored with his father from 1960 to 1968, and it has had a history that goes back some 113 years, just after the *period of Reconstruction* in the United States of America. I think this church has been *noted* because of the bravery of Dr. King, and that kind of brave action is to be seen in the fact that he started in Montgomery, Alabama to try to break down the walls of segregation in transportation, and he was successful in doing that without any guns, without any violence. And the method of social change which he *advocated* was one that *called upon* us to *appeal to* the conscience of people, realizing that there is in everybody the desire to do good, and once you appeal to conscience and *decency*, he thought this nation would change.

Did Martin Luther King think education was important? Pastor Joseph L. Roberts explains.

'He was one who thoroughly believed in educational opportunities and was well educated himself. He thought that education should always *spill over into* some action that helped people. He was a *peace advocate*. But I think Dr. King has always been concerned about the fact that we must make sure that religious expression is allowed, even if one does not agree with it, because if you stand against that, then you're not ever going to be able to have a land of freedom and a land of justice. So this church has always stood for religious freedom, for the integrity of the individual and the *sacredness* of human personality and for the right for people to stand for what they believe in without guns, and realize that, in the final analysis, it is conscience that shall win and not military arms.'

Working with the text

I. Answer the questions on the text. Use your own words as far as possible.

1. Why is Joseph Roberts's church so famous?
2. What important event happened in Montgomery, Alabama?
3. How did Martin Luther King think that social change would come about in the USA?
4. Why was the freedom of religious expression so important for Martin Luther King?

II. What do the underlined words in the text refer to?

1. … and it has had a history that goes back some 113 years (line 4)
2. … and he was successful in doing that without any guns (line 9)
3. … even if one does not agree with it (line 20)

III. Find the word in the text which means …

1. separating one group of people from another
2. the awareness of what is right or wrong in your own thoughts and actions
3. being respectable and polite
4. something that is holy and highly respected

IV. Find out more.

1. Joseph Roberts says that Martin Luther King 'brought about a revolution in this country'. What was that revolution exactly?
2. What happened to Martin Luther King in 1968?

Exercises

I. Complete the sentences. Use the words from the box.

conscience ◆ decency ◆ integrity ◆ sacred ◆ segregation

1. You could have the … to apologize for what you did.
2. I lied to him and I shouldn't have. I've got a terribly guilty … now.
3. In how many countries around the world is there still a policy of racial … ?
4. This is a … place so you can't take photographs or talk loudly.
5. She is a woman of the highest … . That's why she was given the job.

II. Complete this text using the correct forms of the words in brackets.

Martin Luther King … (be born) in 1929 in Atlanta, Georgia. Although his father … (be) a banker and the family … (have) a comfortable life, the young Martin … (meet) racism every day. He … (can, not, use) certain buses, he … (not, allowed) to go into certain shops and if he … (go) into the cinema, he … (must) sit upstairs. Once Martin Luther King … (tell) a story about a policeman who … (stop) his father while he … (drive). 'Let me see you driver's license, boy,' the police officer … (ask). Father King … (point) at his son. 'That's a boy,' he … (say). 'I'm a man.' Martin's father … (hate) the laws of … (segregate). 'It's no good … (accept) the system,' he … (explain). 'I'm never going to accept it. I'll fight it until I … (die)!'. Young Martin … (never, forget) his father's words.

III. What happened in Montgomery, Alabama? Put the seven sentences (a-g) into the correct order (1-7) to find out.

a. *When a white man ordered her to give up her seat and move to the back of the bus, she refused.*

b. *On December 1, 1955 a young black woman called Rosa Parks had gotten on a bus in Montgomery, Alabama.*

c. *The black civil-rights movement had begun.*

d. *A group of black activists decided to boycott the Montgomery bus company. They chose Martin Luther King as their leader.*

e. *Feeling tired after a long day's work, she decided to sit down at the front of the bus.*

f. *The driver called a policeman and Rosa Parks was arrested for breaking the city's segregation law.*

g. *The boycott began on December 5, 1955 and continued for 382 days. On December 21, 1956 Montgomery's busses became desegregated.*

Martin Luther King

IV. *Read part of a speech Martin Luther King made in Washington, DC in August 1963. Did his dream come true? In what way was the US constitution changed in 1964? (If you don't know, try and find out.)*

'I have a dream that one day on the red hills of Georgia, the sons of former slaves and the sons of former slave owners will be able to sit down together at the same table. I have a dream that my four little children will one day live in a nation where they will not be judged by the color of their skin, but by the content of their character.'

V. *These two young people have just visited the Martin Luther King Center. What did they think of it?*

Young black man: *I'm from New York, you know. My name is David. I feel like the Martin Luther King Center has a very major purpose, you know. It's like ... not many things are done for the African-American community, so as far as this is going on, it's like giving back to the community, and it's highly appreciated. I mean, anything that is done wholeheartedly you can awesomely respect. Period. Thank you very much.*

Young black woman: *I thought it was very emotionally moving. Some of the stuff that I learned in the Center today was stuff that I hadn't been taught in school. So it was just a nice learning experience, I think it's something that I think each black person needs to see. You know you hear about it, you see it, you see the speech, but, you know, it's a different thing when you come here and you actually see it for yourself, you see his home and everything, so it was a nice experience.*

Overview

anchorman, anchorwoman	Nachrichtenmoderator(in)
to have an anchoring job	als Nachrichtenmoderator(in) arbeiten
to adapt	sich einleben
everyday encounters	Alltagssituationen
to pastor	als Pastor/Prediger tätig sein
segregation	Rassentrennung
aviation	Luftfahrt

7A Jonathan Mann and Raissa Vassileva

professional program	Studioproduktion
to put sb on the air	jmdn. (im Fernsehen oder Hörfunk) auftreten lassen, auf Sendung gehen lassen
to try out for sth	sich um etw. bemühen, bewerben

7B Major Vida Longmire

emissions testing	Emissionstest (von Abgasen)
PT (Physical Training) test	Fitness-Test
abs	Bauchmuskeln
to score high	viele Punkte machen
to be in good/bad shape	in Form/nicht in Form sein
to stick with sth	bei etw. bleiben

7C Pastor Joseph L. Roberts, Jr.

period of Reconstruction	Zeit des Wiederaufbaus nach 1865
to be noted	berühmt, bekannt sein
to advocate	eintreten für, befürworten
to call upon sb	jmdn. aufrufen, zurufen
to appeal to	appellieren an
decency	Anstand
to spill over into	sich ausbreiten auf
peace advocate	Anwalt des Friedens
sacredness	Heiligkeit, Unantastbarkeit

Florida

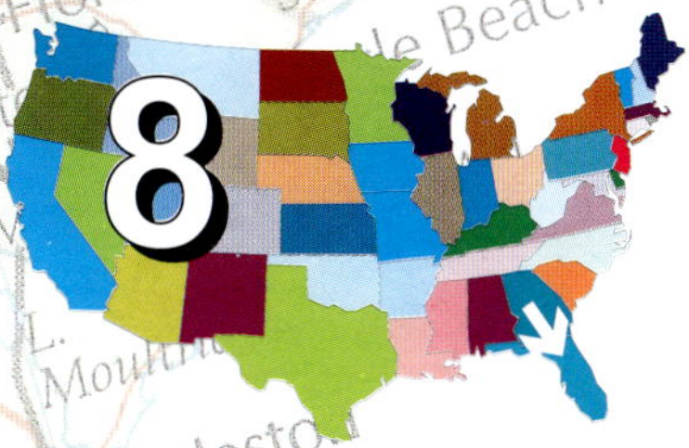

What do you know about Florida? Try this quiz and find out.
(The answers are at the bottom of the page.)

1. **What is the average annual temperature in Miami?**
   a) 12° C b) 24° C c) 32° C

2. **Which are tourist attractions in Florida?**
   a) the Statue of Liberty and Niagara Falls
   b) Kennedy Space Center and Disney World
   c) the Golden Gate Bridge and Disneyland

3. **What is the 'Everglades'?**
   a) a national park b) an expensive hotel c) a famous pop group

4. **'Spring Break' takes place every year at Daytona Beach, Florida. What is it?**
   a) a cheap holiday for elderly people from New York
   b) a waterskiing competition for Floridians
   c) a party for US college students

5. **What sort of people are 'Hispanics'?**
   a) people from Spain
   b) people from countries in Latin America where Spanish is spoken
   c) people who speak Spanish

6. **By how much did Florida's population increase between 1950 and 1970?**
   a) by 14% b) by 45% c) by 145%

7. **What percentage of Miami's population are Cuban-Americans?**
   a) 62% b) 36% c) 16%

Answers: 1. b), 2. b), 3. a), 4. c), 5. b), 6. c), 7. a)

Overview

William Schwartz is a lieutenant in the Miami Police Department. The Department *runs* a *law enforcement operation* based on preventive community *policing* with particular emphasis on trying to get *young people at risk* involved in social activities. Policing in Miami takes place at a personal level. Police officers take responsibility for the neighborhoods that they patrol and make sure that, as far as possible, any *problem* they encounter is *tackled* at an individual level.

One of the officers in the Miami Police Department is **Tommy Sardiña**. Tommy works beats, which means he has special responsibility for a specific area in the city. Tommy explains what his work involves and we see him answering emergency calls, talking to local people and dealing with their problems.

Pablo Canton is the administrator for the Neighborhood *Enhancement* Team (NET) in East Little Havana, an area of Miami. Pablo's job involves trying to solve problems in the community: problems with *garbage*, with public works, with *vagrants* and with the police, for example. Pablo feels NET has made a lot of progress in recent years but he knows there is still a lot to do. One of the projects he is working on at the moment is to instruct local residents, many of whom come from countries in Central America, about the laws in the US.

Anne Davis manages a center for senior citizens in Miami. The center has been in existence since August 1970. At that time the senior citizens' program was only available in the mornings as teenagers used the center in the afternoons. Now the elderly people have the center to themselves every day. Anne runs various programs, including arts and crafts, ceramics, meals, trips, parties and any other recreational activities. Anne thinks it's very important for elderly people to get out of the house and to share their problems with others.

Tom and Barbara Dwyer run a fruit plantation in Miami called Knollwood *Groves*. The farm has been designed for young people. It specializes in citrus fruits but there are also animals – including alligators and *racoons* – a simulated Indian village and a shop where people can buy marmalades and candies made from home-grown produce.

Find out more about ...

William Schwartz in	**8A**	(pages 130 – 133)
Pablo Canton in	**8B**	(pages 134 – 138)
Tom and Barbara Dwyer in	**8C**	(pages 139 – 141)

8A William Schwartz

Does Lieutenant Schwartz enjoy living in Miami?

'As soon as I got here, soon as I got off the plane, as soon as I put my foot on the ground here, I said: "I'm home. This is it. This is where I want to be." I saw the palm trees, I saw the Deco Architecture, I saw blue water, the beaches, and more importantly, I saw the people. There was just such a variety of folks here from all over the world. This truly is the southern melting pot of the United States. And it's a microcosm of the whole world. It's a very, very exciting, dynamic place. You know, many, many people are confused when they think of Miami, they think "Miami Vice". Well, as much as I'd like to say that I live on a houseboat and I have got a crocodile for a pet and I have ten million women chasing me, I have to say that my life is just *a tad* different than that – well, maybe I have the women, I'm not sure!'

What's special about the Miami Police Department?

'It is a very progressive law enforcement operation. We have a chief of police that's just always thinking of new things. We're on the cutting edge of preventive community policing. We have sports programs, we have a boxing program, we have a police athletic league that deals with basketball, everything from basketball actually to dancing. It's a program where we try to reach out to kids at risk and bring them in and get them involved in some sort of pro-social activity on a regular basis. We take ex-gang members, or current gang members, and we try to preach the theory of non-violence. Actually, "preach" is not the right word. We try to show them the theory of non-violence. We have *gang officers* who on Friday are out there arresting gang members and on Saturday are out there playing basketball with gang members. So, in that way, they're establishing a personal *rapport*.'

Working with the text

I. Look at the first part of the text. Mark the correct ending to the sentence.

1. Lieutenant Schwartz … a) comes from Florida originally.
   b) doesn't come from Florida originally.
2. He … a) doesn't mind living in Miami.
   b) enjoys living in Miami.
3. He seems to have … a) no sense of humor.
   b) quite a good sense of humor.

Street life in Miami

II. Mark the correct answer.

1. 'Miami Vice' (line 9) must be …
   a) a name of a person. b) a name of a book. c) a name of a TV program.
2. If your life is a 'tad' (line 11) different from other people's lives it is …
   a) a lot different from theirs.
   b) a little different from theirs.
   c) not different from theirs.
3. If policing is 'preventive' (lines 15-16) it makes sure …
   a) crimes can't happen during the day.
   b) crimes don't take place at all.
   c) crimes stay within a neighborhood.
4. A 'current' gang member (line 20) is somebody who …
   a) was in a gang. b) is in a gang. c) would like to be in a gang.

III. Which word or expression in the text means …

1. an animal you keep at home?
2. to run after somebody?
3. the latest stage in the development of something?
4. a group of criminals?
5. to give somebody strong advice about morals/behavior?

IV. Explain the following expressions. Use your own words.

1. a 'variety of folks' (line 5)
2. a 'melting pot' (line 6)
3. a 'houseboat' (line 10)
4. 'community policing' (line 16)

V. Say these words out loud.

1. palm trees
2. microcosm
3. crocodile
4. theory
5. rapport
6. violence

VI. What do you think? Answer the questions.

1. Is getting young people involved in sports a good way of preventing crime?
2. Is personal rapport between police officers and the public important?

Exercises

I. For which game or sport do you need these words?

1. heart – club – diamond – spade
2. bishop – king – pawn – knight
3. hotel – house – jail – free parking
4. backstroke – breaststroke – butterfly – freestyle
5. birdie – par – green – tee
6. headphones – track – volume – bass

II. Write a short text in English (60-80 words) saying what you like to do in your free time.

III. Say these words out loud. (Be careful! There are some letters you don't pronounce.)

1. calm
2. bomb
3. knee
4. pneumatics
5. psychology
6. knife

IV. Explain the difference, if any, between …

1. 'shoplifting' and 'burglary'.
2. a 'victim' and a 'hostage'.
3. 'homicide' and 'murder'.
4. 'arson' and 'assault'.

V. Lieutenant Schwartz talks about community policing in Miami. What do you think of his ideas?

We make our officers go out and take ownership of their neighborhoods that they patrol. I mean, if there is a specific problem, whether it's a serious, serious problem, like armed robberies, or a quality-of-life issue, like someone drinking in public, or panhandling (*Betteln*), we tell our officers: You solve that problem, no, *you* solve that problem. That's your responsibility.

VI. Officer Sardiña sees a man picking up cans on somebody else's property. He stops his car and talks to him. How does he speak to the man? And how well does he handle the situation?

Officer: Come here, buddy. What's going on?

Man: I've been picking up some cans.

Officer: Picking up some cans? As long, as long as the owner of the property says it's OK for you to go onto there, their property, to pick up some of the stuff, I don't have a problem, but my problem comes in when you go into somebody's property and they call us up, and they say: "Listen, he came into my yard without even telling me anything." You know? A lot of times business owners in this area, they'll tell you: "You can pick up whatever you want from there". Because a lot of the stuff is trash for them anyway, which might be important to you, OK, might be worth something to you. Just make sure that, if you're going to pick up something from somebody's property, just knock on their door and let them know. "Listen, if you don't want this, I'll pick it up and I'll take it from you."

Man: I do …

Officer: All right? All right, you have a good day, buddy.

Man: You too.

Officer: All right. You have a good one.

VII. William Schwartz mentions 'Art Deco'? What is 'Art Deco'? Read this and decide which sentence (a-c) comes at the beginning of the text.

a) Art Deco is an expression which is hard to define.
b) Art Deco is a style of design which was popular in the 1920s and 1930s.
c) Art Deco is back. Just look around Miami and you'll see what I mean.

It was used in furniture, jewelry, textiles and interior decor. Although the movement began about 1910, the term 'Art Deco' was not used until 1925.

Art Deco grew out of an effort to simplify the turn-of-the-century Art Nouveau style. Art Deco objects were usually not mass produced, but they often possess qualities found in mass production: simplicity, unvaried repetition and geometric patterning.

8B Pablo Canton

Pablo Canton, the Administrator for the Neighborhood Enhancement Team (NET) in East Little Havana, comes originally from Cuba. How did he get his present job with the city government of Miami?

'I went to University of Miami, graduated in 1969 with a Bachelor in *Business Administration*. I went to the Army for a couple of years as an Infantry officer. As you can see, I was a *paratrooper* with the 101st *Airborne*. After that I came back to Miami and I went back to Florida International University and I have a Bachelor of Science in Construction Management. I went into business in the private field for a few years and I've been working with the city of Miami now since 1987.

Does Pablo think NET has been successful?

'I think in the last few years we have been very effective. We have done a lot of things for the community and you can see the difference. Still, there's a lot to be done. Right now we are trying to educate some of the people. As you know, this area is not only a majority of Cuban citizens, or Cuban nationals that immigrated to the United States, we have a lot of other Central American countries that have residents in the area, largely Nicaraguans, Hondurans, some other countries from Central America. Again, some of these people in their countries do not have the laws that we have here in the United States. So we have to educate them as far as *solid* waste, when they throw the garbage in the streets, the 'pickup days'. Sometimes they throw it anytime of the week and we have specific days where the garbage is picked up. So we have to make sure that everybody follows up the laws otherwise we have garbage all over the streets. Same thing with crossing the streets at the corner or maybe throwing *litter* out in the streets, which is something that we are definitely very much against. We want to keep to the image of Miami as a clean city, and we not only hope that the tourists *abide by* the law, but our own residents should be the first ones that should follow the laws and keep the city clean.'

Working with the text

I. Which sentence(s) in the first part of the text show(s) you …

1. that Pablo Canton has lived in Miami for many years?
2. that he has often been in airplanes?
3. that he's had a job in local government for over ten years now?

II. Join up the two halves of the sentences using the information in the text.

1. He went into	a. a Bachelor in Business Administration.
2. He graduated from	b. throwing litter onto the street.
3. He has	c. the army.
4. He is trying	d. residents – and tourists – to keep the streets clean.
5. He is against people	e. to inform residents about garbage collection.
6. He would like	f. two universities in Florida.

III. Answer the questions on the second part of the text.

1. How does Pablo feel about the work NET has done in East Little Havana?
2. What problem does Miami have with residents in East Little Havana?
3. What is Pablo doing to solve this problem?

IV. What does the underlined word refer to in the text?

1. Right now <u>we</u> are trying to educate some of the people … (line 14)
2. As <u>you</u> know, this area is not only a majority of Cuban citizens … (line 14)
3. So we have to educate <u>them</u> as far as solid waste … (line 20)
4. … and <u>we</u> have specific days where the garbage is picked up (line 21)

V. Explain these expressions using an example or a definition.

1. A 'paratrooper' (line 6) is …
2. A 'Bachelor of Science' (line 8) is …
3. A 'pickup day' (line 21) is …

VI. What's the difference in meaning, if any, between ...

1. a 'Bachelor of Science' and a 'Bachelor of Arts'?
2. a 'Cuban citizen' and a 'Cuban national'?
3. 'litter' and 'garbage'?
4. a 'tourist' and a 'resident'?

Exercises

I. Underline the correct word in the brackets.

- Last night we were [somewhere/anywhere] near your apartment.
- Near our apartment? I didn't see you [anywhere/somewhere]!

- Did you do [anything/something] special on the weekend?
- No, I didn't! It was kind of boring! I didn't do [anything/something]!

- Did [anybody/somebody] see you in the park?
- Yes, [anybody/somebody] from my old school but I don't know his name.

- Have you got [any/some] food for your trip?
- Yes, we've got [some/any] but not enough for everybody.

II. What's the opposite of the underlined word?

1. What <u>is</u> your <u>present</u> job?
2. Is it really such an <u>effective</u> method?
3. I can't see the <u>difference</u>.
4. Are you <u>against</u> speed limits?
5. He got <u>off</u> the bus and said <u>hello</u>.
6. <u>He put his</u> bag <u>on</u> the table.

III. Put the words into the correct columns.

scarf ◆ church ◆ sticky ◆ confused ◆ gloves ◆ scared ◆ sweatshirt ◆ worried ◆ store ◆ sky ◆ windy ◆ cottage

weather	clothes	buildings	feelings

IV. The US space center, operated by NASA, is in Cape Canaveral, Florida. Read the text about the first man on the moon and answer the question below.

On July 16, 1969, the crew of Apollo 11 – Neil Armstrong, Mike Collins and Buzz Aldrin – headed for the moon to attempt the lunar landing. On July 20, Armstrong and Aldrin passed through a connecting tunnel from the command module, Columbia, to the attached lunar module, Eagle. It was a tense (*spannungsgeladen*) moment as Armstrong and Aldrin fired Eagle's rocket to slow the craft into its final descent (*Abstieg*) to the moon's Sea of Tranquillity.

Suddenly an overloaded onboard computer threatened to hinder the landing but quick action by experts at NASA allowed the astronauts to continue. Armstrong took over manual control and brought Eagle to a safe touchdown with less than a minute's worth of fuel left. 'Houston,' Armstrong radioed, 'Tranquillity Base here. The Eagle has landed.'

Hours later Armstrong placed his left boot on the powdery lunar surface – the first human footstep on another world. His famous first words on the moon were: 'That's one small step for man, one giant leap for mankind,' but he had wanted to say: 'That's one small step for *a* man, one giant leap for mankind.'

On July 24 the three astronauts returned to the earth carrying 22 kilograms of lunar rock and soil. NASA had shown that humans were capable of leaving their home world and traveling to another.

The first man on the moon

Translate these sentences into German.

1. 'That's one small step for man, one giant leap for mankind,'
2. 'That's one small step for a man, one giant leap for mankind.'

V. Florida is famous for its hurricanes. What happened when Hurricane Floyd arrived? Read this article and find out.

Two million flee from hurricane

Nearly two million people fled from the Florida coastline yesterday as Hurricane Floyd, one of the biggest storm systems ever recorded off the American coast, roared across the Caribbean towards the US mainland.

A state of emergency was declared in Florida. Tourists there were facing disruption as airports at Miami, Orlando and Tampa were closed after all major flights in and out of the state were cancelled. Jeb Bush, Florida's Governor, said: 'This is a monster storm. It is large, ferocious and it is scary.'

Jerry Jarrell, director of the National Hurricane Centre, gave warning that if Floyd hit a populated area, 'then it's off the scale in terms of damage. This is a really intense beast. This is enough to really scare us out of our wits.' Disney World at Orlando, visited by some 200,000 tourists a day, shut its doors for the first time in its 28-year history and staff said it would not reopen until tomorrow at the earliest.

More than 12,000 workers at Cape Canaveral – the Space Shuttle launch pad – were moved inland as a skeleton crew tried to save equipment. Four Shuttles were secured in hangars, but the buildings were designed to withstand winds of no more than 105 mph to 125 mph.

Floyd is almost four times the size of Hurricane Andrew which caused around £19 billion damage – the costliest natural disaster in US history. It left 40 dead and 140,000 homeless when it hit south of Miami in August, 1992. The winds at the core of Hurricane Floyd were clocked yesterday at 155 mph, the same velocity as Andrew's, establishing both storms as Category 4 hurricanes.

An aerial view of Miami

8C Tom and Barbara Dwyer

Tom and Barbara Dwyer are not only plantation owners. Both have teaching certificates, too, so it was natural for them when they bought Knollwood Groves to want to develop it into a place where young people could have a learning experience.

Tom: We're small, very small, family, little farm. We don't *ship* to supermarkets. Our juice is all sold only at the *retail store* here. As you noticed, we make the apple pies. We have our animals, our *deer*, our pigs, our *coons*, our fox – all this is part of our operation. Barbara takes care of our shipping part of it here, the gifts ...

Barbara: We take oranges and ship them in boxes to individual families. Your customers come down, your visitors come down, they want to send a gift of citrus Florida back north. That's what we do. We pack everything and ship it up as an individual gift. And we also ship different salad dressings, different marmalades, candies, anything that says: 'This is Florida. This is a gift from Florida.'

Tom: We're, so to speak, 30 acres right in the middle of the city here, so, as a result, people come out here, relax under the trees. They'll spend a day of fun here with their children, with the shows, and everything else, and the tour's every hour on the hour. We have a tour going throughout the grove.

Say 'Cheese'

Working with the text

I. *Are the following statements true or false according to the text? If they are false, correct them.*

1. Tom and Barbara Dwyer own and run a plantation.
2. The plantation is in Miami.
3. The Dwyers' plantation is open to visitors.
4. The farm produce can be bought all over the US.

II. *Which sentence(s) in the text show(s) you …*

1. that the Dwyers are qualified to teach?
2. that they sell food and drink in their farm store?
3. that their plantation has lots of visitors from outside Florida?
4. that their plantation is in the city?

III. *Replace the underlined words with words of the same (or similar) meaning.*

1. As you <u>noticed</u>, we make the apple pies … (line 7)
2. Barbara <u>takes care of</u> our shipping part … (line 9)
3. We're, so to speak, 30 acres right in the <u>middle</u> of the city … (line 16)
4. … so, <u>as a result</u>, people come out here, relax under the trees … (line 17)

IV. *Mark the best ending to the sentence.*

1. A 'retail store' (line 6) is a shop where …
   a) any member of the public can buy goods.
   b) only tourists can buy goods.
   c) only US citizens can buy goods.
2. A 'gift' (line 9) is another word for …
   a) a large box. b) a present. c) a kilo of oranges.
3. An example of a 'citrus fruit' (line 12) is …
   a) a melon. b) a lemon. c) a strawberry.
4. The word 'acre' (line 16) is used when talking about …
   a) the size of plantations. b) the size of land. c) the size of stores.

V. *Describe or define these expressions using your own words.*

1. juice (line 6)
2. salad dressing (line 14)
3. marmalade (line 14)
4. candy (line 14)

VI. *Do you remember the film? Which animal – and which man – is the special attraction at Knollwood Groves?*

VII. What do you think? Answer the questions.

1. Could you imagine living in Miami permanently? Say why/why not.
2. Are you affected by the weather? Does a warm sunny day make you feel good? Write three or four sentences saying how the weather influences your mood.

Exercises

I. Take a piece of paper and write down, in English, the name of …

1. … six types of fruit.
2. … six types of vegetable.
3. … six animals.
4. … six birds.
5. … six flowers.
6. … six types of shop.

II. Martin Twofeather, a Native American who also works at Knollwood Groves, talks about the Battle of the Little Bighorn. Why was this battle so important in US history? Complete this text to find out.

After they … (guarantee) their own reservation in South Dakota, the Sioux Indians … (accept) peace with the US government. In 1875, however, gold … (discover) in the Black Hills and white settlers … (begin, move in). The Indians, for whom the Black Hills were a sacred place, … (order, return) to their reservations. If they … (not, return), the US government … (consider) them hostile.

Sitting Bull … (set up) camp in the valley of the Little Bighorn River where, one night, he … (perform) the Sun Dance. When he … (wake up) from his trance, he said he … (see) US soldiers falling like grasshoppers from the sky.

Soon Sitting Bull's vision … (become) reality. When on June 25, 1876 Lieutenant Colonel George Custer … (ride) into the valley, he and all his men … (kill) in the Battle of the Little Bighorn.

The Sioux … (manage, win) many battles against US troops but they … (can, not, succeed, win) the war.

III. Find out more about the Sioux Indians. What happened in 1890 at Wounded Knee Creek in South Dakota?

Overview

to run	durchführen
law enforcement operation	*etwa im Sinne von: eine Operation (ein Einsatz) mit dem Ziel, dem Gesetz Geltung zu verschaffen*
policing	Kontrolle, Überwachung
young people at risk	gefährdete Jugendliche
to tackle a problem	ein Problem angehen, anpacken
enhancement	Verbesserung
garbage	Müll, Abfall
vagrant	Land-/Stadtstreicher
groves	Wäldchen, Hain
racoon	Waschbär

8A William Schwartz

a tad	ein bisschen
gang officer	*Polizeibeamter mit spezieller Zuständigkeit für die Jugendgangs*
rapport	Beziehung

8B Pablo Canton

Business Administration	Betriebswirtschaft
paratrooper	Fallschirmjäger
Airborne (troops/soldiers)	Luftlandetruppen
solid	fest (im Gegensatz zu „flüssig“)
litter	Abfall
to abide by	sich halten an

8C Tom and Barbara Dwyer

to ship	liefern
retail store	Einzelhandelsgeschäft, Laden
deer	Hirsch, Rotwild
(ra)coon	Waschbär

Canada
0 200 miles
0 200 km
ATLANTIC OCEAN
PACIFIC OCEAN
Beaufort Sea
Baffin Bay
Davis Strait
Labrador Sea
Hudson Bay
Hudson Strait
Foxe Basin
Gulf of Alaska
Greenland
Arctic Circle
C A N A D A
U S A
Alaska USA
Yukon Territory
Northwest Territories
Nunavut
British Columbia
Alberta
Saskatchewan
Manitoba
Ontario
Québec
Newfoundland
New Brunswick
Nova Scotia
P.E.I.
Banks Island
Victoria Island
Melville Island
Bathurst Island
Devon Island
Sommerset Island
Prince of Wales Island
Boothia Peninsula
Baffin Island
Melville Peninsula
Southampton Island
Peninsule d'Ungava
Labrador Peninsula
Anticosti I.
Vancouver Island
Queen Charlotte Islands
Alexander Archipelago
Amundsen Gulf
Great Bear Lake
Great Slave Lake
Lake Athabasca
Reindeer Lake
Lake Winnipeg
Lake Superior
Lake Michigan
L. Huron
L. Ontario
L. Erie
St. Lawrence R.
Yukon R.
Mackenzie R.
Athabasca R.
Back R.
Fraser R.
Missouri R.
Snake R.
ALASKA RANGE
MACKENZIE MTS.
COAST MOUNTAINS
ROCKY MOUNTAINS
Mt. McKinley 6194
6050 Mt. Logan
Mt. Robson 3954
Anchorage
Valdez
Fairbanks
Central
Bay
Dawson
Whitehorse
Haines
Skagway
Watson Lake
Inuvik
Yellowknife
Hay River
Fort Smith
Fort Nelson
Hazelton
Prince Rupert
Prince George
Dawson Creek
Grande-Prairie
Fort McMurray
La Loche
Lynn Lake
Gilliam
La Ronge
Jasper
Edmonton
Port Hardy
Kamloops
Banff
Vancouver
Victoria
Calgary
Prince Albert
Saskatoon
Regina
Lethbridge
Brandon
Winnipeg
Pickle Lake
Geraldton
Thunder Bay
Timmins
Sault Ste Marie
Chibougamau
Chicoutimi
Rimouski
Québec City
Montréal
Ottawa
Oshawa
Toronto
London
Sherbrooke
Saint-John
Halifax
Sydney
Gaspé
Havre-St-Pierre
Labrador City
St. Anthony
Channel-Port-aux-Basques
St. John's
Iqaluit
Seattle
Spokane
Portland
Great Falls
Billings
Bismarck
Fargo
Duluth
Minneapolis
Milwaukee
Detroit
Syracuse
Boston
Providence
New York
Sioux Falls
Rapid City
Casper
Boise
Eureka
Sacramento
Reno
Salt Lake City
Washington
Oregon
California
Idaho
Nevada
Utah
Montana
Wyoming
North Dakota
South Dakota
Nebraska
Minnesota
Iowa
Wisconsin
Michigan
New York
Pennsylvania
Vt.
N.H.
Mass.
Maine

Quebec

What do you know about Quebec? Try this quiz and find out.
(The answers are at the bottom of the page.)

1. **What is Quebec?**
   a) the name of a city in Canada
   b) the name of a province in Canada
   c) the name of a province and a city in Canada

2. **Why does Quebec have a special status within Canada?**
   a) It is the largest province in the country.
   b) It has its own parliament.
   c) It is a French part of an English-speaking country.

3. **Which is the largest city in the province of Quebec?**
   a) Ottawa b) Montreal c) Vancouver

4. **What percentage of Quebec's people are of French descent?**
   a) About 30% b) About 50% c) About 80%

5. **What's the name of the main river in Quebec?**
   a) Hudson River b) Fundy River c) Saint Lawrence River

6. **In which year was Quebec City, the capital of Quebec, founded?**
   a) 1608 b) 1708 c) 1808

7. **The Quebec coat of arms has the words 'Je me souviens' on it. What does this mean?**
   a) I find b) I remember c) I seek

Answers: 1 c), 2 c), 3 b), 4 c), 5 c), 6 a), 7 b)

Overview

Tracy Martineau works in the Office of External Relations and Public Information at the headquarters of the International Civil Aviation Organization (ICAO) in Montreal, Canada. ICAO, a specialized organization of the United Nations, has a council of 33 member countries. The council is responsible for creating international standards in international civil aviation. These are distributed to the 185 ICAO member countries, whose responsibility it is to *incorporate* them into their own national legislation and to *enforce* them *on* their *carriers* and their *manufacturers*. As Tracy explains, the purpose of ICAO is to ensure the safety, security and the regularity of international civil aviation worldwide.

Priscille LeBlanc is the Director for Corporate Communications for Air Canada in Dorval, Quebec. Priscille talks about the history of Air Canada, the role it played in the economic development of Canada and the service it offers today. The company started life in 1937 as Trans Canada Airlines and now operates 600 flights in 239 aircraft daily. Canada is a large country so there is also a need for Air Canada to provide service between regional communities. Air Canada's regional airline network consists of three carriers: Air Nova, operating in the Atlantic provinces and Quebec, Air Ontario, operating in Canada's largest province, and Air DC which serves the West.

André Maesscheart is the District Manager for Avis rent-a-car in Montreal. Avis has been in Canada for 42 years. Today the company is located in 150 cities across the country, employing 1200 people and having approximately 16,000 cars on rent at any one time. André says that Avis *puts* great *emphasis on* high levels of customer satisfaction. One way of achieving this is by training staff to treat customers *properly* and effectively. Avis makes sure it employs people from a diverse cultural background so that customers can be served at the *counters* in many different languages.

André Paré is a physical education teacher in College Mont Notre-Dame in Cherbourg near Montreal. The school is for girls between the ages of 12 and 18. Students learn three languages – French, English and Spanish – and enjoy a broad education including activities outside the classroom such as ecology, sports and theatre. André thinks it's not always important what the students do at school but how they do it. Sport, in André's view, is not about winning. It's about participating.

Betty Eitner is the Director of Marketing and Sales for Citadelle *Maple* Syrup Producers Co-operative. Betty describes the production processes at Citadelle. First the syrup is gathered from the maple trees and stored in barrels. Then each barrel is tested by a government inspector. Afterwards the syrup is filtered, pasteurised and stored in stainless steel tanks. Later it is bottled. Betty emphasises that maple syrup is one of the few sweeteners in the world that is 100% natural. It is becoming increasingly popular around the world especially for people who are looking for natural products in their diets.

Find out more about ...

Priscille LeBlanc in **9A** (pages 148 – 151)
André Maesscheart in **9B** (pages 152 – 157)
Betty Eitner in **9C** (pages 158 – 161)

9A Priscille LeBlanc

How did Air Canada begin?

'Air Canada was born of very *humble* origins. Its *predecessor* was Trans Canada Airlines which started service on September 1st 1937 between Vancouver and Seattle. On that historic day a small ten-seater L 10A aircraft flew between Vancouver and Seattle with two passengers and many sacks of mail. Since that day Trans Canada Airlines played a very active role in the economic development of Canada. Canada is a very large country and very dependent on air transportation for its economic growth. Therefore, the airline soon became government owned and operated for many years in a heavily regulated environment. The government had much say into the routes we flew, the *fares* we charged, and the frequency, and the type of network that we had.'

What about Air Canada's operation today?

'*As the years evolved* Air Canada grew to become Canada's major airline and became a leader in world transportation as well. In 1969 the name was changed to Air Canada formally. Today Air Canada provides passenger service to 17 Canadian cities, 34 cities to the United States and 22 cities in Europe, Asia, the Middle East and the Caribbean. We operate over 600 flights a day, in 239 airplanes ranging from the 50-seat Canada Air regional jet to the 234-seat Airbus 340. In 1998 we carried almost 15 million passengers. Our strong international network is further strengthened by our Star Alliance partnership. In 1997 we formed Star Alliance with Lufthansa, Thai Airways, Varig, SAS and United Airlines.'

Does Air Canada serve the regions within Canada?

'What is different about air transportation in Canada is that there is a need for service between many regional communities as it would not be possible for *freight* and goods to be carried by train through these long distances, not to mention essential air travel for passengers. Therefore, Air Canada has a very strong regional airline network, formed of three carriers: Air Nova which operates in the Atlantic provinces and Quebec, Air Ontario which operates in Canada's largest province, and Air DC which serves the West. These three regional carriers serve over 30 smaller Canadian communities bringing passengers and goods into Air Canada's network at the major cities. The regional carriers carry over 3 million passengers each day and operate almost 600 flights a day.'

Working with the text

I. Are these statements true or false according to the text? If they are false, correct them.

1. Air Canada only operates in Canada.
2. Air Canada's full name is Trans Canada Airlines.
3. Air Canada flies people and freight.

II. Which line(s) in the text shows(s) you that ...

1. Air Canada was once dependent on the Canadian government?
2. Air Canada works together with other airlines?
3. Air Canada flies to many regional communities?

III. Answer these questions. Use your own words as far as possible.

1. Why did the Canadian government become interested in Air Canada?
2. Which foreign country does Air Canada fly most frequently to?
3. Why does Air Canada serve so many regional communities in Canada?

IV. Which word from the text is it?

1. the person or thing that came before something else
2. letters and parcels
3. the cost of a trip on a plane, train or bus
4. goods which are transported by plane, train or ship

V. Replace the underlined words with words of the same (or similar) meaning.

1. Canada is a very large country ... (line 7)
2. The government had much say into the routes we flew ... (line 10)
3. As the years evolved Air Canada grew to become ... (line 13)
4. ... not to mention essential air travel for passengers ... (line 27)

VI. Make verb-noun partnerships.

1. to charge	a. excellent service
2. to fly	b. millions of passengers
3. to become	c. high fares
4. to provide	d. a major airline
5. to carry	e. long-distance routes

VII. What about you? Answer the questions.

1. Do you enjoy flying? Say why/why not.
2. Have you ever been to Canada? If so, what was it like? (If not, would you like to go and what would you like to do there?)

Exercises

I. *Say these pairs of words out loud. Which pair is not said in the same way? Use the words in sentences to show their meanings.*

1. fair	–	fare	4. freight	–	fright
2. route	–	root	5. mail	–	male
3. air	–	heir	6. through	–	threw

II. *What's the opposite of the underlined words or expressions?*

1. It's a very long flight between Vancouver and Seattle.
2. We have a number of minor problems at the moment.
3. There's been a huge reduction in the number of domestic flights.
4. The government wants to regulate the market.
5. Trans Canada Airlines's predecessor was Air Canada.

III. *Form word partnerships.*

1. goods and	a. exit
2. entrance and	b. domestic
3. passenger and	c. charter
4. international and	d. services
5. scheduled and	e. freight

IV. *Put the lines of this dialogue into the correct order (1-12). Start with a. and finish with g.*

a. *Hello. Can I see your ticket and passport, please?*

b. *Non-smoking and an aisle seat if possible.*

c. *Oh, good.*

d. *OK. Can you put them on the scales, please? Smoking or non-smoking?*

e. *OK. Did you pack the suitcases yourself?*

f. *Right. Here's your boarding card. It's Gate 23. Boarding at 11.45. Have a nice flight.*

g. *Thank you.*

h. *That should be no problem. The plane's only half full.*

i. *Two. And this is hand luggage.*

j. *Yes, I did.*

k. *How many items of luggage are you taking with you?*

l. *Yes, of course.*

V. Look at these population statistics for Germany and Canada. What differences are there between the two countries? Write four or five sentences in English.

	Germany	**Canada**
Population:	82,071,765	28,846,761
Population density:	230 persons/km^2	3 persons/km^2
Urban/Rural:	87% urban 13% rural	78% urban 22% rural
Largest cities:	Berlin 3,447,900 Hamburg 1,703,800 Munich 1,251,100	Toronto 4,680,349 Montreal 3,326,510 Calgary 933,726
Ethnic groups: (* einheimisch, Ur-)	German 95% Other 5%	British 35% French 25% Other European 20% Asian 10% Indigenous* peoples 3% Black 2% Other 5%

VI. Read this text and put the five numbers into the correct position.

59 ◆ 25 ◆ 3 ◆ 300 ◆ 75

Although Canada has a very low population density of … persons per square kilometre, this is a misleading statistic. Actually the population is highly concentrated, with about … per cent of all Canadians living within about … km of the US border. Canadians are concentrated into about … metropolitan areas. The last census (*Volkszählung*) showed … per cent living in such areas.

9B André Maesscheart

André Maesscheart works for Avis rent-a-car in Montreal. The company has been in existence since 1957 and has over 150 *locations* across Canada, with 1200 employees and approximately 16,000 cars on rent at any one time.

What role does customer satisfaction play in Avis's work and employee training?

'We've been a major business partner to a lot of the leading corporations and we've achieved this through good service to our customers. High levels of customer satisfaction and customer loyalty are our goal. Primarily we have to make sure that we train and teach our people the right way of doing things and the right way of treating our customers. One of the *key phrases* that we use is called "*Sense* and *Response*", which means the employees are trained to sense the needs of each individual customer and then respond as best as they can with all the *tools* available. As an example, we have a lot of foreign visitors that come to Canada to visit the country and when they arrive at our rental counters, we would help them out, especially someone who's never been here before and might be nervous. We would help them out with driving directions, driving tips on how to drive the vehicle, which would be on an audio tape, you could insert into the vehicle while they're driving it, traffic rules, all sorts of helpful advice that would make his experience less stressful and more pleasant during his stay in Canada.'

How does Avis deal with the different languages its customers speak?

'We've hired employees from a great diverse cultural background. It enables our employees to serve our customers at the counter in many languages. Some of the languages include Punjabi as an example or Cantonese or Mandarin or even German, French, English, Italian. Diversity is part of the *cornerstone* on which Avis is built on. In addition to that, for the people who we can't serve in their native language, we have many, many foreign languages, including some even *obscure* languages, in which we have our printed material, so that we can provide the customer with the information they require when visiting Canada.'

Working with the text

I. Complete the sentence using the information in the text.

1. Avis has been in Canada for … .
2. It now has offices … .
3. Avis employees are taught to … .
4. Avis likes to hire employees from different cultural backgrounds because …

II. Answer the questions using complete sentences. Use your own words as far as possible.

1. How many cars does Avis have on average at each of its locations in Canada?
2. What is the idea behind the phrase 'Sense and Response'?
3. What sort of help and advice does Avis give to foreign customers renting cars?
4. In what way does Avis try and help customers who speak unusual languages?

III. Make adjective-noun partnerships. (The text will help you.)

1. key	a. language
2. native	b. stay
3. helpful	c. phrase
4. pleasant	d. background
5. diverse	e. material
6. printed	f. advice

IV. Explain the following expressions using your own words as far as possible.

1. 'leading corporations' (line 5)
2. 'key phrase' (line 9)
3. 'driving directions' (line 15)
4. an 'obscure language' (line 26)

V. Say these words and expressions out loud.

1. employee 2. vehicle 3. audio tape 4. diversity

VI. What do you think? Answer the questions.

1. What can make driving in a foreign country stressful?
2. How much emphasis do you yourself put on being served properly?
3. Why is customer satisfaction and customer loyalty so important to companies?
4. Why does a company like Avis, with offices in Canada, depend so much on having employees who speak many different languages?

The Three Courthouses in Montreal

Exercises

I. Look at the sentences below. Which time, which meaning and which if-pattern can you identify?

Time:	past – present – future
Meaning:	advice – offer – possibility – promise – warning – wish
If-pattern:	I – II – III

Example: *If we left early, we'd get there on time. – future time, a possibility, if-pattern II*

1. I'll take you to the airport if you want.
2. If I were you, I'd go and see a doctor.
3. I would have told you the answer if I'd known it.
4. If you touch that, you'll set off the alarm.
5. If he came now, we could start the meeting.
6. If I could save some money, I'd go on holiday to Canada.

II. Read the sentence and think of an explanation.

Example: *Bill invited Jane to dinner at eight. It's nine o'clock and Jane hasn't come.* → *She must have forgotten about the invitation.*

1. The roads are wet but everybody has put their umbrellas away.
2. John is wearing sports clothes. He's very red in the face.
3. There is a traffic jam. You can hear an ambulance.
4. Philippa's phone has just rung. She's still wearing headphones.
5. Mike usually cycles to work. Today his bike is at home.
6. You come back home after work and you see that your PC is on.

III. Match the underlined expressions (1-6) to the correct translation (a-f).

1. Traffic is moving slow inbound … → e.
2. Traffic is jammed …
3. A fender bender is causing problems …
4. There's construction work at the interchange …
5. We've got a gaper's delay at …
6. Drivers should be careful on the off-ramp …

a. Unfall mit geringem Schaden
b. Autobahnausfahrt
c. Autobahnkreuz
d. staut sich
e. stadteinwärts
f. Verkehrsstau wegen Schaulustiger

IV. Look at this information about renting a car. What sort of service is being advertised here? Who is it aimed at? How can you go about getting this service?

AVIS **Programs & Services**

- **Rates & Reservations**
- **The Fleet**
- **Rental Locations**
- **Programs & Services**
  - Preferred Services
  - Wizard Number
  - One Way Rentals
  - Rate Programs
  - Rental Services
  - Travel Agents
  - Travel Partners
- **Maps & Directions**
- **Corporate Information**
- **Talk To Us**

AVIS "On Call"

Avis "On Call" is an exclusive telephone assistance service offered only to Avis renters while on the road in 21 countries (16 in Europe) via toll-free telephone numbers which are answered by Avis representatives in the U.S. 24 hours a day, 7 days a week. This service can offer you help on a variety of issues relating to travel abroad.

How to obtain this service

Avis renters must call Avis "Know Before You Go" at 1-800-297-4447 prior to departure from the U.S. to obtain and carry with them the country-specific toll-free numbers as they are NOT available anywhere in Europe.

You must give your Rental Agreement number to access Avis "On Call" assistance during your rental period.

What kind of help can I expect?

Avis "On Call" connects you to a trained agent in the U.S. who can help you solve a myriad of travel hassles, which can mar a vacation. Examples of help categories include:

- Refilling prescriptions for medication (or eye glasses)
- Medical assistance (to nearest qualified English speaking doctor)
- Finding lost luggage (enroute with airline, left at a hotel etc.)
- Simultaneous language translation (French, German, Spanish & Italian)

V. Complete this text about the early history of Quebec. Use the words in the box before each paragraph.

banks ◆ monopoly ◆ rights ◆ death ◆ settlers

In 1608 the French explorer Samuel de Champlain established a trading post on the … of the Saint Lawrence River at what is now Quebec City. New France, as the colony was called, grew slowly. France granted companies … to the territory. These companies were supposed to bring out … in return for a … on the fur trade. However, at the time of Champlain's … in 1635 the colony was still very small.

dispatched ◆ offered ◆ determined ◆ made ◆ encouraged

In the 1660s King Louis XIV of France was … to transform the colony into a prosperous province of the French empire. Responsibility for government was … a direct concern of the Crown. A brewery and a shipyard were built and agriculture was … . Even a regiment of French troops was … . To stimulate immigration, bonuses were …, and single women, the famous 'filles du roi', were sent to become brides for the young men who had settled New France.

from ◆ on ◆ about ◆ of ◆ over

Beginning in 1689 France and Britain were involved in a century-long series of wars … the control of the fur trade. Both nations received military assistance … colonists but they also relied … the help of the indigenous peoples. By 1713 the French influence in North America was not as great as the British. French colonists numbered … 12,000 while there were almost 1 million British colonists. As a result Great Britain took control … Hudson Bay and part of the French colony known as Acadia (now New Brunswick, Nova Scotia and Prince Edward Island).

however ◆ still ◆ in addition to

The first half of the 18th century were years of peace in New France. Economic development was rapid. … capital acquired through the fur trade, money came from the French government. … , although the population grew steadily there were few new immigrants and by 1754 the number of French colonists was … only 50,000.

capture ◆ freedom ◆ support ◆ half ◆ control

In the second … of the 18th century the Anglo-French struggle concentrated on the Saint Lawrence River. The … of Quebec in 1759 by the British led to the French colony coming under British … . Later, with the passing of the Quebec Act (1774), the British government tried to win the … of the people in its newest colony by guaranteeing the use of the French legal code in civil cases and the … of the Roman Catholic Church. It also gave Quebec control over all the land north of the Ohio River.

loyalist ◆ Constitutional ◆ Lower ◆ French ◆ little

The American Revolution (1775-1783) had … effect on Canada but it did bring … British settlers into Quebec. This, in turn, led to the division of the … colony. By the … Act of 1791, Quebec was divided into Upper Canada (now Ontario) and … Canada (now Quebec).

Château Frontenac in Quebec

9C Betty Eitner

Betty Eitner, Director of Marketing and Sales for Citadelle Maple Syrup Producers Co-operative, answers some questions about maple syrup and maple syrup production.

How popular is maple syrup?

'Maple syrup is one of the few sweeteners in the world that is 100 per cent natural. It is boiled down from the *sap* of a tree into a syrup, as it is further boiled down it becomes a maple *spread*, and further down it becomes a maple sugar. There is no refining techniques, there are no techniques other than a pure natural product. It is the only sweetener in the world that does contain minerals, calcium, *potassium* and magnesium. It is a slow absorption product, therefore – similar to honey – it is acceptable for diets, for people who cannot absorb refined sugars in their system. It is becoming a very, very popular product around the world and it seems it is becoming more and more popular, especially for people who are looking for natural sweeteners and natural products in their diets.'

How is maple syrup produced?

'When we bring the product into the facility, the first thing we do is each barrel is tested by a government inspector for clarity, for flavor and is *graded*. We, in turn, later, will filter this product, we will pasteurise the product and store it in stainless steel tanks with a nitrogen barrier which will keep its springtime flavor until we further *process* it. At that point what we do is we pump it into units which will reheat the product to over 85° Celsius and it will go through a bottling facility. Our bottling facility then bottles at 85° Celsius to make sure that the product is completely bacteria free and as pure as nature intended it to be. With our special system of *capping* on metal caps, no oxygen can enter into the bottles as oxygen is the biggest enemy of maple syrup which would cause, more than usual, cause flavor changes or which could cause color changes. So we guarantee that the product you get is as pure and as fresh as the product the Indians *harvested* many, many years ago.'

Working with the text

I. Mark the correct ending to the sentence.

1. One of the reasons why maple syrup is so popular is that it is …
   a) cheap to produce.
   b) a natural product.
   c) good for people who want to lose weight.
2. Maple syrup comes from maple trees but it …
   a) has to be refined before it can be eaten.
   b) has to be sweetened before it can be eaten.
   c) has to be processed before it can be eaten.

II. Continue these sentences using the information in the text.

1. Maple syrup is considered a healthy product because … .
2. If maple syrup is not processed properly it … .

III. Put these production steps into the correct order (1-7).

a. The syrup is bottled.
b. The syrup is collected in barrels.
c. The syrup is graded.
d. The syrup is pasteurised.
e. The syrup is reheated.
f. The syrup is stored in tanks.
g. The syrup is tested.

IV. *Find a word in the text which means …*

1. a substance, like gold or salt, that is found naturally in the earth
2. to heat a liquid (and then cool it) in order to kill harmful bacteria
3. a chemical element in the air which is necessary for all forms of life
4. a type of metal that does not normally rust

V. *Explain these words and expressions by continuing the sentence.*

1. Your 'diet' (line 11) is … .
2. A 'government inspector' (line 18) is … .
3. If you 'grade' (line 18) a product you … .
4. A 'bottling facility' (line 23) is … .

VI. *Say these words out loud.*

1. technique
2. diet
3. calcium
4. bacteria
5. nitrogen
6. oxygen

VII. *What about you? Answer the questions.*

1. Are you careful with what you eat? Explain.
2. Where do you do your food shopping? Do you choose the things you buy carefully?

Exercises

I. *How would you describe the following? Use the words from the box.*

bitter ◆ salty ◆ sweet ◆ sour ◆ spicy ◆ tasteless

1. Indian curry
2. an unripe apple
3. a mug of coffee with six lumps of sugar
4. white bread
5. sea water
6. raw courgettes

II. *Link the beginning and end of Betty's sentences.*

1. In Canada we produce over	a. to produce one single litre of maple syrup.
2. We at Citadelle have over	b. six million maple trees in our plantation.
3. We will harvest over	c. 80 per cent of the world's maple syrup.
4. There are over	d. four million kilos of sap.
5. The products we ship	e. 3,000 people that gather the sap.
6. It takes forty litres of sap	f. around the world are 100 per cent pure.

Harvesting the sap

III. Read these questions and choose an answer. Then check your answers by reading the text below.

1. What percentage of Canada's population are French Canadians?
   a) 25% b) 40% c) 80%
2. In which part of Canada are the largest Francophone communities?
   a) Alberta and Manitoba
   b) Quebec and Ontario
   c) Newfoundland and Prince Edward Island
3. What percentage of Quebec's population are French Canadians?
   a) 25% b) 40% c) 80%

The term 'French Canadians' refers to the residents of Canada who speak the French language, especially the descendants of settlers from France who immigrated to the colonies of New France in North America between 1604 and 1760.

About 25 per cent of Canada's total population are French Canadians. Most of them live in the province of Quebec. In fact 82 per cent of the province's 6.8 million citizens are French speaking. Quebecois control the province's legal, political, economic and social institutions.

French Canadians also live in Canada's other provinces and territories. The French-speaking residents of Ontario, or Franco-Ontarians, form the largest Francophone community outside Quebec.

IV. In 1995 there was a referendum on the independence of Quebec. What was the result of this referendum? Try to find out.

Overview

to incorporate into	aufnehmen, integrieren in
to enforce sth on sb	jmdm. etw. aufzwingen
carrier	Fluggesellschaft
manufacturer	Hersteller
to put emphasis on sth	etw. betonen
properly	richtig, korrekt
counter	Schalter
maple	Ahorn

9A Priscille LeBlanc

humble	bescheiden
predecessor	Vorgänger
fare	Flugpreis
as the years evolved …	mit der Zeit …, im Laufe der Zeit …
freight	Fracht

9B André Maesscheart

location	Standort, Niederlassung
key phrase	Schlüsselsatz, Slogan
sense	Gespür
response	Reaktion, Erwiderung
tools	Mittel
cornerstone	Eckpfeiler
obscure	unklar, unverständlich, verworren *hier:* selten, ungewöhnlich

9C Betty Eitner

sap	Saft
spread	(Brot-)Aufstrich
potassium	Kalium
to grade	klassifizieren
to process	verarbeiten
to cap	etw. mit Deckel versehen
to harvest	ernten

Ontario

What do you know about Ontario? Try this quiz and find out.
(The answers are at the bottom of the page.)

1. Which is the largest city in Ontario?
a) Hamilton b) Scarborough c) Toronto

2. The capital of Canada also lies in Ontario. Which city is it?
a) London b) Ottawa c) Toronto

3. What do some Ontarians call their province?
a) The Central Province b) The Empire Province c) The Head Province

4. On which parliamentary system has the Canadian parliament modelled itself?
a) on the British system b) on the German system c) on the US system

5. What is 'Hudson Bay'?
a) a type of wine b) a huge inland sea c) a famous ship

6. What attracts millions of tourists to Ontario every year?
a) Hudson Bay
b) Point Pelee National Park
c) Niagara Falls

7. What is 'The Globe and Mail'?
a) the name of a newspaper
b) the name of a horse race
c) the name of a comedy duo

Answers: 1. c), 2. b), 3. b), 4. a), 5. b), 6. c), 7. a)

Overview

Christine Trauttmansdorff is a *clerk* at the House of Commons in Ottawa where she is responsible for recording the decisions of the members of parliament during debates. Christine talks about the system of government in Canada, how legislation comes about and the purpose of 'question period'. She also mentions that the proceedings in the House are broadcast across the country and made available to the public on the Internet both in English and French.

Ali Rahnema is Vice-President of Marketing at 'The Globe and Mail', one of Canada's national newspapers. Ali talks about the paper's *circulation*, its readers and some of the challenges it faces publishing nationally in a country as large as Canada.

Brenda K. Hobbs is the Manager of Records and Historical Information at the Hudson's Bay Company. Her job came about as part of an agreement with the Canadian government in which the Hudson's Bay Company would look for new information within the company's history and make that available to the public. Brenda tells the story of how the Hudson's Bay Company was founded and how it first traded with *aboriginal* communities in Canada.

David Crisp is also with the Hudson's Bay Company. As Senior Vice-President of *Human Resources* and Public Affairs he is primarily responsible for keeping the public informed of the history of the Company. David says that the Hudson's Bay Company has had customers in Canada for over 330 years and that the history of the Company is closely *tied to* the history of Canada.

Jim Orban works for Corel Corporation in Ottawa as Executive Vice President of Sales and Marketing. Corel is a young, dynamic company with employees from very different backgrounds. Corel's main challenge is to try to work out what consumers need from their software and from their computers two or three years into the future.

One of the members of the staff at Corel is **Erich Forler**. Erich shows us how important his computer is for him to communicate with people inside and outside the company and to organise his day. Erich relies heavily on email as a mode of communication but when he needs to discuss new ideas in detail he still uses the telephone.

Are Americans and Canadians basically one and the same? Some visitors to Niagara Falls seem to have differing opinions. **Mel and Carol Beatty**, for example, have mixed feelings. On the one hand they prefer Canadian gun laws to US gun laws and feel safer at home. On the other hand they think the standard of living is higher in the States than in Canada.

Find out more about ...

Christine Trauttmansdorff in **10A** (pages 166 – 169)

Ali Rahnema in **10B** (pages 170 – 174)

Brenda K. Hobbs in **10C** (pages 175 – 179)

10A Christine Trauttmansdorff

Christine Trauttmansdorff, *Deputy Principal Clerk* at the House of Commons in Ottawa, describes the structure of parliament in Canada. There are two houses: the Upper House, or Senate, and the Lower House or House of Commons. The other component of parliament is the Queen or the Crown who is represented in Canada by the Governor General. The 301 members of parliament are elected to the House of Commons by the citizens of Canada. Each one represents a *constituency*.

How many parties are there in the House of Commons?

'We have five political parties here in the House right now and that presents us with a rather diverse group of members of parliament, a very diverse number of points of view and opinions. The majority party forms the government. Right now we have a Liberal government and there's 156 members of the Liberal government. The official opposition is the Reform Party and we have three other parties also in the House. The government members sit on the Speaker's right, so over on this side of the House, and the Opposition sits on the Speaker's left. The official opposition sits usually closest to the Speaker and then the other opposition parties towards the back of the chamber.'

How does legislation *come about*?

'The legislation comes to the House in the form of a *bill*. Most of the bills that are dealt with are introduced by the government and they represent the measures that need to be put into place in order to *implement* the government's policies. Each bill comes to the House sponsored by a Minister of the Crown, a member of the cabinet, and it's debated over a series of reading stages, and then is eventually passed, and sent to the Senate, where it is again considered at numerous stages and finally goes to the Governor General to receive royal *assent*, and then becomes a statute or a law and is *enacted*.'

Apart from television how can people *keep track of* what is happening in the House of Commons?

'We also have the official record of the House and the debates … the *verbatim* transcript of the House called Hansard, which is … recorded every word that is spoken in the House, whether it's in English or in French – which are our two official languages – are translated into the other language, printed and not only made available to the members here the next morning but also published on an Internet site. And so anyone anywhere in the world can access that Internet site and read what the members of parliament, what the government, has said or decided about any particular issue.'

The House of Commons

Working with the text

I. Mark the best ending to the sentence.

1. The Canadian parliament consists of …
   a) two components. b) three components. c) four components.
2. The members of parliament in the House of Commons are elected by …
   a) the Governor General. b) the Senate. c) the people.
3. The government in Canada is formed by …
   a) the party which wins the most votes in an election.
   b) the party which has the most members in the Senate.
   c) the party which sits closest to the Speaker.
4. Before a bill becomes a law in Canada …
   a) the Crown must think it's a good idea.
   b) it must go through at least three stages in parliament.
   c) it is discussed with the Governor General.
5. If people want to find out exactly what has happened in the House of Commons …
   a) they can go and visit parliament themselves.
   b) buy Hansard.
   c) look at the House of Commons' Internet site.

II. *Answer the questions. Use your own words as far as possible.*

1. What are the components of the Canadian parliament?
2. What function does the Governor General have?
3. How many parties are there in the House of Commons at present? Where do they sit in the chamber?
4. Which stages must a bill go through before it becomes a law?
5. What exactly is 'Hansard'?

III. *Which word from the text is it?*

1. a voting area
2. the person who is in charge of the debates in the House of Commons
3. a plan for a new law
4. a formal word for an agreement
5. a written copy of spoken words

IV. *Replace the underlined words with words of the same (or similar) meaning.*

1. The other <u>component</u> of parliament is the Queen or the Crown … (line 4)
2. We have five political parties here in the House <u>right now</u> … (line 8)
3. The official opposition sits usually <u>closest</u> to the Speaker … (line 15)
4. … to be put into place in order to <u>implement</u> the Government's policies … (line 20)
5. … what the government has said or decided about any particular <u>issue</u> … (line 35)

V. *Say these words and expressions out loud.*

1. constituency
2. member of parliament
3. the government's policies
4. an official record of the debates
5. to access the Internet site
6. points of view

Exercises

I. *Complete this text. Fill in the missing words.*

chambers ◆ constituency ◆ election ◆ majority ◆ MPs ◆ opposition

Parliament in Canada consists of two … : the Senate and the House of Commons. In the House of Commons there are 301 …, each representing one … . The ruling party in the Commons is the one which gains a … of seats in the … . The other parties form the … .

II. Choose the correct word in the brackets.

1. The previous MP died. That's why there was a [vote/referendum/by-election].
2. Is she [running/sitting/walking] for parliament in the next election?
3. His father was [voted/stood/elected] MP in 1986.
4. What is Canada's defense [politics/policy/politician]?
5. Do you think Trudeau can be called a [politician/statesman/president]?
6. How many voters live in this [area/constituency/district]?

III. Explain the difference, if any, between ...

1. ... an 'ambassador' and an 'embassy'.
2. ... a 'mayor' and a 'prime minister'.
3. ... a 'chamber' and a 'cabinet'.
4. ... a 'bill' and a 'law'.

IV. Match the Latin expressions on the left (1-5) with their English equivalents on the right (a-e). Then add the German translations.

1. eg	a. compare
2. am	b. that is to say
3. ie	c. in the afternoon
4. pm	d. for example
5. cf	e. in the morning

An aerial view of Toronto

10B Ali Rahnema

One of only two national newspapers in the country, 'The Globe and Mail' was established in 1844 and is one of Canada's oldest newspapers. Based in Toronto, it has a circulation of 390,000 on a Saturday and 330,000 on a weekday and enjoys a readership of about 1,100,000 every day.

What challenges faces a newspaper published in a country like Canada?

'Today you have certain parts of this country, especially on the West coast, where you have close to 60 per cent of some of the areas near Vancouver and Western Canada that speak an Oriental language. There's been huge waves of migration from different parts of the world at different periods and so that has led to a cultural diversity that's one of the great *trademarks* of this country, but also linguistically a challenge. In a city like Toronto which is, according to all the statistics, the most multicultural or diverse city in the world in terms of the number of ethnicities represented, the latest statistics indicated that over 50 per cent of the people that live in Toronto today were not born in Canada, which is absolutely a *staggering* statistic.'

Is 'The Globe and Mail' an English-language publication?

'The issue of language, of course, is in the public domain, and the major issue has always been around English and French. Already we have the challenges of producing this paper in the context of a country as vast as Canada in eight printing zones, *printing plants* across the country, … bureaus in every province etc. If we were to take that work and then have to do it in French as well because printing a daily newspaper and producing a daily newspaper involves more than just taking content and translating it into another language. We have a very strong readership in Quebec, both Anglophone and Francophone and so clearly we're doing the right thing with an English product.'

What about the situation in Quebec?

'There are challenges. One of the big issues in Quebec, for example, is advertising. Because there have been over the years several laws that have been passed *barring* the use of the English language in advertising in Quebec. And the only exception to that is a cultural product that produces only in English. If we had a French edition we would have to do advertising in French in Quebec, but because we are only an English language newspaper, we are allowed to advertise from billboards to direct marketing to other magazines in Quebec, we are allowed to advertise in English, and that is a major *bone of contention* in Quebec itself.'

Getting the papers ready for delivery

Working with the text

I. Are these statements true or false according to the text? If they're false, correct them.

1. 'The Globe and Mail' is a weekly newspaper.
2. Its readership is greater than its circulation.
3. It is only printed in Ontario.
4. It appears in English and French.
5. It is not available in Quebec.

II. Answer these questions.

1. Which languages are spoken in Canada?
2. What is special about the city of Toronto?
3. What effect does the size of Canada have on the production of 'The Globe and Mail'?
4. What special status does 'The Globe and Mail' enjoy in Quebec?

III. Mark the correct ending to the sentence.

1. A 'staggering' (line 15) statistic is …
   a) interesting. b) surprising. c) worrying.

2. Language in the 'public domain' (line 17) is …
   a) language used on the Internet.
   b) language used in parliament.
   c) language used everywhere outside the home.
3. A 'billboard' (line 33) is …
   a) a large board for advertisements.
   b) a poster in a train.
   c) a part of a newspaper.
4. A 'bone of contention' (line 34) is …
   a) something which people don't want to pay for.
   b) something which people disagree about.
   c) something which people don't want to eat.

IV. Explain or define these words by completing the sentences.

1. The 'circulation' of a newspaper (line 2) …
2. A 'wave of migration' (lines 8-9) …
3. A 'Francophone' readership (lines 24-25) …
4. If you 'bar' something (line 29) you …

V. What about you? Answer the questions.

1. What sort of problems does 'The Globe and Mail' face that newspapers in your country do not face?
2. Do you read a daily newspaper? Which part of it do you read first? Which part of it do you enjoy most? (If you don't read a newspaper, say why you don't.)

Exercises

I. Look at a map of Canada. (See page 143 in this book). Check the names of the 3 territories and 10 provinces. One province is missing in this grid! Which is it?

Atlantic Provinces	4	New Brunswick, Newfoundland, Nova Scotia, Prince Edward Island
Central Provinces	2	Ontario, Quebec
Prairie Provinces	3	Alberta, Manitoba, Saskatchewan
Northern Territories	3	Northwest Territories, Yukon Territory, Nunavut Territory

II. Use the information in exercise I to complete these sentences.

1. 'The North' is another expression for the … .
2. 'Central Canada' is another term for the … .
3. The 'Maritimes' are the four Atlantic Provinces except … .
4. The 'West' refers to the four provinces west of Ontario. That means the three … and British Columbia.
5. The letters 'NFLD' must stand for … .

III. Some pairs of words are written in the same way but are stressed differently and have different meanings. Look up these pairs of words in your dictionary.

Are you con<u>tent</u> with your job?
The <u>con</u>tent of his speech was OK but the delivery was terrible.

1. re<u>fuse</u> – <u>re</u>fuse
2. mi<u>nute</u> – <u>mi</u>nute
3. <u>fre</u>quent – fre<u>quent</u>
4. ob<u>ject</u> – <u>ob</u>ject

IV. Which is the odd word out? Can you say why?

1. an editor – a librarian – a columnist
2. a crossword – a critic – a foreign correspondent
3. a tabloid – a horoscope – an editorial
4. a crossword – a small ad – a letter

V. Explain what these headlines mean using normal English.

CHANCELLOR CUTS INTEREST RATES

PRIME MINISTER TO VISIT TORONTO

BOMB BLASTS CENTRAL LONDON

AIRPORT BLAZE FOURTEEN DEAD

VI. Read this advertisement. Who is saying 'thank you'?

Of the 76 million words 'The Globe and Mail' published for our readers over the past year, these may well be the most important two.

Thank you!

VII. How is the population of Canada distributed? Look at the figures (in per cent) in the box. Can you guess where they go in the grid?

8 ◆ 62 ◆ 17 ◆ 0.5 ◆ 12.5

Region	%
Alberta, Manitoba and Saskatchewan	
British Columbia	12.5
Newfoundland, Prince Edward Island, Nova Scotia, New Brunswick	
Quebec and Ontario	
Yukon Territory, Nunavut Territory, Northwest Territories	

VIII. Link the names of the time zones to the numbers on the map.

Atlantic Standard Time ◆ Central Standard Time ◆ Eastern Standard Time ◆ Mountain Standard Time ◆ Newfoundland Standard Time ◆ Pacific Standard Time

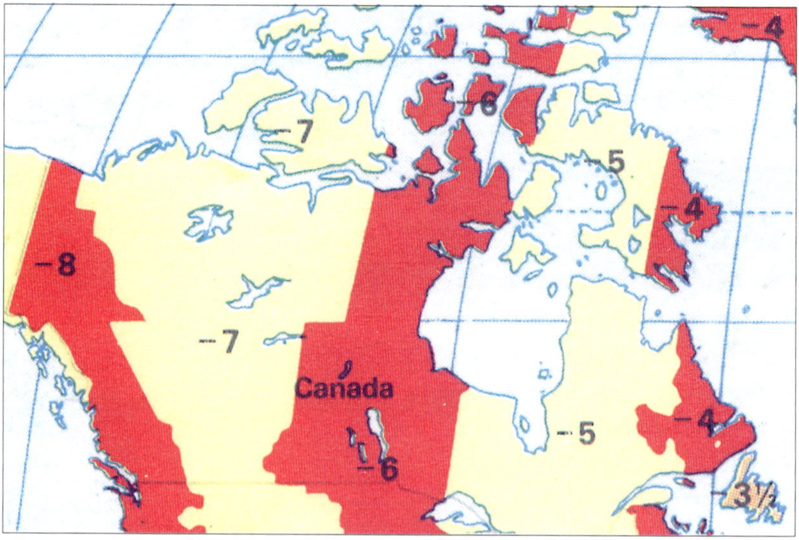

Note: Clock times are shown behind Greenwich Mean Time.

10C Brenda K. Hobbs

Brenda K. Hobbs, Manager of Records and Historical Information at the Hudson's Bay Company in Toronto, talks about fashion, the discovery of Hudson Bay and the Hudson's Bay Company.

'I like to think of the Company as having always been in the fashion business because in around the early sixteen hundreds the whole finding of North America was an accident. They were looking, of course, for another route to the East. They were looking for silks, spices and Asian items and instead Henry Hudson, who has no relationship to our company at all other than that the bay is named after him – the bay that we have the territories from. When they came, they *wound up* finding these fabulous, fabulous furs: beaver, *marten*, fox. And that was also something that was incredibly valuable for early sixteen hundred fashion.'

How did the Hudson's Bay Company begin?

'At that time they gave the authority for all of the land that flowed, any river that flowed into the Hudson's Bay and the James Bay became part of the ownership of the Hudson's Bay Company. And they had rights to farm it, *trap* it, anything like that. So that was the start of the Company. From there Radisson came through on the Nonsuch – it's a ship also very important in our history – and they continued trapping. They would be in settlements all along the bays and then the aboriginal community would come in to trade. That would be where they would start getting some of their items.'

What role did the aboriginal communities play in the growth of the Company?

'One of the major items that the aboriginal community was interested in were Hudson's Bay *blankets*. That was probably the primary item they traded for because it provided them with warmth. It was something that they could sew, they could cut into their clothing, they could use as tents. So they worked very hard to collect furs and then what happened was, it was very difficult to know how many furs it took for each blanket so what they started doing was putting little black stripes on a blanket showing how many furs it would take to purchase that blanket. And so they would have like a three-and-a-half point, a six-point, an eight-point blanket. So what happened was that the blanket was developed the first time in 1685. The exact same process, the same blanket is still sold in our stores today.'

Working with the text

I. Complete these sentences using the information in the text.

1. Explorers found North America by accident because … .
2. These people discovered something that was very precious: … .
3. The Hudson's Bay Company was very lucky because it … .
4. To buy the Hudson's Bay Company's blankets aboriginal communities … .
5. The Hudson's Bay Company's blankets had stripes on them so that … .

II. Look at the word 'they' in the text. Who does Brenda mean exactly?

1. They were looking, of course, for another route to the East … (line 6)
2. At that time they gave the authority for all of the land that flowed … (line 14)
3. And they had rights to farm it, trap it … (line 16)
4. It was something they could sew … (line 25)
5. … so what they started doing was putting little black stripes … (line 28)

III. Which ending to the sentence is best?

1. If you 'trap' land you …
   a) catch the animals on it. b) farm it. c) sell it.
2. A 'spice' is something like …
   a) gold and silver. b) ginger and pepper. c) beef and lamb.
3. If you 'wind up' doing something …
   a) you work hard to do something.
   b) you enjoy doing something.
   c) you end up doing something.

IV. Replace the underlined words with a word of the same (or similar) meaning.

1. … who has no relationship to our company at all … (line 8)
2. When they came, they wound up finding these fabulous, fabulous furs … (line 10)
3. That was probably the primary item they traded for … (line 24)
4. … showing how many furs it would take to purchase that blanket … (line 29)

V. Say these words out loud.

1. silks
2. beaver
3. valuable
4. aboriginal community
5. to sew
6. stripes

VI. What does the underlined word refer to in the text?

1. … other than that the bay is named after him … (line 9)
2. … it's a ship also very important in our history … (line 18)
3. … because it provided them with warmth … (line 25)
4. … the same blanket is still sold in our stores … (line 33)

Exercises

I. Replace the underlined word with the correct form of 'take' together with a preposition or adverb (multi-word verb).

1. Delivery will be delayed if we accept any more orders.
2. I hope I'm not occupying too much of your time.
3. What time does the plane depart?
4. She resembles her father, doesn't she?

II. Replace the underlined word with the correct form of 'turn' together with a preposition or adverb (multi-word verb).

1. Our request for more pay has been rejected.
2. Don't worry. I'm sure everything will be fine.
3. If he doesn't come soon, we'll have to start without him.
4. How long does it take the bus to reverse direction?

III. Read this advertisement for the Hudson's Bay blanket.

There are few items so richly entwined in the history of Canada as the Hudson's Bay Blanket. This blanket was one of the trade goods most highly prized by the Natives in exchange for beaver pelts. Much more than a superb virgin wool blanket, its outstanding craftsmanship, luxurious texture, superior warmth and the long-lasting beauty of its colours have earned the Hudson's Bay Blanket a unique place in Canadian history. Please see the selection box for product prices. Please note we cannot guarantee Christmas delivery for US orders at this time.

IV. The first sentences of the three paragraphs in the text on page 179 have been removed. Read the text and put the sentences into the correct position.

- For almost a century this monopoly was unchallenged.
- However, a monopoly that was so profitable could not be held for long.
- Hudson's Bay Company, formed in 1670, was originally an English corporation.

A It held a monopoly over trade in the region watered by rivers which flowed into Hudson Bay. In this huge territory the Company had the power to establish laws, to build forts, to maintain ships of war, and to make peace or war with the native peoples.

B The Company had grown slowly. By 1760 it had five coastal forts and 120 employees. The annual trade consisted of three or four shiploads of British goods in return for an equal weight of furs and skins.

C In 1783 a group of speculators formed the North West Company of Montreal and competed fiercely with the Hudson's Bay Company. Eventually, in 1821, the two great companies merged, with a combined territory that was extended by a license to the Arctic Ocean on the north and the Pacific Ocean on the west. In 1859, however, the trade monopoly was abolished and trade in the region was opened to any entrepreneur.

Niagara Falls, a waterfall in western New York and south-eastern Ontario is one of the biggest tourist attractions in North America

Overview

clerk	Schriftführer(in)
circulation	Auflage
aboriginal	Ureinwohner-
human resources	Personalwesen
to tie to	verbinden mit

10A Christine Trauttmansdorff

deputy principal clerk	stellvertretende(r) Hauptschriftführer(in)
constituency	Wahlkreis
to come about	zu Stande kommen
bill	(Gesetzes)entwurf
to implement	durchführen, vollziehen
assent	Zustimmung
to enact	verfügen, erlassen
to keep track of sth	auf dem Laufenden bleiben
verbatim	wortwörtlich

10B Ali Rahnema

trademark	Warenzeichen
staggering	verblüffend
printing plant	Druckerei
to bar	untersagen, verbieten
bone of contention	Zankapfel

10C Brenda K. Hobbs

to wind up	enden, landen
to wind up doing sth	am Ende etw. tun
marten	Marder
to trap	Fallen stellen
blanket	Decke

Alberta

What do you know about Alberta? Try this quiz and find out.
(The answers are at the bottom of the page.)

1. **In which year did Alberta become a province in its own right?**
   a) 1705 b) 1805 c) 1905

2. **Between which two provinces is Alberta situated?**
   a) Saskatchewan and British Columbia
   b) Ontario and Quebec
   c) New Brunswick and Nova Scotia

3. **Which are the two major cities in Alberta?**
   a) Burnaby and Vancouver
   b) Calgary and Edmonton
   c) Halifax and Sydney

4. **Which important international sporting event took place in Alberta in the 1980s?**
   a) the Superbowl b) the Winter Olympics c) the World Cup

5. **Which mountain range runs through the south-west corner of Alberta?**
   a) the Appalachian Mountains
   b) the Mackenzie Mountains
   c) the Rocky Mountains

6. **Which annual event is the city of Calgary famous for?**
   a) a marathon b) a rodeo c) a ski-jumping competition

7. **What does Alberta supply the rest of Canada with?**
   a) milk and butter b) oil and gas c) water

Answers: 1. c), 2. a), 3. b), 4. b), 5. c), 6. b), 7. b)

Overview

Ron Casey is Mayor of Canmore, a small community located 100 kilometres west of Calgary, in Alberta. Canmore was originally a mining town but in 1979 the mines closed and Canmore turned to tourism as its main source of income. Since 1988 Canmore has developed at an enormous rate. Despite this rapid growth the town has not neglected the environment. *Wildlife corridors* have been built so that enough green space is available for animals to move around without being disturbed.

G. Brooke Carter runs a printing company in Calgary. Brooke talks about the beginnings of his business, how T-shirts and other items of clothing are printed and what sort of investments are necessary to ensure that the company can grow and *prosper*.

Robert Ollerenshaw's grandfather came from England to Canada in 1913 and bought the farm where Robert was born and raised. Now Robert owns and runs the farm himself. Although he is not very optimistic about the future of farming Robert seems determined to keep going.

Earl Mennie, Robert Ollerenshaw's farm manager, talks about the work on the farm. From fall to spring it's mainly cattle work. In spring it's land work, including the preparation of the land, *fertilizer* application and seeding. At the end of August harvesting begins.

Jean Séguin and Manon McSween-Séguin are both members of the Royal Canadian *Mounted Police* (RCMP). In fact that's where they met. Jean's work involves examining crime scenes and *recovering forensic evidence* and fingerprints. Jean and Manon talk about the high quality of training given to cadets at the RCMP. Today the training is centralised so wherever cadets go eventually, the training they receive will be the same across the country.

Dr. Bruce Naylor is Director of the Royal Tyrrell Museum of Palaeontology in Drumheller, Alberta. The museum contains a magnificent collection of fossils and dinosaur bones. Recently the museum discovered a complete skeleton of a juvenile Albertosouras, a flesh-eating dinosaur named after the Canadian province. Apart from carrying out *fieldwork* and scientific research, the museum is also open to the public.

Jim Cabe, who also works at the Tyrrell Museum, has been spending some time getting a *specimen* ready for display in the museum. He is pleased with the progress he has made so far and is confident that the job will be finished in five or six months' time.

Find out more about ...

Ron Casey in **11A** (pages 184 – 188)

G. Brooke Carter in **11B** (pages 189 – 191)

Dr. Bruce Naylor in **11C** (pages 192 – 195)

11A Ron Casey

Ron Casey is the mayor of Canmore, a small community just on the edge of the Rocky Mountains and close to Banff National Park.

How has Canmore developed in the last 100 years?

'Initially Canmore was located here because of our coal mining. There are large coal deposits on the mountain *slopes* around us and so initially for the railroad the coal was needed to supply the trains moving back and forth through the mountains. But as time went on the need for our coal diminished and so in 1979 on July 13th our mine closed so that left Canmore *in a bit of a spot* because always being a mining town the people were worried, well what will we do in the future, what can we do to *sustain* ourselves? And so being so close to Banff National Park and to the ski areas of Banff we turned to tourism naturally. The Canmore Nordic Centre was built in 1988 to accommodate the Olympic Games and that really *put* Canmore *on the map*.'

How quickly has Canmore developed and what is being done to protect the environment as the town grows?

'As development has occurred in Canmore it has come at an alarming rate. It has, … we've been growing anywhere from 7 per cent to 12 per cent per year and so in municipal terms, that's extremely high. In a *municipality* if you had 3 per cent growth, that would be incredible growth. So 7 or 12 per cent growth is amazing growth. But one of the things that we've done all the time that we've been growing is that we've always put the environment out in front of us. We were always lucky to be surrounded by the natural environment but that also included herds of *elk*, grizzly bears, black bears, wolves, deer, cuckoos. So there was *an abundance of* wildlife around us. And so it was very clear right from the beginning that if we were to develop as a *destination resort*, or if we were going to develop for tourism, we wanted to be able to maintain that wildlife. We didn't want the development within the town of Canmore to destroy what we've always enjoyed about the area. So one thing that we've done particularly in Canmore is we've built wildlife corridors into all our developments and so there are *setbacks* from these environmentally sensitive areas. And we've made sure that there's enough green space that the animals can move through the town and around the town, hopefully without being too greatly disturbed.'

Canmore with a view of the Rockies

Working with the text

I. Mark the best ending to the sentence using the information in the text.

1. Canmore first grew as a town due to …
   a) Banff National Park.
   b) the recreational activities it could offer.
   c) its coal deposits.
2. In 1979 the mines around Canmore closed …
   a) because the coal was no longer required.
   b) because tourism became more important.
   c) because coal mining was bad for the environment.
3. In the 1990s Canmore …
   a) built a wildlife park.
   b) became a tourist resort.
   c) hosted the Olympic Games.
4. In recent years Canmore has been careful …
   a) not to grow too quickly.
   b) to protect the environment.
   c) to use its coal deposits.

II. Answer the questions. Use complete sentences.

1. What was Canmore's coal used for?
2. Which event helped Canmore to become well known?
3. How fast has Canmore's growth been in comparison to other towns?
4. What has been done in Canmore to protect the wildlife?

III. Which verb in the text means ...

1. to become less and less?
2. to keep oneself alive or in existence?
3. to provide room for somebody or something?
4. to take place?

IV. Mark the correct ending to the sentence.

1. If you are 'in a bit of a spot' (lines 8-9) you are ...
   a) in a fortunate position.
   b) in a difficult position.
   c) in an envious position.
2. If something 'puts you on the map' (line 13) it ...
   a) puts you under pressure.
   b) makes you poor.
   c) makes you famous.
3. If something grows at 'an alarming rate' (line 16) it ...
   a) grows normally. b) grows quickly. c) grows slowly.

V. What do you think? Answer the questions.

1. Ron talks about the Canmore Nordic Centre. What sports are done at a Nordic centre?
2. What else must Canmore offer if it accommodates an event like the Olympic Games?

Exercises

I. Replace the underlined word with the correct form of 'give' together with a preposition or adverb (multi-word verb).

1. He has <u>resigned from</u> his job.
2. I've no idea what is in the drawer but it's <u>emitting</u> an awful smell!
3. When are you going to <u>stop</u> smoking?
4. The chair <u>collapsed</u> under his enormous weight.

II. Replace the underlined word with the correct form of 'call' together with a preposition or adverb (multi-word verb).

1. Thanks for ringing. I'll telephone as soon as I have the information.
2. The management's offer persuaded the union to stop the strike.
3. If you're in the area, why don't you visit us? We'd love to see you!
4. The company have asked people to return all the cars with the faults.

III. Join the animals (1-6) to their noises (a-f).

1. Horses	a. croak
2. Pigs	b. howl
3. Frogs	c. neigh
4. Wolves	d. hoot
5. Owls	e. roar
6. Lions	f. grunt

IV. People can be compared to animals. Do these adjectives describe positive or negative characteristics? Look them up in a dictionary!

1. catty
2. sheepish
3. ratty
4. cocky

V. What sort of skiing can you do in Canmore?

SKI THE ROCKIES

JASPER AREA
BANFF AREA
KANANSKIS COUNTRY
LAKE LOUISE AREA
CANMORE NORDIC CENTRE

Banff Trail – This is the only trail at the Nordic Centre recommended for beginning skiers. This two way trail runs 6 km through the centre of the site to the boundary of Banff National Park. Skiers using this trail may turn around at any point. But please, for your safety and the safety of others, always keep to the right hand set of tracks.

Beyond the western boundary of the Canmore Nordic Centre the trail is not maintained or easily identifiable and is suitable for ski touring only. From this point it is 14 km to the Banff Springs Golf Course.

Recreational 2.5 km Loop – This trail is lighted for night skiing and utilizes part of the biathlon race course. You may see biathletes with rifles while skiing this trail, but the rifles are safe (bolts removed) and cannot be fired. The trail has a full range of degrees of difficulty.

VI. Did Manitoba, Alberta, Saskatchewan and British Columbia become part of Canada in the same year? What is special about Manitoba? Read this text and find out.

The British North America Act of 1867 created the Dominion of Canada (Quebec, Ontario, New Brunswick and Nova Scotia) and made it possible for other British possessions to join the four existing provinces.

Canadians began to look north and west to the huge territory between the Great Lakes and the Rocky Mountains. In March 1869 the Canadian government came to an agreement with the Hudson's Bay Company and British authorities. The Hudson's Bay Company would surrender (*übergeben, herausgeben*) its claim on the land in return for compensation in cash and real estate (*Immobilien*) and Britain would transfer the territory to Canada.

Plans for the Canadian takeover were upset (*durcheinander bringen, umwerfen*) in autumn 1869 however, when the Métis, an indigenous people living in the Red River colony (the region around the present-day city of Winnipeg), organized a resistance movement and prevented Canadian officials from entering the territory. The Canadian government was forced to offer guarantees for Métis property and other rights. As a result, the Red River region entered Canada as a province, called Manitoba, in 1870.

Beyond the prairies and the Rockies lay the province of British Columbia. In 1871 it too joined the Confederation, giving Canada a coast on the Pacific Ocean and allowing the railroad system to be extended across the continent. The federal government promised to pay off British Columbia's huge public debt and invest heavily in its economic development.

Meanwhile, settlement of the prairies had begun. By 1905 the population was large enough for local self-government. That year, two new provinces, Alberta and Saskatchewan, were established in the region between Manitoba and the Rocky Mountains.

VII. Why is July 1st a special day in the Canadian calendar? Try and find out!

11B G. Brooke Carter

G. Brooke Carter runs a company called 'Wheat Buckley and his Talking Horse Screenworks' in Calgary, Alberta. How did Brooke first get into the printing business?

'This is a company that my wife and I have been working in for the last almost 30 years. We started this company in 1970 in a very small space, about 1200 square feet, and just the two of us. Well, the Olympics came along and we sold 35,000 T-shirts in about 10 days. It was an extremely good thing for our company and as a result we were able to buy more machinery. Well now, 1999, we have 30 employees and our space is about 12, 15 times bigger.'

What sort of printing jobs can Brooke's company do?

'Sometimes people only want 12 shirts, 24 shirts. Well, on a job like that, there's no point in using the big automatic presses and we use the small manual presses. Or if we're doing complicated work, something like printing on sports bags or golf bags or *screening* things like bathing suits, we do those with the manual so that the people printing can be very careful and do a good job on them. We also have three automatic presses. One of them will print up to six colours, one will print up to ten colours and the other one which we put in when we expanded the building will print up to 14 colours. And it's one of the biggest T-shirt presses made and it was quite expensive I have to add. But it was very helpful for us because we have several customers that want very good artwork. One of our customers is a company called Canadian Pacific and they have a whole *bunch* of hotels all across Canada which are all very historic sites and we have done T-shirts from the old posters that were made up many years ago. So this historic line of T-shirts sells very well across the whole country for us. The only way that we could do that was to have a press that was large enough to print as many colours as we needed to do these really nice designs.'

How exactly are T-shirts printed?

'We use a simple *mesh* that is like a screen. It used to be made out of silk. That's why the process was called silk screening. Now it's made out of polyester. It's much stronger. But the process is exactly the same. We cover it with an emulsion. We put the ink through the holes in the screen directly onto the T-shirt. After the T-shirt has been printed it goes through a dryer which *cures* the ink and it takes about 30 seconds. So after the T-shirt has been printed, 30 seconds later, you can wear it!'

Working on T-shirt designs

Working with the text

I. *Are these statements true or false or does the text not say?*
Tick the appropriate box in the grid.

	T	F	N
1. Brooke has been very successful with his printing business.			
2. He employs members of his – and his wife's – family.			
3. His company only prints T-shirts and sweatshirts.			
4. All the printing is done automatically.			

II. *Answer these questions using complete sentences.*

1. Why were the Olympics so important for Brooke's business?
2. Why does the company have manual and automatic presses?
3. What is the advantage for Brooke of having machines that can print 14 colours?
4. How do you know that Brooke is doing business all over Canada?

III. *What does the underlined word refer to in the text?*

1. <u>It</u> was an extremely good thing for our company … (line 7)
2. One of <u>them</u> will print up to six colours … (line 16)
3. … and <u>they</u> have a whole bunch of hotels all across Canada … (line 21)
4. … <u>it</u> goes through a dryer which cures the ink … (line 32)

IV. Find another word in the text which is pronounced in the same way as the words in this list.

1. feat
2. bye
3. hole
4. sight
5. threw
6. where

V. Read what Brooke says towards the end of the film sequence. What problem do you think he has in his company?

'But it's a good business. And it's a very complicated business. And it takes lots of training. We have to get the people to be able to produce the quality of work that we like to do.'

VI. What do you think? Answer the questions.

1. What impression do you have of Brooke? Does he still enjoy his work after 30 years in the business?
2. Was it clever of Brooke to choose such an unusual name for his business? Say why/why not.

Exercises

I. Which adjective (a-f) describes what these objects (1-6) feel like?

1. a wet bar of soap	a. prickly
2. branches on a rose bush	b. glossy
3. the surface of a mirror	c. jagged
4. an expensive fashion brochure	d. rough
5. broken glass	e. slippery
6. a tree trunk	f. smooth

II. Use four words from the box to complete these sentences.

dim ◆ dazzling ◆ glaring ◆ hollow ◆ polished ◆ shady ◆ vivid

1. Can you turn off that light, please! It's … me!
2. If the torch light is a bit … you probably need some new batteries.
3. Did you like the way she looked at the audience with her … blue eyes?
4. It's so hot on the terrace! Let's go and sit in a … corner of the garden.

III. When were the Winter Olympics held in Calgary, Alberta?

a) 1984 b) 1988 c) 1992

11C Dr. Bruce Naylor

Bruce Naylor talks about the Royal Tyrrell Museum of Palaeontology in Drumheller, Alberta.

'One of the unique aspects of what we do is we can go out our back door and find dinosaurs, *fossil mammals*, fossil birds, any of the great diversity of *extinct* animals that used to inhabit our province. Recently we discovered a complete skeleton of a juvenile Albertosouras, which is a flesh-eating dinosaur named obviously for our province and this specimen was *magnificent* because it's complete from the tip of the nose right down to the very end of the tail.

The museum obtained its royal *designation* when Queen Elizabeth II visited our province some years ago and it was a great honour to receive this designation. In addition to doing fieldwork, scientific research, we are also a public museum, we *boast* upwards of 400,000 visitors annually. We run public programs, we encourage visitors to participate in *field digs* and explorations and we basically present to the public of the province and the world what Alberta's fossil history is about.'

Working with the text

I. *Answer these questions using complete sentences.*

1. Why is the Tyrrell Museum where it is?
2. What two main things does the museum exhibit?
3. What was so special about the recent discovery that was made?
4. Why is the museum called the 'Royal' Tyrrell Museum?
5. What other work takes place at the museum besides showing exhibits?
6. What shows you that the Tyrrell Museum is popular?

II. *Replace the underlined words with other words of the same (or similar) meaning.*

1. … diversity of extinct animals that used to <u>inhabit</u> our province … (line 5)
2. <u>Recently</u> we discovered a complete skeleton … (line 5)
3. … this specimen was <u>magnificent</u> because it's complete … (line 7)
4. … we boast upwards of 400,000 visitors <u>annually</u> … (line 12)

III. *Put the words in the box into the correct category.*

addition ◆ Alberta ◆ complete ◆ dinosaur ◆ extinct ◆ fossil ◆ history ◆ museum ◆ research ◆ royal ◆ skeleton ◆ unique

oO	Oo	Ooo	oOo

IV. *What does the underlined word refer to in the text?*

1. One of the unique aspects of what <u>we</u> do … (line 3)
2. … named obviously for <u>our</u> province … (line 7)
3. … because <u>it</u>'s complete from the tip of the nose … (line 8)
4. … it was a great honour to receive <u>this designation</u> … (lines 10-11)

V. *What do these expressions mean? Explain them using your own words.*

1. … we can go out our back door and find … (lines 3-4)
2. … we encourage visitors to participate in field digs … (line 13)

Exercises

I. Use 'used to' + a verb which fits in.

1. John … the piano but now he just listens to his CDs.
2. We often … to the movies but now we watch videos instead.
3. Before they got their PC they … their letters by hand.
4. Fiona … a lot but now she mostly stays at home in the evenings.
5. Some years ago we … tennis every other day. Now we don't do any sport.
6. My brother … cigars until recently.

II. Say these sentences making sure to pronounce the underlined words correctly.

1. She likes to <u>use</u> her time wisely.
2. We <u>used</u> your CD player last night.
3. They didn't <u>use</u> to have a video recorder.
4. Did you <u>use</u> my Walkman yesterday?
5. They <u>used</u> to watch a lot of violent films.
6. He <u>used</u> to have a TV in his room.

III. What is the difference between 'to be used to' + gerund and 'used to' + infinitive? Translate the following sentences into German.

1. She used to live in a village.
2. She is used to living in the city now.
3. He used to work for a Canadian company.
4. He was used to speaking English at work.

- Which word describes something you no longer do?
- Which word means you do (or did) something easily because you do (or did) it so often?

IV. Read these mini-dialogues. What do the expressions signal? Choose an answer from the box.

– being more precise	– giving yourself more time
– indicating an afterthought	– introducing an explanation
– making a suggestion	– signalling the end of the dialogue

1.
- It's cold, isn't it?
- Yes, very.
- *Having said that*, it is January so it's not surprising.

2.
- What's your new phone number?
- *Let me see*, I've written it down somewhere.
- You can give it to me another time if you want.

3. • I need to fix my car but I haven't got the right tools.
   • *Look*, why don't you let me repair it for you?
   • Would you? That'd be great.

4. • So you live in Canmore, do you?
   • *Well*, near Canmore, actually.
   • It's not Banff, is it?

5. • I'm afraid I can't come to your party next Saturday.
   • Oh, dear. That's a pity.
   • *Anyway*, thanks for the invitation.

6. • Theresa speaks English well, doesn't she?
   • Yes. *Mind you*, she did spend a year in Canada.
   • Did she really? When?

V. Read this newspaper article. Four sentences in it don't make sense. Can you find them?

Briton escapes as bear raids camp in Rockies

A grizzly bear attacked six tourists in a camp site in the Canadian Rockies, destroying their tents and almost killing two of them. A British tourist in a nearby tent had to run for his life. The 300lb she-bear entered the site near Lake Louise in Banff National Park at about 3am on Monday. There had been a lot of snow at the weekend. It rolled on the first tent, flattening it and terrifying the German couple inside.

'They started to scream and the bear bit and slashed at anything that was moving underneath,' said Bob Haney, the park's chief warden. How dare you say such things about me? The bear then went on to do the same to two Americans and then two Australians in the next tent. The fireworks were spectacular and memorable. A British tourist, Steve Edgington of London, was awakened by his fellow campers' screams and ran from his tent.

'There was lots of scratching and ripping and it was so close that I just thought, "Well, my tent's next!",' Mr Edgington said. 'So I opened my tent, turned the other way and just ran.'

Four people were injured, two seriously. The position will involve international travel. An Australian and a German are 'fair' in a Calgary hospital. The other two were released after treatment in a local clinic.

The bear and her 100lb cub were later trapped and shot.

Overview

wildlife corridors	Lebensräume für wild lebende Tiere
to prosper	wachsen, gedeihen
fertilizer	Dünger
mounted police	berittene Polizei
to recover	sicherstellen
forensic	gerichtsmedizinisch
evidence	Beweis
fieldwork	Feldforschung
specimen	Exemplar

11A Ron Casey

slope	Abhang, Hang
to be in a bit of a spot	in Schwierigkeiten sein, in der Klemme sitzen
to sustain	erhalten, unterhalten
to be put on the map	bekannt werden, einen Namen bekommen
municipality	Stadt, Gemeinde
elk	Elch
an abundance of	eine Überfülle von
destination resort	Erholungsziel
setback	*hier im Sinne von: Rückzugsmöglichkeiten*

11B G. Brooke Carter

to screen	im Siebdruckverfahren bedrucken
bunch	Haufen
mesh	Netz-, Gittergewebe
to cure	haltbar machen durch Trocknen

11C Bruce Naylor

fossil	fossil, versteinert
mammal	Säugetier
extinct	ausgestorben
magnificent	großartig, prachtvoll
designation	Ernennung, Bezeichnung
to boast	sich rühmen
field digs	Feldausgrabungen

British Columbia

What do you know about British Columbia? Try this quiz and find out.
(The answers are at the bottom of the page.)

1. Who gave British Columbia its name?
a) George Washington b) Henry Hudson c) Queen Victoria

2. How many people live in British Columbia?
a) 4 million b) 40 million c) 400 million

3. Which is British Columbia's capital?
a) Vancouver b) Vernon c) Victoria

4. Mount Fairweather is the highest mountain in British Columbia. How high is it?
a) 2663 m b) 4663 m c) 8663 m

5. How many US states border on British Columbia?
a) none b) two c) four

6. How far is Vancouver from the US border?
a) 42 km b) 420 km c) 4200 km

7. About 15 per cent of the population of Vancouver speak a language which is not English. Which language is it?
a) French b) Chinese c) Punjabi

Answers: 1. c), 2. a), 3. c), 4. b), 5. c), 6. a), 7. b)

Overview

Dorothy Grant belongs to the Raven Clan of the Higher Nation, a group of *First Nations people* from the northern part of British Columbia. Dorothy is a fashion designer who has used her *ancestral* roots to create a new form of art and design in fashion. Dorothy's work is known throughout Canada and in many parts of the United States.

Peter Mitchell is Director of the British Columbia Film Commission in Vancouver. He describes how the Commission tries to attract the film business to Vancouver. If a film producer in the US, for example, has a project and is searching for suitable *locations* he might send the film scripts to Vancouver. The Commission will then try to match the locations in the script to locations in British Columbia. If the producer and the director like what the Commission can offer they will come to British Columbia and look at the locations themselves. If everything goes well, the *film* will *be shot* in Canada.

John F. Timms is the community relations co-ordinator for Translink, the operator of SkyTrain, the driverless train in Vancouver. John describes how regional planners first came together in Vancouver to find ways of reducing pollution in the city. Their solution was the SkyTrain, a fully automated regional train service. Although the service is driverless, it is very safe. Apart from hundreds of cameras monitoring the system there are also alarm systems on the trains and in the stations providing passengers with a quick and effective method of asking for help.

David E. Park, Chief Economist and Assistant Managing Director for the Vancouver *Board of Trade*, is considering some issues concerning urban transportation. David is concerned about public reaction towards the cost of SkyTrain following a decision to expand the network. He would therefore like to prepare a *policy statement* for the Board of Trade which can be issued as a statement to the public.

Glenn Voung is an independent businessman who *chairs* the Community Affairs Committee at the Vancouver Board of Trade. The committee deals with issues such as transport, healthcare and crime. Glenn is hoping to advise David Park on the issue of the SkyTrain.

Firoz Rasul is President and *Chief Executive Officer* (*CEO*) of Ballard Power Systems, a company that is involved in the development of *fuel cell* technology. Firoz explains that fuel cell technology is an environmentally clean power source which can be used in a large range of applications.

Find out more about …

Peter Mitchell in **12A** (pages 200 – 204)
John F. Timms in **12B** (pages 205 – 209)
Firoz Rasul in **12C** (pages 210 – 213)

12A Peter Mitchell

British Columbia is the third-largest film and television production centre in North America. How do film and TV producers come to choose British Columbia as a location for their productions? Peter Mitchell, Director of the British Columbia Film Commission in Vancouver, explains.

'If you're a producer with the five elements that are needed to create a film, which are the script, the producer and the director, and the star and the money, and you come *prancing* down the steps of Paramount with this great 50 million dollar project, which is the size of the average US *feature film* these days, you will send that script to a number of film commissions. So perhaps British Columbia, Ontario, Washington State, Norway and Egypt. And we along in competition with the other commissions will take that script and *break* it *down* to locations. We will then go to our film library of *still photos* actually, and we will try and match the locations in the script to locations in British Columbia, so if they need a cabin on a lake in the woods with a mountain in the background we have a selection of those kind of *locales*, plus a *gritty* urban alley where someone might be involved in a car chase or a *shootout*. So we will put together a package of different alternatives, will send that back to the producer … to him in Los Angeles and they compare those different *bids*, if you will, all of which are associated with a price tag. And, fortunately for us right now, British Columbia is very, very cheap in terms of our international pricing, so we get quite a bit of the work coming here.'

Why is British Columbia so popular with film producers at the moment?

'The reasons that people come to British Columbia to shoot, particularly from Los Angeles, are numerous but the key one is the *exchange rate*. People come here because their exchange rate is favourable and they can get a better value for their money here in Canada than they can elsewhere. They stay because of the experience. And the experience is that we are only two and a half hours away by plane from Los Angeles, we're in the same time zone, we have very good crews, we have the infrastructure, we have *stages* that have been built to accommodate all the production. And the *overall* experience that people have here tends to bring them back again and again.'

Working with the text

I. Mark the best ending to the sentence using the information in the text.

1. Peter Mitchell is …
   a) a film director.
   b) the head of an organisation that does business with film companies.
   c) the boss of a film studio.
2. The British Columbia Film Commission …
   a) makes films in British Columbia.
   b) produces films in British Columbia.
   c) attracts film makers to British Columbia.
3. The British Columbia Film Commission has competitors …
   a) in British Columbia. b) in Canada. c) all over the world.
4. One of the reasons the Commission has been so successful is …
   a) the good price that they can offer.
   b) the good weather that they can offer.
   c) the good infrastructure that they can offer.

II. Which line(s) in the text show(s) you that …

1. British Columbia is an important part of the North American film industry?
2. British Columbia can offer very different film locations?
3. filming in British Columbia is not as expensive as in other parts of the world?
4. Vancouver is close to the centre of the US film industry?

III. Answer these questions. Use complete sentences, please.

1. What, according to Peter, are the five things needed to make a film?
2. How does the Film Commission start looking for locations?
3. What one thing is particularly favourable for British Columbia at present?
4. What advantages are there for Californian film producers if they shoot their films in British Columbia?

IV. Explain the meaning of these words and phrases.

1. a script (line 6)
2. a director (line 6)
3. a car chase (line 16)
4. a favourable exchange rate (line 25)

V. What about you? Answer the questions.

1. When did you last go to the movies? What did you watch? Did you enjoy it?
2. Do you watch a lot of television? What sort of programmes do you like best?

Exercises

I. Replace the underlined word with the correct form of 'put' together with a preposition and/or adverb.

1. The crew has made a claim for a shorter working week.
2. We refuse to tolerate this sort of behaviour.
3. My husband broke his wrist so we'll have to postpone our holiday.
4. We'll have to work a lot of overtime to finish this production.

II. Replace the underlined word with the correct form of 'look' together with a preposition and/or adverb.

1. I'm trying to find their bid.
2. He'll take care of the post while we're away.
3. We will investigate the matter as soon as possible.
4. He's very popular and all the crew respect him.

III. What's the difference, if any, between ...

1. a 'director' and a 'conductor'?
2. a 'cabin' and a 'house'?
3. a 'library' and a 'bookshop'?
4. 'Ontario' and 'Ottawa'?
5. a 'million' and a 'billion'?

The Rocky Mountains

IV. Read out the text making sure you say the numbers correctly.

'Last year, in 1998, we did 808 million dollars' worth of production, and that is a figure that has grown at a rate of more than 20 per cent per year over the last twenty years. In fact, last year we grew 28 per cent. We are only second to New York and Los Angeles now in terms of our relative size in North America. The overall economic impact of the film and television industry in BC is over two billion dollars and it employs more than 25,000 people.'

V. Ask and answer these questions.

1. How many hours of TV do you watch a week?

- Less than 5 hours?
- 6 - 15 hours?
- More than 15 hours?

2. Do you watch TV ...

- at the weekend?
- in the evening?
- in the morning?
- alone?

3. If you have a video recorder at home, do you ...

- hire videos from a shop and watch them?
- record TV programmes and watch them?
- exchange videos with friends?

4. Do you switch the TV on ...

- only when you know what is on?
- when you don't know what is on?

5. When your favourite programme is over, do you ...

- switch the TV off immediately?
- see what is on the other channels?

6. Which of the following programmes do you like watching most? Name three in order of preference.

- news
- sports programmes
- chat shows
- documentaries
- comedy programmes
- music programmes
- soap operas
- films

7. Does watching TV affect other activities you do or not? Does it or does it not affect ...

- listening to the radio?
- going to the cinema?
- listening to music?
- going to bed?
- reading?
- getting up?

VI. Read this article. What does it say about Vancouver?

Switzerland comes out top

London ranks 34th in the world for quality of living, ahead of New York but behind Berlin, Paris and Tokyo.

The survey, conducted by William M. Mercer, one of the world's largest human resources consultancies, judged the cities according to a set of 10 criteria each marked out of 10. These *ranged from* political, economic and social environment, *through* healthcare and educational provision *to* recreation and transport infrastructure.

Each city was scored with New York used as the base city with a score of 100 which put it in 50th place. Overall US cities suffered on the grounds of high crime rates and unfavourable personal security issues. The highest ranked US city was Honolulu with 104 points.

London was marginally ahead of New York with 101.5. It scored maximum points for the personal freedom allowed its residents and freedom from 'troublesome and destructive animals and insects'. Its poorest scores – six out of 10 – were awarded for its climate and traffic congestion. Behind London were Glasgow, with 99 points, and Birmingham, with 98, ranked 55th and 60th respectively.

Albert Bore, leader of Birmingham city council, was pleased with his city's performance. He said: 'We were particularly pleased to compare so well with modern *vibrant* cities like Chicago, New York, Barcelona and Madrid.'

In joint 1st place were Vancouver, Berne, Vienna and Zurich while Sydney, Geneva, Auckland and Copenhagen *tied for 2nd*. Swiss cities occupied three of the top 10 *slots* making it the single most successful country of all those surveyed.

VII. Which is your favourite city? Write a short text (60–80 words) giving some reasons for your choice.

to range from … through … to	reichen von … über … bis
vibrant	dynamisch
to tie for 2nd place	sich den 2. Platz teilen
slot	Position

12B John F. Timms

SkyTrain is a fully automated train which operates on a 29-kilometre-long, rapid transit line in Vancouver. It carries about 140,000 passengers per day and has been *in operation* since 1986. John F. Timms, Community Relations Coordinator for Translink, the operator of the SkyTrain system, explains how regional planners decided on this system of public transport for their city.

'The SkyTrain system's history goes back about 25 years ago when the regional planners of the Greater Vancouver area were looking for a creative way that they could reduce the number of cars that come from the suburban areas into the *downtown core*. At that time we had all of the employment, all of the cultural activities, the theatres, the restaurants, everything within downtown Vancouver. Downtown Vancouver was surrounded by 18,000 square kilometres of what we call '*bedroom communities*'. This is where people live. People live in the suburbs. They commute to Vancouver to work. About 25 years ago we first noticed that we were having problems with the quality of our air. We were noticing an increase in air pollution. Vancouver is not an industrial city. Close to 80 per cent of that pollution came from private automobiles. So the regional planners came together to look at ways they could reduce the number of cars coming into the city.'

SkyTrain is driverless so how can Translink ensure that passengers can enjoy a safe ride?

'We have about 300 cameras on our system. Most cameras are used to monitor the stations, to watch the stations to see if perhaps there is a passenger in a wheelchair that might need assistance. On the platform we also have a number of alarm systems. In the *emergency cabinets*, and every station has at least two emergency cabinets, we have emergency telephones. Above the telephone there is a red button. This button will allow passengers to stop the automatic movement of trains. They can close the station. If someone or something falls down into the track, all of the red area, all of the plates on the track, if they are disturbed, this will also stop the automatic movement of the train. The yellow line above the window, above the seats along the middle of the window, is a silent alarm. If passengers reach up and touch this yellow strip this sends a silent electronic message to the control room. This is an indication that there is a problem on board of the train.'

Working with the text

I. *Are these statements true or false according to the text? If they are false, correct them.*

1. SkyTrain is a driverless train.
2. It first operated 25 years ago.
3. The aim of SkyTrain is to stop people taking their cars into Vancouver.
4. Although SkyTrain is fully automated, it is very safe.

II. *Answer the questions. Use full sentences, please.*

1. What effect did the 'bedroom communities' have on the pollution levels in Vancouver?
2. What two ways are there for SkyTrain passengers to ask for help?
3. Can passengers actually stop the trains? If so, how?
4. What is the function of the yellow strip inside the trains?

III. *Find a word or expression in the text which means …*

1. someone who travels on a train
2. an area on the edge of a city
3. to travel to work and back every day
4. part of a station where you wait for the train

IV. *Replace the underlined words with words of the same (or similar) meaning.*

1. About 25 years ago we first <u>noticed</u> that we were having problems … (line 14)
2. <u>Close to</u> 80 per cent of that pollution came from private automobiles … (line 16)
3. So the regional planners <u>came together</u> to look at ways … (line 17)
4. This is an <u>indication</u> that there is a problem on board the train. (line 32)

V. *Say these sentences out loud.*

1. 'It carries about 140,000 passengers per day.'
2. 'Downtown Vancouver was surrounded by 18,000 square kilometres of what we call "bedroom communities".'
3. 'Close to 80 per cent of that pollution came from private automobiles.'
4. 'We have about 300 cameras on our system.'

VI. *What do you think? Answer the questions.*

1. What's your opinion of SkyTrain?
2. Are you concerned about pollution levels in the place where you live and work?

The SkyTrain

Exercises

I. What's the opposite of the underlined words? Say the complete sentence.

1. The number of cars going into the city has increased.
2. There was a sudden increase in pollution levels.
3. Above the telephone is a red button.
4. 25 years ago people were aware of the problems.

II. Complete the sentences. Use the correct form of the verb (gerund or infinitive) in brackets.

1. He mentioned (see) a similar train somewhere in the States.
2. I look forward to (hear) from you in the near future.
3. We avoided (use) an expensive design.
4. They are attempting (maintain) the present level of air pollution.
5. The Board of Trade want the bank (lend) them more money.
6. We have asked Mr Timms (come) as soon as possible.
7. The trains start (run) at 5am.
8. I advise you (consult) a specialist before reaching a decision.
9. We agree (pay) on receipt of the goods.
10. His boss refused (let) him take his holidays in August.

III. Vancouver has an opera company, a ballet company, orchestras and dance companies. But what about the theatre? Read this text. Would you say the theatre is popular in Vancouver?

The ***Vancouver Playhouse Theatre Company*** *is dedicated to producing live theatre of the highest quality – to presenting a stimulating and challenging repertoire of plays of enduring value and relevance that speak to today's audience.*

An Overview: *The Vancouver Playhouse Theatre Company was founded in 1962 to provide the people of British Columbia with professional live theatre. The Playhouse raised the curtain on its very first production, The Hostage by Brendan Brehan, in 1963. Since that time The Vancouver Playhouse Theatre Company has grown from a core of volunteers operating out of basement offices into one of the country's leading regional theatre companies, presenting an outstanding selection of plays produced by the very best actors, directors, designers and craftspeople from across the country. The company has a rich history of premiering original Canadian plays, including the highly-acclaimed Ecstasy of Rita Joe by George Ryga, Herringbone, the musical by Tom Cone, If We Are Women by Joanna McClelland Glass, and The Overcoat by Morris Panych and Wendy Gorling.*

Programming: *The Playhouse recently expanded its programming to produce a seven-play season which runs from September through May. The company offers a five-play Mainstage subscription series, and will also stage two limited engagement productions for the next season. All Mainstage performances are held at the Vancouver Playhouse Theatre, a civic theatre located at Hamilton and Dunsmuir in the heart of the city's entertainment district. Each Mainstage production has a run of approximately 30 performances over a four week schedule. Special performances are held for students through the Student Matinee Series, and for seniors through two Wednesday Tea Matinees. The Artistic Director selects the plays, guest directors and leading roles for the season.*

mainstage production	Vorstellung im eigenen Haus
subscription	Abonnement
to stage	aufführen
engagement production	Gastspiel
run	Laufzeit

IV. Read this text about immigration into Canada. One piece of information in it is wrong. Can you guess which it is?

Immigrants make up about 16 per cent of the population of Canada. For most of post-colonial history people from Europe were favoured but in the 1960s this practice was replaced by new rules which classified immigrants into three groups:

- refugees fleeing political persecution
- family members of Canadian citizens
- independent immigrants

Independent immigrants are admitted into Canada under a point system (level of education, experience in the labour market, knowledge of one or both official languages, etc). Those with enough points are allowed to become permanent residents and, ten years later, Canadian citizens.

V. Look at these statistics showing which part of the world people entering Canada in the 1990s came from. Why do you think the figure for Asia is so high? Read the text below to find out.

Source	**%**
Asia	47
Europe	26
South America / Caribbean	12
North / Central America	9
Africa	6

The top ten source countries in the 1990s were Hong Kong, India, the Philippines, China, Sri Lanka, Taiwan, Bosnia and Herzegovina, England, the United States and Pakistan. Migration from Hong Kong was especially prominent during the 1990s due to the concern in Hong Kong over the return of the colony to China in 1997.

12C Firoz Rasul

Firoz Rasul is the President and Chief Executive Officer of Ballard Power Systems in Vancouver. Ballard is involved in the development of fuel cell technology. Why is fuel cell technology so important?

'Fuel cell is an environmentally clean *power generation device*. It is a way of making electricity without pollution and making electricity in a way that is highly efficient, and can be used in many, many different applications. The fuel cell originally came from the space programme. It was used by NASA in the Gemini space programme, which was before Apollo, and did not have any commercial applications until the last ten years.'

What applications are there for fuel cells?

'Over the last ten years the fuel cell has been demonstrated in many different areas; not just for cars, buses and trucks, but also in power generation devices for homes, for buildings, for ships, for trains, but also in what we call small *portable* power generation devices that can be used in a boat or in a *recreational vehicle* or for *remote power*, like a small generator that can be used in a picnic or camping and so on. So a fuel cell has as many applications as your imagination will allow you to think about. And we are now getting ready to develop prototypes with our *automotive* partners and customers. And we have customers that include not just DaimlerChrysler and Ford, but also General Motors, Nissan, Honda, Volkswagen, Volvo who are beginning to evaluate fuel cells as the next-generation technology for *powering* vehicles.'

What makes fuel cell technology so exciting?

'Fuel cells will be the technology of the next hundred years because it is a revolutionary technology which will replace not only the internal *combustion engine*, but other conventional power technologies and we will see it all over the world in as many different applications, as I said, if your imagination will allow you to think about. And the only thing that will be limiting is how creative we can be in thinking about the applications for the future.'

Working with the text

I. Finish these sentences using the information in the text.

1. The future of fuel cell technology looks promising because … .
2. The idea for the fuel cell came first … .
3. There's a whole range of areas where fuel cells can be used such as … .
4. For Ballard there are commercial applications for the technology including … .

II. Which part of the text does the underlined word refer to?

1. <u>It</u> was used by NASA in the Gemini space programme … (line 7)
2. … also in what <u>we</u> call small portable power generation devices … (line 13)
3. … in as many applications, as <u>I</u> said, if your imagination … (line 26)
4. … how creative <u>we</u> can be in thinking about the applications … (line 28)

III. Say these words and expressions out loud.

1. fuel
2. vehicle
3. prototype
4. imagination
5. next-generation technology
6. engine

IV. What do you understand by the following expressions? Explain their meaning.

1. space programme (line 7)
2. recreational vehicle (lines 14-15)
3. prototype (line 18)
4. revolutionary technology (line 24)

V. What do you think? Give answers and add some reasons.

1. What do you do on a day-to-day basis to help reduce air pollution?
2. Will the next hundred years see the conventional car engine being replaced by alternatives?

Vancouver harbour

Exercises

I. Shorten the sentences by using a present participle.

1. Mike first became interested in the environment while he was helping out on his uncle's farm.
2. Before he left college, he joined Our Earth, an environmental pressure group.
3. He started a job in a chemical company soon after he had completed his studies.
4. After he had been with the firm for two years, Mike decided to do something completely different.
5. 'I opened my own fruit and vegetable shop – but not before I'd informed myself about organically-grown food.'
6. 'I read a lot and while I read,' he explained, 'I make notes.'
7. In the week before he opened his shop, Mike was not sure what people's reaction would be.
8. 'After they had tasted the difference between my apples and the supermarket's, I knew my customers would buy my produce,' Mike said and smiled.

II. Translate these sentences bringing out the difference in meaning.

1a. Living in a small village, Jack's girlfriend had to drive him to the station every morning.

1b. Living in a small village is not everybody's wish.

2a. Not having his own car, Mark had to borrow his sister's whenever he could.

2b. Not having your own car is becoming fashionable for young people.

III. Which word (or words) is it? Write it (them) down.

1. cars, trains, planes:
2. cauliflower, peas, Brussel sprouts:
3. Monday, Thursday, Friday:
4. pineapple, cherries, pears:
5. summer, fall, winter:
6. hydrogen, oxygen, nitrogen:
7. tea, apple juice, coffee:
8. archery, judo, javelin:
9. waistcoat, gloves, tie:
10. ballet, opera, pantomime:

IV. Complete this text. Use the correct form of the words in brackets.

With the world's population … (grow) by 90 million every year, more and more energy … (require). When energy sources such as coal, oil and gas … (use up), they … (can, not, renew). This is why many countries … (now, develop) renewable energy sources. The amount of energy which the Earth … (receive) from the sun, for example, is enormous. With the benefit of modern technology … (science) have developed ways of … (use) this energy to produce power. One of the world's … (large) solar power plants … (can, find) in the Mojave desert in California. The plant itself … (surround) by hundreds of mirrors. The mirrors … (reflect) the sun's … (hot) to a central boiler, … (contain) water. The water boils, … (give off) steam and this drives a turbine … (link) to an electricity generator. The electricity … (produce) by the power plant is enough … (provide) 2000 homes with all their energy needs. Solar energy is … (particular) popular with … (environment) because they consider it to be the … (reliable) and … (clean) source of energy available to man.

An aerial view of Vancouver

Overview

First Nations people	Einheimische, Urbevölkerung
ancestral	Ahnen-, Vorfahren-
location	Drehort (*Film*)
to shoot a film	einen Film drehen
Board of Trade	Handelskammer
policy statement	Grundsatzerklärung
to chair	den Vorsitz haben
Chief Executive Officer (CEO)	Vorstandsvorsitzender
fuel cell	Brennstoffzelle

12A Peter Mitchell

to prance	tänzeln, herumhüpfen, -tanzen
feature film	Kino-, Spielfilm
to break down a script	Drehbuchauszüge erstellen
still photo	Standfoto
locale	Schauplatz (einer Handlung, eines Films)
gritty	Schotter-
shootout	Schießerei
bid	Angebot
exchange rate	Wechselkurs
stages	Produktionsstätten
overall	allgemein

12B John F. Timms

to be in operation	im Einsatz sein
downtown core	Stadtkern
'bedroom communities'	„Schlafstädte"
emergency cabinet	Notrufsäule

12C Firoz Rasul

power generation device	eine Möglichkeit / ein Mittel, Energie zu erzeugen
portable	tragbar
recreational vehicle	Wohnmobil, Großraumlimousine
remote power	*im Sinne von: eigene Energieerzeugung für abgelegene Orte*
automotive	selbstfahrend, mit Selbstantrieb
to power	betreiben
combustion engine	Verbrennungsmotor

Nova Scotia

What do you know about Nova Scotia? Try this quiz and find out.
(The answers are at the bottom of the page.)

1. **What does the word 'Nova Scotia' mean?**
   a) 'New Scotland' b) 'New Settlement' c) 'New Strait'

2. **What is the capital of Nova Scotia?**
   a) Dartmouth b) Halifax c) Sydney

3. **What is the population of Nova Scotia?**
   a) About 1 million b) About 5 million c) About 10 million

4. **What is Nova Scotia's nickname?**
   a) Canada's Fishing Paradise
   b) Canada's Gates
   c) Canada's Ocean Playground

5. **Port Royal (now called Annapolis Royal) was the first French colony in North America and is Canada's oldest settlement. When was it founded?**
   a) 1605 b) 1705 c) 1805

6. **The Micmac are a First Nations tribe living in Nova Scotia. How many Micmac live in the province?**
   a) 1,400 b) 14,000 c) 140,000

7. **What was the word the French used in the 17th century to describe what is now known as Nova Scotia?**
   a) Acadia b) Evangeline c) Pierre du Gua

Answers: 1. a), 2. b), 3. a), 4. c), 5. a), 6. b), 7. a)

Overview

Wayne Melanson guides visitors around a reconstruction of the first French colony in North America, at Port Royal on the coast of Nova Scotia. Wayne goes through some of the rooms – the blacksmith's shop, the kitchen, the community room, the *artisan*'s workshop, the apothecary's room and the Governor's room – and talks about some of the objects *on display*.

Greg Carlin is a superintendent at the Annapolis *tidal generating station* at Annapolis Royal, Nova Scotia. Greg talks about how the oil crises of the 1970s led to a search for alternative energy sources and in particular renewable energies. He goes on to explain how the tidal generating system at Annapolis Royal works. Using the large *range* in the *tides* (10 metres from high to low) water can be passed into the turbine and generate electricity. The generator is able to power approximately 4,000 homes.

Sherman Pace works in the port of Halifax, Nova Scotia. He's a *longshoreman*, which means he is responsible for loading and unloading ships. Sherman talks about his work and the training involved.

Alan Syliboy is a Micmac artist from Truro, Nova Scotia. Alan talks about Micmac art and culture and its place in Canada today. He also mentions some of the problems he encountered at school growing up as a Micmac in an English-speaking environment.

Ralf Getson is the Curator of Education at the Fisheries Museum of the Atlantic at Lunenburg, Nova Scotia. Ralf talks about the importance of fishing for Nova Scotia and how fishing practices have changed through the centuries.

Find out more about ...

Wayne Melanson in	**13A**	(pages 218 – 221)
Alan Syliboy in	**13B**	(pages 222 – 225)
Ralf Getson in	**13C**	(pages 226 – 230)

13A Wayne Melanson

Wayne Melanson takes us through the reconstruction of a French settlement established in 1605 in Port Royal, Nova Scotia.

The Blacksmith's Shop

'The blacksmith was the most highly paid man here at Port Royal. He was getting 150 *livres* a year as opposed to the pharmacist, Louis Hébert, who was getting 100. He had to be *versatile* because as well as being a blacksmith sometimes he would also, when his work was finished, he would also be able to do some hunting, do some gardening, do other things as the governor saw fit.'

The Kitchen

'And this was where all the meals were prepared so it was very much a communal style of life here at Port Royal. There were two methods of cooking, you can see the open hearth here with a *spit* and some meat would be roasted on there. At times they would also use *charcoal* and spread it over the stones on the floor and put *Dutch ovens* there and cook the meals there as well. Now again here in the kitchen, you'll notice all the copper and iron cooking utensils. These are actually antiques as well that date back to the early 1600s. All the *pottery* and the *pewter* has been reproduced.'

The Community Room

'This is where all the men would gather for their meals as well as for meetings. The central dining table here would be where the gentlemen would sit and on the sides even more tables and the working class like myself would eat on the side. Now this is where the Order of Good Cheer would have been held, a social club started by Samuel de Champlain to try to improve the *morale* as well as the *diet* of the men. So during the winter months they'd take their turns in organising a big feast for the rest of the company. For some there was a competition among the men to see who was the best chef and this way they were always ensured of good food and fewer men would die of *scurvy*. And then they'd have singing and story-telling and music, to give the men something to look forward to, to pass away the long evenings without their families.'

Working with the text

I. Are these statements true or false according to the text? If they are false, correct them.

1. The blacksmith at Port Royal had a special position in the colony.
2. If you go into the kitchen you will see the original utensils that were used in the 1600s.
3. In the community room there were – and still are – beds and washing facilities.

II. Answer the questions. Use complete sentences.

1. Why did the blacksmith have to be versatile?
2. What two methods of cooking were used in the kitchen?
3. What was the idea behind the Order of Good Cheer?

III. Mark the correct ending to the sentence.

1. A 'blacksmith' (line 3) works …
   a) with wood. b) with iron. c) with leather.
2. 'Pewter' (line 17) is a metal used for making …
   a) knives. b) saucepans. c) cups and dishes.
3. Your 'diet' (line 34) is …
   a) how much food you eat.
   b) the type of food you eat.
   c) how often you eat.
4. 'Scurvy' (line 37) is …
   a) a lack of food.
   b) not enough sleep.
   c) a disease of the blood due to a lack of vitamin C.

IV. Say these words out loud.

1. pharmacist
2. versatile
3. hearth
4. morale
5. pewter
6. scurvy

V. Use a dictionary if you wish. Say what the difference is between …

1. 'moral' and 'morale'.
2. a 'pharmacist' and a 'farmer'.
3. a 'chef' and a 'chief'.
4. 'pottery' and 'pewter'.
5. 'meal' and 'meat'.

Exercises

I. What are the opposites of the underlined words? Say the complete sentence.

1. They said goodbye through the window before getting on the bus.
2. 'Don't be early,' he said.
3. They turned left into a large room.
4. Slowly they walked up the hill.
5. It was cold so she put on her anorak.
6. Who was at the front of the plane?
7. 'I can see everything!' she said.
8. After dinner they packed their suitcases.

II. Match the two halves of the dialogue.

1. Are you all right?	a. You're welcome.
2. What's the weather like?	b. Oh, not too bad.
3. Have fun at the weekend.	c. I don't mind!
4. Thanks for your help.	d. Yeah, I'm fine.
5. I'm sorry I'm late!	e. It's lovely!
6. How's work going?	f. Thanks!

III. Complete the dialogues. Put in 'been', 'did', 'was' or 'were'.

1. • So what have you … doing in Canada?
   • I've … staying with my pen pal.
   • Pen pal?
   • Yes, she lives in Montreal.
2. • And … you have a good time?
   • Yes, it … lovely.
   • … it your first visit?
   • Yes, it … .
3. • … you travel around a lot?
   • Yes, we … .
   • And … you homesick?
   • Well, I … at the beginning. But I'm not anymore!

IV. Form pairs. Then say them out loud.

1. envelopes and …	a. newspapers
2. milk and …	b. addresses
3. names and …	c. forks
4. hats and …	d. stamps
5. books and …	e. gloves
6. knives and …	f. sugar

V. Read what Judy Pearson, another guide at Port Royal, says about the Micmac. Try and find some more information about the Micmac before you look at Unit 13B.

'Before the coming of the Europeans the Micmac had inhabited this land for over 10,000 years. They were very versatile. They had their own way of life, their own religion and their own culture. The French were the first to inhabit these lands, the first Europeans, and they first settled here at Port Royal in 1605. In 1710 the English came in to Nova Scotia and they renamed this land New Scotland.'

Houses at Port Royal

The Atlantic coastline

Halifax

13B Alan Syliboy

Alan Syliboy is a Micmac artist from Truro, Nova Scotia. He was born on the Nova Reserves and still lives there.

What does Alan do and what is important for him?

'My whole life *revolves around* my culture and I like to think that my work will bring the ancient designs, the symbols, forward and keep them current. They're part of what I am today. I'm not trying to *replicate* the past or trying to be someone that, you know, lived a hundred years ago. The reality is that I'm a modern Micmac in this modern time but I never forget my roots and where I come from. And so it's extremely important that the symbols are *preserved* in that even ourselves as Micmac people live to see what our own designs or ancestors did, and understand the work, what it *entails* and the purpose of it.'

Has life changed for the Micmac in recent years?

'From the time I was going to school to this time I think life has changed a lot as far as Micmacs go in that we're more *visible*. Before I went to school I spoke no English at all. I spoke Micmac, my language. But *assimilation* was forced on us. We had to start talking English. It was, you know, that you couldn't do well at school. The Micmac language held you back if you didn't speak good English and that's how it was sort of given to us and that's how we went but in that process, I think, we sort of got lost, too. We've lost our identity and who we are and I think that was also damaging to us and we're trying to *regain* that. And we're searching for our identity and I think that's sort of a life-long process. And I think you have to know who you are to find your *footing* in this world. I think that's why I was put here as an artist to tell a story of my people. And I think, you know, it's good for all of us.'

Working with the text

I. Mark the best ending to the sentence using the information in the text.

1. Alan …
   a) seems unhappy about being a Micmac.
   b) is proud to be a Micmac.
   c) wants to live somewhere where there are no Micmac.
2. Alan would like the Micmac to …
   a) learn to appreciate their history and their art.
   b) forget their history and art.
   c) reinvent their history and art.
3. When Alan went to school he …
   a) wanted to learn English.
   b) was forced to learn English.
   c) forgot how to speak English.
4. Alan thinks that the Micmac need to …
   a) find their identity again.
   b) speak better English.
   c) move away from their reserves in Nova Scotia.

II. Answer the questions. Use complete sentences and your own words as far as possible.

1. Why are Micmac symbols so important to Alan?
2. In what way did Alan dislike his school days?
3. How does Alan feel about the position of the Micmac in society today?
4. What does he say about his own work as an artist?

III. Explain the meaning of these words or expressions.

1. ancestors (line 15)
2. visible (line 22)
3. assimilation (line 24)
4. to find your footing (line 35)

IV. What does the underlined word refer to in the text?

1. <u>They</u>'re part of what I am today. (line 5)
2. … what it entails and the purpose of <u>it</u> … (line 17)
3. But assimilation was forced on <u>us</u> … (line 25)
4. I think <u>that</u>'s sort of a life-long process … (line 34)

V. Put the words into the correct column according to their stress pattern.

ago ◆ also ◆ amazing ◆ ancestor ◆ ancient ◆ damaging ◆ design ◆ extremely ◆ important ◆ language ◆ today ◆ visible

Oo	oO	Ooo	oOo

VI. What do you think? Write down your answers.

1. Alan says (lines 13-15): '… even ourselves as Micmac people live to see what our own designs or ancestors did … '. Is Alan criticising other Micmac people when he says this? Explain.
2. At the end of the text Alan says (line 36): 'It's good for all of us.' What does he mean exactly? And do you agree with him?

Exercises

I. Complete these sentences. Put in 'a', 'an', 'some' or 'any'.

1. There are … letters for you.
2. I bought … magazine and … chewing gum.
3. They live in … old house near the sea.
4. Have you read … poems by Henry Wadsworth Longfellow?
5. There are … flowers in our garden but there aren't … trees.
6. I'll give you … money to buy a souvenir.
7. She hasn't got … time to write postcards.
8. Let's go out and get … fresh sea air!

II. Which letter in these words do you not pronounce? Underline it.

1. t h o u g h t	3. c l i m b	5. h a l f
2. w a l k	4. k n e e	6. b o m b

III. What's the middle word? Put it in.

1. first, … , third	3. breakfast, … , dinner
2. past , … , future	4. thirty, … , fifty

IV. Construct a short text about the Micmac by putting the sentences (a-g) into the correct order (1-7). Start with sentence b. When you have finished, make three paragraphs with your sentences.

a. *The clans were nomadic, fishing in summer and hunting in winter.*

b. *The Micmac are a First Nations tribe who lived in eastern Canada at the time of early European settlement.*

c. *Today descendants of the Micmac clans live in Nova Scotia, New Brunswick and on Prince Edward Island.*

d. *The Micmac had several clans, each with its own leader.*

e. *Their dwellings also varied with the season: open-air wigwams were used in summer, while birch-bark-covered wigwams provided shelter in winter.*

f. *They were allies of the French, fighting against the English in numerous battles.*

g. *They were finally pacified by the British at the end of the 18th century.*

13C Ralf Getson

Ralf Getson is Curator of Education at the Fisheries Museum of the Atlantic at Lunenburg, Nova Scotia.

Has fishing always been important for the people on the east coast of Canada?

'For 500 years they've been fishing on this coast and the fish that they've been after has been the *cod*. Cod was the most important fish in the days before refrigeration. When it's caught and cleaned it can be salted and dried and you have a product that will last for a long period of time. It was a very important source of protein for the poor of Europe, for the armies of Europe and, when we have settlement in the New World, for colonies in the West Indies and South America.'

How long has Lunenburg been a fishing community?

'Codfish, known as the beef of the sea in Nova Scotia, we call it the bread of the sea. And Lunenburg has been involved in the fishery for a long period of time. The town was settled in 1753 by foreign Protestants, people who were farmers, *peasants*, tradesmen but when they got to the New World found that farming was very *poor* here. A lot of stones. It was all right if you were farming granite but not very good *soil*. So they were versatile enough in that they could turn to the fishery. And they started very early on to the nearshore banks and, beginning in 1873, to the Grand Banks off of Newfoundland.'

How did fishing develop in the 20th century?

'After the war they started the modern fishery, fishing with large nets and bringing the fish in and selling it fresh. Instead of packing it in salt they packed it in ice. And that really was the beginning of the modern fishery. Many changes took place in the 1950s and 60s. New equipment. They went into cooked fish, fishsticks … from this building here in the 1950s.'

Working with the text

I. Continue these sentences using the information in the text.

1. People have been fishing off the coast of Atlantic Canada for … .
2. At that time fish was important because … .
3. The first people to settle in Lunenburg didn't fish at first. They … .
4. Fishing changed in the 20th century. Technological advance meant that … .

II. Answer these questions.

1. Which came first? Fishing in Lunenburg or the arrival of European settlers in Lunenburg? Explain.
2. Why was farming difficult for the first settlers in Lunenburg?
3. Which invention of the 20th century had the greatest impact on the fishing industry?

III. What does the underlined word refer to in the text?

1. For 500 years they've been fishing on <u>this</u> coast … (line 4)
2. <u>It</u> was a very important source of protein … (line 7)
3. So <u>they</u> were versatile enough in that they … (line 17)
4. Instead of packing <u>it</u> in salt … (line 22)

IV. Say these sentences making sure to pronounce the numbers and dates properly.

1. For 500 years they've been fishing on this coast.
2. The town settled in 1753 by foreign Protestants.
3. How did fishing develop in the 20th century?
4. Many changes took place in the 1950s and 60s.

V. Say these words out loud.

1. source 2. protein 3. peasants 4. granite

VI. Answer these questions.

1. What do we mean when we refer to the 'New World'?
2. What do you understand by the expression 'bread of the sea'?

Lunenburg

Exercises

I. Past simple or present perfect? Complete the sentences.

1. I'm an artist. I … (live) in Nova Scotia when I was a child.
2. I'm an artist and I … (live) in Nova Scotia all my life.
3. I … (have) two exhibitions last year.
4. I … (have) two exhibitions so far this year.
5. I … (win) two prizes for my work so far. I hope I can win a third.
6. I … (win) my first prize last year.

II. Which small word is missing? Put it in.

1. Our neighbours are … vacation.
2. Can I stay with them … a week?
3. I've never been … Canada.
4. Are you going to be … the airport?
5. Yesterday she got an email … her aunt in New Brunswick.
6. Have you been thinking … the summer?
7. She appeared … over forty films.
8. Do you like listening … music?

III. What's the difference, if any, between …

1. 'North America' and the 'USA'?
2. the 'New World' and 'New Brunswick'?
3. 'South America' and 'Central America'?
4. an 'artist' and an 'artiste'?
5. a 'peasant' and a 'pheasant'?

IV. Which word in the brackets is the correct one? Underline it.

1. She applied for a [job/work] as a personnel officer.
2. Some employees have a long [journey/travel] to work every day.
3. The cost of [life/living] has gone up again.
4. Please send precise [measurements/measures] when ordering.
5. We expect prices to [raise/rise] by at least five per cent.
6. We only exchange goods if you produce a [receipt/recipe].
7. I must [remember/remind] the boss about that meeting this afternoon.
8. Can you [say/tell] the difference between these two products?
9. The company is extremely [sensible/sensitive] to any criticism.
10. There's some more paper in the [stationary/stationery] cupboard.

V. *Find out more about one of Canada's most famous writers. Put the paragraphs (a-g) into the correct order (1-7) to make a text about Lucy Montgomery.*

a. *After working as a teacher for three years and as a newspaperwoman on the* HALIFAX DAILY ECHO *for one year, Montgomery, who had been writing since childhood, began publishing stories and poems in newspapers and children's magazines.*

b. *Anne, the heroine, is a spirited, independent orphan with an active imagination who wins the hearts of the elderly brother and sister who adopt her.*

c. *Her first novel,* ANNE OF GREEN GABLES *(1908), was an instant success in Canada and the United States and is now considered a classic of children's literature. It has been made into several motion pictures and a popular television series.*

d. *Lucy Maud Montgomery (1874-1942) is a Canadian writer best known for her novels set on Prince Edward Island.*

e. *Montgomery chronicled her heroine Anne's career, marriage and family in five additional novels.*

f. *Montgomery was educated at Dalhousie University in Halifax, Nova Scotia, and Prince of Wales College in Charlottetown, Prince Edward Island.*

g. *She was born in Clifton (now New London), Prince Edward Island and raised by her grandparents after her mother died and her father moved to Prince Albert, Saskatchewan.*

VI. *Read this passage from Anne of Green Gables. Anne, the heroine, is going to find out if she has won a scholarship (an 'Avery') to go to college. Which part of the book do you think this excerpt comes from – the beginning or the end?*

On the morning when the final results of all the examinations were to be posted on the bulletin board at Queen's, Anne and Jane walked down the street together. Jane was smiling and happy; examinations were over and she was comfortably sure she had made a pass at least; further considerations troubled Jane not at all; she had no soaring (hochfliegend) *ambitions and consequently was not affected with the unrest attendant thereon. For we pay a price for everything we get or take in this world; and although ambitions are well worth having, they are not to be cheaply won, but exact* (fordern) *their dues* (Anteil) *of work and self-denial, anxiety and discouragement. Anne was pale and quiet; in ten more minutes she would know who had won the medal and who the Avery. Beyond those ten minutes there did not seem, just then, to be anything worth being called Time.*

'Of course you'll win one of them anyhow,' said Jane, who couldn't understand how the faculty could be so unfair as to order it otherwise.

'I have no hope of the Avery,' said Anne. 'Everybody says Emily Clay will win it. And I'm not going to march up to that bulletin board and look at it before everybody. I haven't the moral courage. I'm going straight to the girls' dressing-room. You must read the announcements and then come and tell me, Jane. And I implore you in the name of our old friendship to do it as quickly as possible. If I have failed just say so, without trying to break it gently; and whatever you do don't sympathize with me. Promise me this, Jane.'

Jane promised solemnly; but, as it happened, there was no necessity for such a promise. When they went up the entrance steps of Queen's they found the hall full of boys who were carrying Gilbert Blythe around on their shoulders and yelling at the tops of their voices, 'Hurrah for Blythe, Medallist!'

For a moment Anne felt one sickening pang of defeat and disappointment. So she had failed and Gilbert had won! Well, Matthew would be sorry – he had been so sure she would win.

And then!

Somebody called out:

'Three cheers for Miss Shirley, winner of the Avery!'

'Oh, Anne,' gasped Jane, as they fled to the girls' dressing-room amid hearty cheers. 'Oh, Anne, I'm so proud! Isn't it splendid?'

And then the girls were around them and Anne was the centre of a laughing, congratulating group. Her shoulders were thumped and her hands shaken vigorously. She was pushed and pulled and hugged and among it all she managed to whisper to Jane:

'Oh, won't Matthew and Marilla be pleased! I must write the news home right away.'

Overview

artisan	Handwerker
to be on display	ausgestellt sein
tidal generation station	Gezeitenkraftwerk
range	Reichweite
tides	Gezeiten
longshoreman	Hafenarbeiter

13A Wayne Melanson

livre (*French*)	Pfund (*alte frz. Währung*)
versatile	vielseitig
spit	Bratspieß
charcoal	Holzkohle
Dutch oven	*eine Art großer Kessel*
pottery	Töpferwaren, Keramik
pewter	Zinn(geschirr)
morale	Moral
diet	Nahrung, die Art, sich zu ernähren
scurvy	Skorbut

13B Alan Syliboy

to revolve around	sich drehen um
to replicate	nachbilden
to preserve	bewahren
to entail	mit sich bringen, verbunden sein
visible	sichtbar
assimilation	Anpassung, Integration
to regain	zurückgewinnen
footing	Stand, Halt

13C Ralf Getson

cod	Kabeljau
peasant	Bauer
poor	unergiebig
soil	Erdreich, Boden

A brief history of the USA

1492 Christopher Columbus sailed across the Atlantic and reached the West Indies.

1565 Spain founded the first permanent European settlement in what is now the United States at Saint Augustine, Florida. However, Native Americans had lived on the continent for thousands of years previously.

1607 The first permanent British settlement in America was established at Jamestown, Virginia.

1763 Great Britain gained control of eastern North America at the end of the Seven Years' War, known in America as the French and Indian War.

1770s Boston became a center of growing American discontent with British rule. At the 'Boston Tea Party' (1773) American settlers protested against the English tax on tea. The American Revolution began nearby in 1775.

1776 The Continental Congress adopted the Declaration of Independence at Philadelphia.

1781 American forces decisively defeated the British at the Siege of Yorktown. Two years later, in the Treaty of Paris, Great Britain recognized the independence of the former colonies as the United States of America.

1787 The Constitutional Congress met in Philadelphia and wrote the Constitution of the United States. All 13 states ratified the Constitution by 1790.

1803 The area of the United States nearly doubled in size after President Thomas Jefferson acquired the territory of Louisiana from France in a transaction known as the Louisiana Purchase.

1812-1815 The War of 1812 between Great Britain and the United States helped end British interference in American affairs.

1823 In the Monroe Doctrine, President James Monroe warned Europeans against interfering in the affairs of any country in the western hemisphere.

1848 The United States gained large amounts of territory as a result of winning the Mexican War. The new land, coupled with the acquisition of the Oregon country in 1846, extended the western border of the United States to the Pacific Ocean.

1861 Several Southern slave states seceded in January and formed the Confederate States of America. The American Civil War broke out in April.

1865 The Confederacy surrendered, bringing an end to the Civil War. Slavery was abolished throughout the United States. President Abraham Lincoln was assassinated.

1867 The United States purchased Alaska from Russia.

1870-1890 The last Native American tribes were defeated by government forces and pushed onto reservations.

1886 The American Federation of Labor was formed to fight for workers in an increasingly industrialized country.

1898 The United States won the Spanish-American War and gained territories in the Caribbean and the Pacific. Hawaii was annexed the same year.

1914 The United States completed construction of the Panama Canal, providing a link between the Atlantic and Pacific oceans.

1917-1918 The United States fought in World War I, confirming its status as a world power.

1920 Women gained the right to vote. The manufacture and sale of alcohol was banned, ushering in the era of Prohibition.

1929 Wild speculation led to a stock market crash, triggering the Great Depression.

1933 Franklin Roosevelt became president and introduced a series of economic and social reforms known as the New Deal. Prohibition was repealed.

1941 Japan attacked US forces at Pearl Harbor, Hawaii, pulling the United States into World War II.

1945 The United Nations was established in New York.

1947 The Truman Doctrine was established to help nations resist Soviet influence. Anti-communist tensions escalated as the Cold War began.

1950-1953 US troops fought in the Korean War.

1962 The United States and the Union of Soviet Socialist Republics narrowly avoided war during the Cuban Missile Crisis.

1963-1964 Important civil rights reforms were passed by Congress, outlawing discrimination in voting and jobs.

1965-1973 US forces fought in the Vietnam War, which sparked widespread protests in the United States.

1969 US astronauts became the first people to land on the moon.

1974 In the wake of the Watergate scandal, Richard M. Nixon became the first US president to resign from office.

1980s The US economy emerged from a recession but was faced with increasing federal and foreign trade deficits.

1990-1991 US forces led a multinational coalition against Iraq during the Persian Gulf War.

1994 The Republican Party swept the November elections and won control of both houses of Congress for the first time since 1954.

1995 Terrorists detonated a bomb outside the Alfred P. Murrah Federal Building in Oklahoma City, causing more than 170 deaths and largely destroying the building.

1999 Bill Clinton was acquitted after becoming the second US president to be impeached following accusations of lying under oath.

A brief history of Canada

about AD 1000 Vikings explored the coast of Newfoundland.

1497 John Cabot discovered the rich fishing grounds off Canada's Atlantic coast.

1534 Jacques Cartier claimed Canada for France.

1604 French colonists founded the first settlement in Canada, in present-day Nova Scotia. They developed thriving fish and fur trades.

1670 The Hudson's Bay Company, an English company, opened its first fur-trading posts in Canada.

1760 The English captured Montreal during the French and Indian War. France formally surrendered its Canadian lands in 1763.

1775 An American invasion of Canada during the American Revolution failed. Many American Loyalists moved to Canada in the following years.

1791 Great Britain divided Canada into predominantly French Lower Canada and predominantly English Upper Canada.

1837 Revolts against the colonial government failed in both Lower and Upper Canada.

1867 The British North America Act was passed, creating the Dominion of Canada.

1885 The Canadian Pacific Railroad was completed, uniting Canada.

1931 Canada achieved complete independence from Great Britain.

1939-1945 Nearly 1.5 million Canadians fought in World War II. After the war, a new wave of European immigrants helped transform Canada into an industrial power.

1980 Quebec voters rejected a proposal to negotiate their province's independence from the rest of Canada.

1990 The Meech Lake Accord, which sought to win Quebec's acceptance of the new constitution while guaranteeing the rights of French Canadians, was rejected by Manitoba and Newfoundland.

1992 A second attempt at constitutional revision, the Charlottetown Accord, was defeated in a nationwide referendum.

1994 Canada entered into the North American Free Trade Agreement (NAFTA) along with Mexico and the United States.

1995 A second referendum on the independence of Quebec was voted down by a narrow margin (50.6 per cent) of Quebec voters.

Key to the exercises

1 Massachusetts

1A Working with the text

I. 1. a) – **2.** c) – **3.** c)
II. 1. She made a cover showing a person's arm in the shape of Cape Cod. – **2.** It showed an arm with lots of images and writing which looked like tattoos. – **3.** She had to scan images and use a font which looked like handwriting.
III. 1. Cape Cod – **2.** a word out of the story – **3.** the computer file – **4.** images (like fish)
V. 1. the front page – **2.** one time every year – **3.** interesting and amusing
VI. 1. Because people would not have been able to read it. – **2.** It's the name of a software program. – **3.** Because it's so large (and contains so many images).
VII. *Examples:* **1.** Yes, I think she does. She certainly sounds interested in talking about the cover she did. – **2.** No, not really. I'm not a very artistic person and I don't know much about computers.

1A Exercises

I. 1. business section – **2.** sports pages – **3.** letters to the editor – **4.** editorial – **5.** foreign news – **6.** horoscope – **7.** advertisements – **8.** home news – **9.** obituary – **10.** cartoons
II. Sentence 2.
III. 1. If she had been a bit more careful she would not have had the accident. – **2.** They would have lent their daughter some money if she had been more sensible. – **3.** If the train had not been late, he would probably have got to work on time. – **4.** If they had told us they were coming, we would certainly have waited for them. – **5.** We would have driven over and visited you if we had had the time. – **6.** I would have helped you if you had asked me. Really! – **7.** Nobody would have been able to read the poster if we had done it by hand. – **8.** She would have gone on vacation if she had been able to afford it.
IV. 1. had – **2.** had – **3.** would – **4.** would
V. Newspapers: Chicago Tribune – New York Times – USA Today – Wall Street Journal – Washington Post
Magazines: Ebony – Reader's Digest – Sports Illustrated – Time – Vanity Fair
VI. … influence … prevent … rights … scenes … .
… example … resigned … administration. … attention … Affair … country.
VII. The Watergate Affair began in June 1972 when five men broke into the Democratic Party's campaign headquarters at the Watergate apartment and office complex in Washington, DC. The men's arrest eventually uncovered a White House plan of spying against political opponents led by the Republican president, Richard Nixon. In order to avoid impeachment Nixon resigned on August 9, 1974, the first president in the history of the US to do so. Watergate showed that in a nation of laws no one is above the law, not even the president. Richard Nixon died in 1994.

1B Working with the text

I. 1. True – **2.** False. She's a management expert. – **3.** False. She's written a book on management and leadership. – **4.** False. She enjoyed working with artists and script writers on her multimedia project.
II. 1. What made the project complex was the different sort of people she had to work with. – **2.** It's a

flexible product because you can use it when – and where – you want to but it remains interactive. – **3.** It was exciting for Linda Hill to discover how to exploit the interactive quality of a multimedia project. – **4.** Actors were needed to act out the different cases described in the book. They were important because they could give the user a much better picture of the diverse people and the various emotions that you are confronted with at work.

III. 1. range – **2.** began – **3.** work out – **4.** major characters

IV. 1. d. – **2.** f. – **3.** b. – **4.** h. – **5.** a. – **6.** g. – **7.** c. – **8.** e.

V. 1. … sell it to companies and businesses. – **2.** … fun but informative. – **3.** … you pay them to do a job. – **4.** … you begin to understand how they feel.

VII.

Ooo	oOo
management	advantage
media	adventure
quality	emotion
video	idea

VIII. *Examples:* **1.** I like to work by myself. I find I can work best when I can concentrate fully on the job. I'm a morning person. I don't find it difficult to get up and start work quite early. I usually find it's my most productive part of the day. It's nice when you've achieved a lot and there's still so much of the day left. Of course I need a break at lunchtime. And I do admit that I sometimes feel quite tired in the afternoon!

2. I get up quite early. I don't have much for breakfast. I'm not usually very hungry in the morning. I get the train to work. It leaves at 7.20 from the local station. I get to my office at about 8.15. There's always a lot to do and usually I have no time to chat to my colleagues. I take my lunchbreak at 12.15. If the weather's OK I go out and get some fresh air. The day finishes at about 5 o'clock but I have flexitime so I can choose when I want to leave the office. I'm usually back home at about 6. I don't go out during the week. I'm usually too tired. I prefer to stay at home. I listen to music, read or play with my cats!

1B Exercises

I. 1. As soon as – **2.** because – **3.** When – **4.** so – **5.** Although – **6.** but

II. 1. The book was not in the library because **(c.)** someone had stolen it. – **2.** It was difficult to get home because **(a.)** it had been snowing all afternoon. – **3.** We weren't able to meet them because **(b.)** they had already gone home. – **4.** We missed the train because **(e.)** we had overslept. – **5.** I felt a bit worried because **(d.)** I had never been on TV before.

III. 1. … of using … ? – **2.** … for not paying … . – **3.** … on waiting … . – **4.** … about (on) becoming … ? – **5.** … to meeting … . – **6.** … from learning … ?

IV. … had … children, … expected his sons to prepare … . … were encouraged … . … was never allowed. … the most famous … . … became … . … did not last … . … riding … was shot … killed. … also entered … advisor. … was assassinated. … read … had been written … . … harder … . … have done … he used to say, … .

V. d. – **e.** – **a.** – **c.** – **b.**

Heading: John F. Kennedy, Jr. feared killed

1C Working with the text

I. 1. … in the Computer Museum in Boston. – **2.** … how things in the natural world happen. – **3.** … build a fish and determine its behavior. – **4.** … traffic jams and fluctuations at the stock market.

II. 1. hungry – **2.** full – **3.** small – **4.** terrified – **5.** friendly – **6.** swim

III. 1. If the fish is hungry or full, relaxed or terrified, friendly or shy, if he likes bubbles or not, if he likes bright objects or not and where in the tank he likes to swim. – **2.** A tag is a label and is a way of identifying fish as they swim around in the tank.

V.

▫□	□▫	▫□▫	▫▫□
decide	govern	determine	entertain
enjoy	happen	develop	interact
explain	study	remember	understand

VI. 1. the most recent developments – **2.** created by a computer – **3.** a long line of traffic that can't move – **4.** the bottom of the sea

1C Exercises

I. 1. tiny – **2.** forget – **3.** cause – **4.** dull – **5.** surface – **6.** practical
II. 1. dry – **2.** stale – **3.** rare – **4.** tough – **5.** hot – **6.** alcoholic
III. 1 g. – **2** c. – **3** a. – **4** h. – **5** f. – **6** d. – **7** b. – **8** e.
IV. 1. jam (on your bread) - jam (= lots of cars) – **2.** study (= to work at university) - study (= a room where you work) – **3.** fine (weather, day) - fine (= the money you pay when you've done sth wrong) – **4.** bright (child) - bright (light)
V. 1. The weather's terrible. I don't know whether he's coming. – **2.** There's a tennis court behind our house. He caught the ball. – **3.** Who's that man over there? This is John and Jackie. And this is their son, Joel. – **4.** It's very cold. The dog's black but its tail is white.
VI. The statue shows John F. Kennedy, US president from 1961-1963. Both sides of Kennedy's family came from Boston. His mother, Rose Kennedy, was the daughter of John F. Fitzgerald, who was mayor of Boston. His father, Joseph Kennedy, was the son of Patrick Kennedy, a successful businessman and a prominent Boston politician. John F. Kennedy was born on May 29, 1917, in Brookline, Massachusetts.
VII. Paragraph 1: In search of a new beginning – **Paragraph 2:** Disagreements with England – **Paragraph 3:** War breaks out – **Paragraph 4:** The birth of the United States

2 Pennsylvania

2A Working with the text

I. 1. False. She's still at high school. – **2.** False. Her favorite sports are softball and skiing. – **3.** True. – **4.** False. She's a qualified ski instructor.
II. 1. She usually plays on two teams. – **2.** If she has worked as a ski instructor for four years she must have learnt to ski some years before that.
III. 1. b) – **2.** b) – **3.** b) – **4.** a) – **5.** b)
IV. 1. brother – **2.** tomorrow – **3.** to pass – **4.** to win – **5.** not enough – **6.** in the past
V. 1. registered – **2.** hard physical exercise – **3.** the normal softball team (but outside high school) – **4.** a local competition
VI. *Examples:* **1.** Yes, I did. I played football, basketball and in the winter I went skiing. – **2.** I don't do sports very much now. I sometimes go running near my house. I can do that all year round.

2A Exercises

I. 1. future – **2.** present – **3.** future – **4.** present – **5.** future – **6.** present
II. 1. When are you leaving for softball camp? – **2.** Which hotel are they staying at in Philadelphia? – **3.** Who are you having a holiday with? – **4.** Who's organizing a Christmas party? – **5.** When is she arriving at the station? – **6.** Where are you driving to at the weekend?
III. 1. second grade = second year of school – **2.** college = higher education establishment (after high school) – **3.** junior = student in the year before the final year at high school – **4.** straight A's = top marks in all subjects
IV. 1. e. – **2.** c. – **3.** d. – **4.** a. – **5.** b.
V. No, he isn't. Football is American football. 'Soccer' is the word Americans use for the British word 'football'.
VI. 1. of – **2.** after
VII. *Example:* These two statements show that Americans are not afraid of saying how proud they are to be able to represent their school. The statements also show how important non-academic activities like sport and music are in high schools.

2B Working with the text

I. 1. No, he works voluntarily. His main job is running a small store. – **2.** No, it also raises its own money at an annual carnival. – **3.** No, they have a long tradition going back two generations. – **4.** Yes, he's got a son-in-law, an uncle, four cousins and a nephew in the fire service.
II. *Examples:* **1.** They receive 400 calls every year which is about one per day. I think that's quite a lot. – **2.** Mark Cooper seems to take his job very seriously so I expect his colleagues do as well. – **3.** At the weekend. – **4.** I doubt it. It has probably become a tradition in many families.
III. 1. d. – **2.** c. – **3.** f. – **4.** a. – **5.** b. – **6.** e.
IV. 1. to get cats that are stuck in trees or on roofs of houses – **2.** when lots of people come – **3.** a fire service in the next community – **4.** when there's an emergency and the firemen have to go to work

2B Exercises

I. 1. grandson – **2.** brother – **3.** nephew – **4.** son – **5.** daughter-in-law – **6.** niece
II. 1. a 'friend' is a man or woman you know and like: a 'boyfriend' is usually a woman's regular male companion with whom she has a romantic/sexual relationship – **2.** 'a friend of mine' is one person's friend: 'a friend of ours' is two people's friend – **3.** if you are a child your 'father' is the man who made your mother pregnant: if you are a child your 'stepfather' is the man who your mother has married after your parents have divorced (or your father has died) – **4.** a 'daughter' is a person's female child: a 'daughter-in-law' is a person's son's wife
III. 1. b. – **2.** e. – **3.** a. – **4.** d. – **5.** f. – **6.** c.
IV. … separation … colonies … . … was written … took … to complete.
V. 'Folgende Tatsachen erachten wir als selbstverständlich: dass alle <u>Menschen</u> gleich geschaffen sind; dass sie von ihrem Schöpfer mit gewissen unveräußerlichen Rechten ausgestattet sind, dass dazu Leben, Freundschaft und das Streben nach <u>Glück</u> gehören.'

2C Working with the text

I. 1. b) – **2.** b)
II. 1. steering an inmate in the right direction – **2.** how many times a week the teacher should help the inmate – **3.** why the inmate wants to study – **4.** the inmate's way of doing math
III. 1. in prison – **2.** wood – **3.** Development – **4.** go to college – **5.** often
IV. 1. helped us – **2.** your other commitments – **3.** just did it how I thought it should be done (without knowing if it was OK) – **4.** learn more

VI. *Examples:* **1.** When the teacher asks the inmate how often he should help him the inmate says 'I have a lot of time here'. Obviously the inmate can study a lot. He can't do much else if he's in prison! – **2.** Yes. It must be very difficult to do carpentry without a basic knowledge of mathematical concepts such as multiplication, division, fractions and so on. – **3.** Mrs Kennedy must be another teacher who is helping the inmate to get his GED. – **4.** Yes, he seems keen to make progress and enjoys learning.

2C Exercises

I. b)
II. *Example:* The writer is talking about his schooldays. It seems that he wasn't a very good student until he taught himself to play the violin. As he got better and better at playing the violin, he began to improve at school and eventually became top of the class. However, he hadn't worked very hard. Without knowing it, he had discovered that you can study much more effectively if you enjoy what you are doing.
III. freshmen – the dormitory – co-ed – junior – cute – off-campus – BS – graduate school – his master's thesis – hunk – No kidding – went out for – NCAA

3 Illinois

3A Working with the text

I. 1. True. – **2.** False. Some trains are quite new. – **3.** False. He's a transportation manager. – **4.** True.
II. 1. passengers – **2.** tracks – **3.** to rent – **4.** to maintain
III. 1. long ago – **2.** At the moment – **3.** jobs / tasks – **4.** happen / take place
IV. 1. every day about half a million people use the CTA – **2.** the tracks were built about 100 years ago – **3.** that means freight trains – **4.** directing trains onto different tracks

3A Exercises

I. 1. … has never been … . – **2.** … lived … . – **3.** … did not have … . – **4.** … I've taken… – **5.** … were … – **6.** … has bought … . – **7.** … did not go … . – **8.** … has seen … .
II. 1. … gone … . – **2.** … been … . – **3.** … gone … . – **4.** … been. – **5.** … gone … . – **6.** … been … ?
III. 1. – How long have they been waiting for us? Not long, I hope!
– For over an hour!
2. – Why has your girlfriend been talking to my boyfriend so secretively?
– Good question. Let's ask them!
3. – What has he been doing all day? I haven't seen him since breakfast!
– Watching TV.
4. – Who have you been writing to all morning? Somebody important?
– My pen pal in Boston.
5. – Why have you been worrying about it so long? It wasn't worth it.
– I don't know. You tell me!
6. – How long has it been making this funny noise?
– I don't know. I've just heard it.
V. … for … through … till … besides … . … in … . … by … on … .
VI. *Example:* I would prefer to do Frank Bernardo's job. I think I'd enjoy being outside and meeting people. I don't like the idea of being a manager and working in an office all day. Of course you would probably earn more money as a manager than as a train driver but that wouldn't bother me. Money isn't everything, is it?
VII. 1. 1 o'clock. – **2.** 12 o'clock. – **3.** daylight. – **4.** Hawaii and Alaska.

3B Working with the text

I. 1. c) – **2.** c) – **3.** a)
II. 1. It's extremely important for her. She really wants to learn. – **2.** She has had a tremendous influence on her. Through her she has learnt that people really do care for others. – **3.** She would like to get medical qualifications and work in a hospital.
III. 1. gave me a chance – **2.** the desire (for more education) is growing all the time – **3.** made it clear to me (that I wanted to learn more) – **4.** it's something that grows day by day
IV. 1. c. – **2.** f. – **3.** a. – **4.** b. – **5.** d. – **6.** g. – **7.** e.
V. *Examples:* **1.** Not always but it certainly does not harm if you have good qualifications. Often luck is involved. You get a good job because you happen to see a vacancy and apply. Another important thing is having good contacts. Often jobs are not advertised in newspapers. People tell you about them. – **2.** Not really. She feels cared for by the teachers at her college so it's natural that she wants to work in a job where she can care for others.
VI. *Example:* Empowerment means to give somebody power. This sentence means that education can give people the power to make choices about their own life.

3B Exercises

I. 1. d. – **2.** b. – **3.** e. – **4.** f. – **5.** a. – **6.** c.
II. What do you do? = What's your job? – What are you doing? = What activity are you performing at the moment?
III. 1. to apply for a job = to try and get a job – **2.** to work freelance = to work for yourself (and not for a company and have a regular income and other benefits) – **3.** to be on maternity leave = not to work because you are expecting – or have just had – a baby – **4.** to work shifts = to work at different times of the day, sometimes during the day, sometimes in the evening and sometimes at night – **5.** to be promoted = to get a job with more responsibility and more pay – **6.** to have flexitime = to be free to decide – within certain limitations – when to start and when to finish your work – **7.** to take early retirement = to stop working earlier than normal, for example at the age of 58 or 60 – **8.** to be made redundant = to lose one's job
IV. 1. a train operator and a nurse wear a uniform: a secretary doesn't – **2.** a carpenter and a plumber work with their hands: an attorney doesn't – **3.** a clown and an actress perform in front of large crowds: a hairdresser doesn't – **4.** a driving instructor and a teacher have to make sure their pupils pass a test: a farmer doesn't
V. 1. *Examples:* I work in a hospital. I'm a nurse. I like working with people and I like caring for people. I work during the day at the moment. If possible, I'd like to work nights so I can earn more money and have more time with my family. – **2.** I'd like to work with animals so it would be good if I could train to become a vet. Let me be realistic, though. I don't think I'll be working as a vet one day. I'm too old to go to university. In any case it's very difficult to get a place studying veterinary science.
VI. g. – d. – i. – f. – e. – j. – b. – c. – h. – a.
VII. … came … had been arguing. … had taken … ordered my mother to cook … . … raised … sold … . … was crying. … to skin … cooking. … was … left … walking … . … cooking … .
… had not come … . … hugged … . … strange … had never behaved … . … waking … . … was screaming. … having to ask … had happened … . … were told … had been killed … . … was … .
VIII. Black Muslims believe in economic cooperation and self-sufficiency amongst black people and follow a strict Islamic code of behavior (diet, dress etc). Members follow Islamic religious rituals and pray five times daily. The Nation of Islam is the most prominent organization within the Black Muslim movement.
Malcolm X was shot on February 21, 1965 while addressing a meeting in New York.
IX. 1. Indiana – **2.** Illinois – **3.** Wisconsin – **4.** Michigan
X. … heart … . … engine … comic book … . … breathtaking. … telescopes … miles … . … suburbs … .

3C Working with the text

I. 1. '… the largest exchange in the world where we have open outcry …' – **2.** '… whether they be in Germany or in London or in New York, Chicago, or in Asia …' – **3.** '… what happens in Germany before I get here is very important …' – **4.** '… the bond pit, which is the most active contract traded in the world …'
II. 1. h. – **2.** d. – **3.** f. – **4.** c. – **5.** a. – **6.** g. – **7.** b. – **8.** e.
III. 1. risk – **2.** the price – **3.** hand signals – **4.** a game
IV. 1. a negotiation of the price – **2.** do business with other companies on behalf of one firm – **3.** of all the contracts the one that is bought and sold the most – **4.** all together as one unit
VI. *Examples:* **1.** In this way it's easier for people to see each other. – **2.** one means selling, the other means buying. – **3.** The bell signifies the beginning and end of trading. – **4.** The jackets are bright so the different companies can be easily recognized. They are light and loose-fitting so that they are comfortable.

3C Exercises

I. 1. He completed the 10-kilometer run in 45 minutes. – **2.** They've got a 30-year mortgage on their house. – **3.** We had a 2-hour flight to Chicago. – **4.** She gave us a new 20-dollar bill. – **5.** I read a 350-page book in a weekend. – **6.** They've just built a new 18-hole golf course in our village. – **7.** Let's have a 5-minute break, shall we? – **8.** The 15,000-member Osage tribe is located in Oklahoma. – **9.** The tribe has a 1.6-million-acre reservation. – **10.** We had a superb 5-course meal.
II. 1. 90¢ – **2.** $63.36 – **3.** $151 – **4.** $6,875
III. 1. c. – **2.** f. – **3.** d. – **4.** a. – **5.** b. – **6.** e.
IV. 1. bull – **2.** assets – **3.** demand – **4.** profit
VI. 1. The Federal Reserve (*Notenbank*) – **2.** a bank account for everyday purposes (*Girokonto*) – **3.** the financial center in New York – **4.** a card you give to other people showing your name, title, company address and phone numbers – **5.** one of a country's leading public companies – **6.** another word for the US dollar bill
VII. He didn't want to go to bed when his mother told him to. – He usually cycled to work. – He became a national hero and was invited to the White House for lunch.
VIII. Prohibition means the ban on the manufacture and sale of alcoholic drinks. The Prohibition era in the US began in 1920 after the 18th Amendment to the Constitution. The amendment banned the sale or manufacture of alcohol. Prohibition ended in 1933 when the 18th Amendment was repealed.
IX. He was very successful but obviously ruthless.
X. Frank Sinatra singing *Chicago! Chicago!*

4 Washington, DC

4A Working with the text

I. 1. Visitor B – **2.** Visitor C – **3.** Visitors B and C – **4.** None of them
II. 1. awestruck – **2.** to grieve – **3.** relatives – **4.** to repeat
III. 1. back to their families in the US – **2.** specific – **3.** people in the military – **4.** lost their lives for no good reason
IV. *Examples:* **1.** They seem very genuine indeed. It's obvious that the Memorial Wall means something to them. – **2.** No, I don't think so. If there is, I have never heard of it.

4A Exercises

I. 1. made – **2.** doing – **3.** made – **4.** do – **5.** made – **6.** do
II. The stress shifts to the other syllable.
III. President Nixon announced that he had a secret plan to end the war. – The average age of a US soldier in Vietnam was 19. – Two days later two students were killed in Mississippi.
IV. 1. d. Jefferson Memorial – **2.** c. Capitol – **3.** e. Lincoln Memorial

4B Working with the text

I. 1. False. She works in Washington, DC. – **2.** True. – **3.** False. It involves informing people about American Indians. – **4.** False. They have many rights and many responsibilities.
II. 1. buffalo roaming the prairie lands – **2.** tribes – **3.** US Americans – **4.** federal government, state government and tribal government
III. 1. main (principal) – **2.** Not long ago – **3.** the job of looking after their territory – **4.** all in all
IV. 1. a special area of land which is protected – **2.** an animal (similar to a cow) – **3.** something like oil or gas which is in the earth – **4.** the government for the whole country, not for just a part of it
V. 1. constitutional – **2.** cultural – **3.** governmental – **4.** linguistic – **5.** legal – **6.** political – **7.** religious – **8.** tribal
VI. *Example:* She thinks people see American Indians as poor people with a lower standard of living than other US citizens.

4B Exercises

I. … settlers … 18th and 19th … . … home. … wagons … westward. … vacant… . … every… . … American … similarly. … 1830s. … give up … . … Cavalry… . … animals and crops … forced … .
II. … buffalo. … meat … fur … clothes. … skins … tents. … bones … tools.
III. 1. the 'capital' is a country's main city: the 'Capitol' is where the US Congress and Senate can be found – **2.** the 'white house' is a house which is white: the 'White House' is the official residence of the US president – **3.** the same – **4.** 'state government' is the government for a specific state: 'federal government' is the government for the whole of the US – **5.** 'Washington, DC' is the US capital: 'Washington State' is a state in its own right – **6.** the same
IV. They were ignorant.
V. c)
VI. … Native Americans. … reservations. … Asian-Americans … Thailand. … Hispanics. … border … . Afro-Americans, … will. … slaves … . … ancestors … life … .
The state with the smallest population is Wyoming.
VII. 1959

4C Working with the text

I. 1. b) – **2.** b)
II. 1. People on both sides had developed strong feelings about defending the ideas they were fighting for. – **2.** It was the question of slavery.
III. 1. ideal – **2.** regiment – **3.** slavery – **4.** human being
IV. 1. the study of war – **2.** the people in our family who come before us – **3.** a person who leaves his or her own country and moves to another country – **4.** an important point
V. *Examples:* **1.** They wanted a better way of life. – **2.** I think they are proud of their ancestors because they fought for their country and what they believed in.

4C Exercises

I. … alphabet … . … lodge … father … region … farmer.
… documents … . … slavery … . … farmowner … . … friends … chance … .
II. 1. Abraham Lincoln – all the other words have something to do with the South in the Civil War – **2.** July 4th – all the other words are connected with the war in Vietnam – **3.** wagon – all the other words have something to do with buffalo – **4.** Liberty Bell – all the other places are in Washington, DC
III. 1. descendants – **2.** emigrant – **3.** tiny – **4.** attack – **5.** minor – **6.** agricultural
IV. a. – **h.** – **e.** – **d.** – **c.** – **b.** – **g.** – **f.**
V. About 58,000 Americans died in Vietnam.
VI. They're celebrating Independence Day (July 4th).

5 Kentucky

5A Working with the text

I. 1. c) – **2.** b) – **3.** a)
II. 1. She races them. – **2.** People say horses thrive on the bluegrass there. – **3.** In the 1940s she used to show horses. After that she bought a farm and raised horses.
III. 1. stallion – **2.** mare – **3.** brood mare – **4.** soil – **5.** limestone – **6.** the forties
IV. 1. b) – **2.** a) – **3.** c) – **4.** a)
V. 1. prepare them for – **2.** to start (off) with – **3.** great/fantastic – **4.** kind
VI. *Example:* She seems to be dedicated to her horses and her farm. She obviously enjoys her work.

5A Exercises

I. 1. He hurt his arm falling off a horse. – **2.** She ran upstairs holding a letter. – **3.** They got home late feeling exhausted. – **4.** We often spend the evening at home listening to country music. – **5.** I stayed in the US for six months working on a farm. – **6.** She looked at the camera trying not to laugh.
II. 1. Did you see that little horse jumping over that huge fence? – **2.** He'd like to have a job offering a regular income. – **3.** The man sat on the park bench talking to himself. – **4.** Do you know about the problems facing farmers in Kentucky? – **5.** They stayed in Paris, Kentucky visiting their daughter-in-law. – **6.** Who is that friendly old woman living in the same road as you?
III. 1. Many people who live in Kentucky love horses. – **2.** Passengers who do not hold a US passport should fill in this form. – **3.** Did you see that dog which was barking at those poor children? – **4.** Drivers who use Interstate 80 can expect delays at the Route 202 interchange in Wings. – **5.** We had a lovely apartment which overlooked the lake. – **6.** Students who want to use the library must first register with the librarian.

IV.

	animal	male	female	young
1.	horse	stallion	mare	foal
2.	duck	drake	duck	duckling
3.	lion	lion	lioness	cub
4.	sheep	ram	ewe	lamb
5.	goat	billy-goat	nanny-goat	kid
6.	goose	gander	goose	gosling

V. 1. buy – **2.** receive – **3.** become – **4.** fetch – **5.** arrive at – **6.** understand

VI. *Examples:* The college principal is Mrs Elisabeth Barton. – He always stands up for his principles. – Do you know where the Sahara Desert is? – Would you like some cheese for your dessert? – It's not fair! You got more than I did! – Please pay your fare when you enter the bus. – If a car doesn't move it's stationary. – Paper and pens are stationery. – The brake is the pedal on the right. – I'm tired. Let's have a break, shall we? – It's late. I'm going home. – That's our neighbor's dog. Its name's Brutus.
VII. The name Frankfort comes from the expression Frank's Ford.

5B Working with the text

I. 1. 'There's nothing I would enjoy any more than to be able to continue farming ...' – **2.** ... I was going to have to do something different than my forefathers ...' – **3.** '... and continue farming as well on the side ...'
II. 1. He thinks the general economic situation in the US has made it difficult for farmers to make a living from farming. – **2.** He gets a regular income and insurance.
III. 1. False. He's a maintenance supervisor in a factory. – **2.** False. He used to be a part-time police officer. – **3.** False. He teaches people how to use concealed weapons.
IV. *Examples:* **1.** He makes sure the machines in the factory are in good running order. – **2.** They feel safer if they know they are carrying weapons. They are concealed, however, in order not to frighten other people.
V. 1. the tough situation for farmers in the US – **2.** raising tobacco
VI. 1. salary – **2.** lb (a pound in weight) – **3.** forefathers – **4.** conceal
VIII. *Example:* The principles on this sign are a sort of 'moral code' for the workers in the factory. Most of them are aimed at the workers' relationship with each other: they should be friendly, cooperative, honest and open for change while at the same time fulfilling any commitments (such as the hours of work, salary etc) they have made to the employer. It's difficult to know how people react to these 'guidelines' but I think if you see them every day you soon begin to ignore them.

5B Exercises

I. 1. Orders placed before 2 pm will be processed on the same day. – **2.** The computers sold in this shop are all made in China. – **3.** Which job offered to you did you accept in the end? – **4.** The people injured in the accident have been interviewed by the police. – **5.** The shop windows destroyed in last week's riots have been repaired. – **6.** Has anybody recorded the program about gun laws shown on CNN last night?
II. 1. Although he was born in Chicago, he was raised in Washington, DC. – **2.** Since he was educated in Louisville, Kentucky, he spoke with a distinct American accent. – **3.** As he had been warned about the problems facing farmers he decided to apply for a job in a factory. – **4.** Before he was offered the job he had to fill out lots of forms. – **5.** As he was pleased with the regular salary he stayed with the company for over ten years. – **6.** When he was offered the chance to return to farming full-time, he immediately agreed.
IV. 1. corporation – **2.** a pay raise – **3.** labor unions – **4.** president – **5.** stockholder
V. 1. An 'employee' works for a company in return for wages: an 'employer' offers work. – **2.** A 'part-time job' is a job you do for part of the working week: a 'full-time job' is for the whole working week. – **3.** To be paid on a 'piecework basis' is to be paid for each individual unit of work you complete (eg. the number of petrol tanks you install into a car): to be paid 'on commission' is to be paid according to the quantity of goods sold (eg. 10%). – **4.** A 'capital-intensive' industry depends on having enough machines and equipment: a 'labor-intensive' industry depends on having enough workers. – **5.** A'white-collar' worker is somebody who works in an office: a 'blue-collar' worker is somebody who works on the shop floor. – **6.** Working 'flexitime' is being able to choose when to start and finish work: 'overtime' is when you work longer than in a normal week.
VI. h. – **d.** – **a.** – **e.** – **g.** – **c.** – **f.** – **b.**

5C Working with the text

I. d. – c. – f. – h. – e. – b. – g. – a.
II. 1. He argued against a law which would have made betting on horses illegal. – **2.** They were grateful because he had helped them to save their livelihood. – **3.** They helped him build a church. – **4.** Yes, they should. It was his hard work that led to the Episcopal church being built.
III. 1. b) – **2.** b) – **3.** c) – **4.** a)
IV. 1. present – **2.** bought – **3.** unpleasant thing to do – **4.** gave

5C Exercises

I. 1. … unless … . – **2.** … nevertheless … . – **3.** … eventually … . – **4.** … so … . – **5.** … despite … . – **6.** … although … . – **7.** … even though … .
II. *Examples:* **1.** money, time – **2.** a cake, a mistake – **3.** homework, a handstand – **4.** horses, money – **5.** for school, for an exam – **6.** your key, your balance
III. 1. d) – **2.** f) – **3.** b) – **4.** a) – **5.** c) – **6.** e)
IV. 1. … present … . – **2.** … provided … ? – **3.** … left … . – **4.** … supplies … . – **5.** … caters … . – **6.** … donate … .
V.
- Martin Luther King Day (3rd Monday in January) celebrates the birth of the civil-rights leader (1929).
- Presidents' Day (3rd Monday in February) celebrates the births of George Washington and Abraham Lincoln.
- Memorial Day (last Monday in May) honors all those who died in US wars.
- Independence Day (July 4th) celebrates American colonies' independence from Britain (1776).
- Columbus Day (2nd Monday in October) marks the anniversary of the day when America is thought to have been discovered (1492).
- Veterans Day (November 11th) honors the veterans of US wars.
- Thanksgiving (4th Thursday in November) celebrates the first Thanksgiving Day by the Pilgrims (1621).

6 South Carolina

6A Working with the text

I. 1. It's because companies from all over the world have settled in the area. – **2.** These are people who have left their home countries to live and work abroad. – **3.** The Mayor enjoys having people from the 'outside' in his community. He doesn't really make a difference between local people and people from other countries.
II. 1. … to lobby the state government. – **2.** … share best practices. – **3.** … tell his colleagues how his city has gained from having a diversified community.
III. 1. upstate – **2.** to lobby – **3.** board – **4.** benefit
IV. 1. worry – **2.** in particular – **3.** mainly – **4.** three months
V. 1. people that come from the 'outside' – **2.** in Spartanburg – **3.** at the meetings: members of the Municipal Association – **4.** the people from Spartanburg: experience with multicultural diversity
VII. He seems to have been well treated by the people in South Carolina.
VIII. He only had his first name (Ulrich) on his overall. This would be unusual in his home country.

6A Exercises

I. 1. postponed – **2.** minutes – **3.** an agenda – **4.** a committee – **5.** unanimously – **6.** abstentions
II. … to elect … … is appointed … … is nominated … seconds … … vote for … … speaks … .

III.

AGENDA
9.00 – 12.00
Room 1018a
April 25, 2002
Sales Meeting (Teams 01, 02 and 03)
1. Apologies for absence
2. Minutes of the last meeting
3. Sales figures 2001
4. Targets for 2003
5. Retirement of James Blackley
6. Any other business

IV. *Example:* In my view most meetings are a waste of time. They often last too long and are unproductive. I find meetings are useful if there is a small number of people and a clear idea of what the meeting is about. It also helps if you set a time limit in advance.
V. (minutes = *Protokoll*)
VI. … born … … parents … … died … … life … .
… town … … role … … aspect … … voice … … determined … .
… actress. … talent … .
… different … … daughters. … incompetent … … world.

6B Working with the text

I. 1. b) – **2.** b) – **3.** c)
II. 1. … parts for the cars could not be delivered to the factory in time. – **2.** … production would stop and cars could not be built. – **3.** … to have another exit ramp near its plant.
III. 1. Amongst other things they need electricity to generate steam. – **2.** In order to dry the paint on the cars.
IV. 1. effect – **2.** forced to sit around and do nothing – **3.** factory … crucial
V. 1. it could affect your output of cars significantly – **2.** we can work for 90 minutes before having to stop – **3.** people in the area are going to be very interested in the question of deregulation
VI. *Examples:* **1.** If you have JIT delivery you don't have to build factories to store all the parts you need. – **2.** BMW's plant has created many jobs and brought a lot of money into the area.

6B Exercises

I. A: Can I close the door? / Is it OK if I close the door?
B: Yes, go ahead. / Yes, please do.
II. past tense (but future time)
III. 1. had a chat – **2.** had a discussion about – **3.** have a look at – **4.** have a critical effect on – **5.** have an increase in – **6.** had a think
IV. 1. The new cars are produced in … . – **2.** A new interstate exit is going to be built … . – **3.** More electricity has to be generated. – **4.** A party of new employees has been invited … . – **5.** The company is being forced to move to the US because of … . – **6.** Your work permit will be renewed … .
V. 1. chairperson – **2.** an underachiever – **3.** the Native Americans – **4.** a flight attendant – **5.** has been forced to downsize – **6.** challenging

6C Working with the text

I. 1. A job at BMW fitted his qualifications and personal goals better. – **2.** He has found German people easy to get on with and open. – **3.** He's taking German lessons. – **4.** His neighbor is German so he speaks German quite often.
II. 1. c) – **2.** b) – **3.** a) – **4.** b)
III. 1. suited – **2.** about – **3.** By chance – **4.** food
IV. *Examples:* **1.** Because that's where BMW has factories in Germany. – **2.** Yes, I could. I would like to live abroad and the climate and way of life in South Carolina would suit me, I think.

6C Exercises

I.

'hello'	**'goodbye'**
Hi there!	Catch you later!
How you doing?	Take care!
How's it going?	See you!
Long time, no see!	So long!

III. 1. d – **2.** f – **3.** e – **4.** a – **5.** c – **6.** b
IV. 1. I'm going to have forty winks. – **2.** It was a piece of cake! – **3.** Let's get down to the nitty gritty. – **4.** He's over the moon!
V. 1. c – **2.** f. – **3.** a. – **4.** b. – **5.** g. – **6.** h. – **7.** e. – **8.** d.
VI. In 1803 President Thomas Jefferson paid Napoleon Bonaparte $15 million for about 2.1 million km^2 of land west of the Mississippi River. This was called the Louisiana Purchase. The huge new territory provided space for the USA and it helped reduce tensions between US settlers and France.

7 Georgia

7A Working with the text

I. 1. He's talking about the city trying to come to terms with two issues: slavery and segregation. – **2.** No. He says the city doesn't have a clear conscience. – **3.** He says: 'there's enormous amounts of immigration, and we're examples of that'.
II. 1. He means there's a lot of building work. – **2.** It means 'high technology' industries, such as computers, information technology or biochemistry. – **3.** I think he means people are not reflecting on themselves and their past. They are thinking more about the future.
III. 1. slavery and segregation – **2.** enormous amounts of immigration – **3.** Jonathan and Raissa – **4.** people in Atlanta
IV. 1. 'I was doing stories about Bulgaria in English …' – **2.** 'Bulgarian TV made me an anchor …' – **3.** 'Are you interested in trying out for an anchoring position? I said, "Of course" … '. – **4.** 'I arrived here six-and-a-half years ago … '
V. 1. … to write and present news reports for TV. – **2.** … are the presenter of a TV show. – **3.** … you give them a job on TV. – **4.** … see if you can get it.
VII. 1. Your 'conscience' is your awareness of what is right or wrong. If you are 'conscious' you are aware of things around you because you use your senses (sight, hearing etc). – **2.** 'Immigration' is when people enter another country to live there. 'Emigration' is when people leave their country to live somewhere else. – **3.** The same. – **4.** The word 'program' is American English. The word 'programme' is British English (except when talking about computers).

VIII. *Examples:* **1.** It means the separation of white people and black people. – **2.** I think it's a bit sad really. It sounds as if he's not interested in the people who he lives and works with.

7A Exercises

I. 1. She was interested in trying out for an anchoring position. – **2.** There are plenty of ways of getting work in Atlanta. – **3.** He's proud of working for CNN International. – **4.** Many people in Georgia are afraid of talking too much about the past. – **5.** The city has succeeded in rebuilding itself. – **6.** Thank you for taking the time to speak to us.
II. 1. d. – **2.** e. – **3.** b. – **4.** f. – **5.** a. – **6.** c.
III. 1. e. – **2.** a. – **3.** d. – **4.** b. – **5.** f. – **6.** c.
IV. Jonathan Mann says this about his colleague, Raissa Vassileva. Yes, I agree with him. I think she has done something very remarkable.
V. … was educated … . … inherited … .
… bought … transformed … transmitting … . … took … .
… launched … to become … achieved … . … sold … retaining … including … . … were shown … was launched … .
… valued … acquired … . … acquisition … . … became … responsibility … containing … .
… donation … . … humanitarian … .

7B Working with the text

I. 1. b) – **2.** a) – **3.** b)
II. 1. She wants to borrow a book but the book has already been lent out. – **2.** She means she's going to do really well in her PT test.
III. 1. You need to complete the form. – **2.** I try as hard as I can. – **3.** You look in good physical shape. – **4.** I haven't given up.
IV. 1. the form in the plastic holder – **2.** the book – **3.** the program – **4.** Major Longmire
VI. *Examples:* **1.** Yes, I think they do know each other well. They seem very friendly and relaxed. – **2.** I think looking good is important for people in the US but not for everybody. There are some people who do a lot of jogging, for example, and spend time looking after their hair and teeth. On the other hand, there are other people in the States who do not seem to worry at all about what they look like. They eat junk food and are overweight.

7B Exercises

I. 1. This is the film I'm interested in. – **2.** This is the man she spoke to. – **3.** This is the fax we were waiting for. – **4.** This is the picture they looked at. – **5.** This is the team she trained with. – **6.** This is the woman you said hello to.
II. 1. I was wondering if you had the book 'Gone with the Wind'? – **2.** I was wondering if I could get some information on emissions testing here? – **3.** I was wondering if you sold newspapers? – **4.** I was wondering when the library closed on Saturday? – **5.** I was wondering if you needed some help? – **6.** I was wondering how this running machine worked?
III. 1. Would you mind lending me your notebook for a day? – **2.** I was wondering if I could borrow your car next week? – **3.** Do you know why I don't lend people my books? I never get them back! – **4.** Hey! Who borrowed my umbrella without asking? Was it you?
IV. 1. OK. I'll open a window. – **2.** Here you are. I'll lend you mine. – **3.** Bye. I'll see you later! – **4.** Don't worry. I'll help you.
V. 1. He's written three letters today. – **2.** He's been writing letters all morning. – **3.** I'm losing my voice because I've been talking all afternoon. – **4.** They're coming to the meeting. I've told them when it is. – **5.** I've never cycled down a mountain. Have you? – **6.** I need to sit down. I've been cycling all

day. – **7.** He's repaired his motorbike and now it works properly. – **8.** He's been repairing his motorbike so I don't know if he can visit us later.
VI. 1. eventually – **2.** formula – **3.** mustn't – **4.** mobile

7C Working with the text

I. 1. It's famous because Martin Luther King pastored it in the 1960s. – **2.** The walls of segregation in transportation were broken down. – **3.** He thought it would come about by appealing to people's conscience. – **4.** He thought that if you didn't allow religious freedom then you wouldn't have a free country.
II. 1. the church – **2.** breaking down the walls of segregation – **3.** allowing religious expression
III. 1. segregation – **2.** conscience – **3.** integrity – **4.** sacredness
IV. *Examples:* **1.** He led the civil-rights movement in the USA which culminated in the Civil Rights Act of 1964. This made racial discrimination illegal in voting, employment and public places. – **2.** He was assassinated in Memphis on April 4th.

7C Exercises

I. 1. decency – **2.** conscience – **3.** segregation – **4.** sacred – **5.** integrity
II. … was born … . … was … had … met … . … couldn't use … was not allowed … went … had to … . … told … stopped … was driving. … asked. … pointed … . … said. … hated … segregation. … accepting … explained. … die. … never forgot … .
III. 1. b. – **2.** e. – **3.** a. – **4.** f. – **5.** d. – **6.** c. – **7.** g.
IV. *Example:* No, his dream did not come true. I think there is still a lot of racism in the US. In 1964 the 24th Amendment was added to the constitution.
V. The young man is pleased that something is being done for the African-American community. The young woman feels it has made a difference to learn something about Martin Luther King in a more direct way by seeing how he lived and what sort of a person he was rather than reading about him in school textbooks.

8 Florida

8A Working with the text

I. 1. b) – **2.** b) – **3.** b)
II. 1. c) – **2.** b) – **3.** b) – **4.** b)
III. 1. pet – **2.** to chase – **3.** cutting edge – **4.** gang – **5.** preach
IV. 1. different kinds of people – **2.** a place where people and ideas are mixed up together – **3.** a small, narrow boat that you can live on – **4.** policing in a small area with direct contact to the people
VI. *Examples:* **1.** Yes, I think so. It keeps them busy and helps them to get rid of some energy and aggression. – **2.** I think so. People always get on better if they know each other. If they see police officers as their friends, as people they can trust, respect and rely on, then I think levels of crime will go down.

8A Exercises

I. 1. cards – **2.** chess – **3.** monopoly – **4.** swimming – **5.** golf – **6.** listening to CDs
II. *Example:* I like to keep fit. I go running as often as I can. I enjoy swimming and I like cycling as

long as it's not too hilly. In the winter, if it's cold enough, I go ice skating on a lake near my house. I like cooking and entertaining but I'm always pleased when somebody offers to do the washing up. What else? I like reading detective stories. I don't mind if they are a bit scary. One day I'd like to read one in English. I also listen to the radio a lot. There are so many interesting programs on. The good thing about the radio is that you can listen and do something else (like ironing) at the same time.
IV. 1. 'Shoplifting' is stealing from shops: 'burglary' is breaking into somebody's house and stealing something. – **2.** A 'victim' is somebody who has been hurt or killed as a result of a crime: a 'hostage' is somebody who is held as a prisoner unless a certain demand is met. – **3.** the same (except 'homicide' is American English and 'murder' is British English) – **4.** 'Arson' is setting fire to a building: 'assault' is attacking somebody.
V. *Example:* I think it's a very good idea. If a police officer is on the streets then he or she can be seen and is part of the community.
VI. *Example:* I think he deals with the situation very well. He explains the problem to the man but he is friendly and polite.
VII. b)

8B Working with the text

I. 1. 'I went to University of Miami, graduated in 1969 …' – **2.** … 'I was a paratrooper with the 101st Airborne.' – **3.** … 'I've been working with the city of Miami now since 1987.'
II. 1. c. – **2.** f. – **3.** a. – **4.** e. – **5.** b. – **6.** d.
III. 1. He's pleased with it but he thinks a lot more could be done. – **2.** The people who live there come from countries where there are not the same laws (for example as regards waste disposal) as in the US. – **3.** He's trying to educate the people to keep the city clean.
IV. 1. NET – **2.** the interviewer – **3.** residents who come from other countries – **4.** the community of East Little Havana
V. 1. … a soldier who is trained to drop from aircraft wearing a parachute. – **2.** … a first university degree in a science subject. – **3.** … the day the community comes around to pick up people's garbage.
VI. 1. A 'Bachelor of Science' is a university degree in a science subject (eg. Physics, Chemistry) and a 'Bachelor of Arts' is a university degree in an arts subject (eg. History, languages) – **2.** A 'Cuban citizen' is a Cuban who lives in Cuba: a 'Cuban national' is a Cuban who probably lives outside Cuba. – **3.** the same – **4.** A 'tourist' visits a country temporarily: a 'resident' lives there permanently.

8B Exercises

I. somewhere – anywhere – anything – anything – anybody – somebody – any – some
II. 1. was, previous – **2.** ineffective – **3.** similarity – **4.** for – **5.** on, goodbye – **6.** She, took, her, off

III.

weather	clothes	buildings	feelings
sticky	scarf	church	confused
sky	gloves	store	scared
windy	sweatshirt	cottage	worried

IV. 1. Das war ein kleiner Schritt für den Menschen, aber ein gewaltiger Sprung für die Menschheit.
2. Das war ein kleiner Schritt für einen Mann, aber ein gewaltiger Sprung für die Menschheit.
V. A state of emergency was announced. Airports were closed, Disney World closed, the Space Shuttle launch pad had to be protected, billions of dollars of damage was done, thousands were made homeless and forty people lost their lives.

8C Working with the text

I. 1. True. – **2.** True. – **3.** True. – **4.** False. It can only be bought on the farm.
II. 1. 'Both have teaching certificates …' – **2.** 'Our juice is all sold only at the retail store … we make the apple pies …' – **3.** '… they want to send a gift of citrus Florida back north.' – **4.** '… right in the middle of the city here …'
III. 1. saw – **2.** looks after – **3.** center – **4.** for that reason
IV. 1. a) – **2.** b) – **3.** b) – **4.** b)
V. 1. it comes out of an orange when you squeeze it – **2.** it's made of oil and vinegar, for example, and you put it on your salad before you eat it – **3.** it's made of citrus fruit such as oranges, lemons and limes, and you spread it on bread or toast – **4.** what children like to eat: British people say sweets
VI. The crocodile and the Native American.
VII. *Examples:* **1.** Yes, I could. I'd enjoy the weather and the Hispanic influence but I'm not so sure I'd like the hurricanes. – **2.** Yes, I think I'm very susceptible to the weather. I don't like the cold and a grey day makes me feel a bit miserable. On a sunny day I like to be outside. I don't mind the heat at all. On the contrary. For me it can never be too hot!

8C Exercises

I. *Examples:* **1.** apple, pear, banana, grape, melon, orange – **2.** potato, carrot, bean, onion, courgette, leek – **3.** dog, cat, horse, hamster, parrot, guinea pig – **4.** robin, sparrow, magpie, blackbird, thrush, blue tit – **5.** rose, daffodil, violet, hyacinth, chrysanthemum, crocus – **6.** baker, butcher, newsagent, chemist, jeweller, greengrocer
II. … had been guaranteed … accepted … . … was discovered … began to move in. … were ordered to return … . … did not return … would consider … .
… had set up … performed … . … woke up … had seen … .
… became … rode … were killed … .
… managed to win … couldn't succeed in winning … .
III. In the 1880s Wounded Knee was the site of a conflict between the local Native American population and the United States government. The Sioux started performing a ghost dance which would result in the return of native lands, the rise of dead ancestors and the disappearance of the whites. White settlers were frightened by the Sioux rituals and asked the US army to intervene. Chief Sitting Bull was arrested in December 1890. As he was being led away, a gunfight erupted. Thirteen people, including Sitting Bull, were killed and his followers fled. The 7th Cavalry pursued the Sioux to Wounded Knee Creek. On December 29, 1890, a shot was fired within the camp and the army began shooting. Accounts of the precise events and the numbers of dead vary but it is likely that the soldiers killed between 150 and 370 Sioux men, women and children, the great majority of whom were unarmed bystanders. Thirty-one US soldiers were killed in action, many of them from fire by their own troops.

9 Quebec

9A Working with the text

I. 1. False. It operates worldwide. – **2.** False. Trans Canada Airlines was its original name. – **3.** True.
II. 1. '… the airline soon became government owned … ' – **2.** '… international network is further strengthened by our Star Alliance Partnership … ' – **3.** '… has a very strong regional airline network … '

III. 1. Because it realised that the country's economic growth depended on air transportation. – **2.** The USA. – **3.** Because Canada is such a large country and people and goods could not be transported huge distances by road or rail.
IV. 1. predecessor – **2.** mail – **3.** fare – **4.** freight
V. 1. an enormous – **2.** decided/influenced – **3.** went by – **4.** vital
VI. 1. c. – **2.** e. – **3.** d. – **4.** a. – **5.** b.
VII. *Examples:* **1.** No, not really. To be quite honest I get a bit nervous when I have to fly especially when the plane takes off. It's not like being in a train or a car. In a plane you're in the air and you can't get out. – **2.** No, I haven't been to Canada but I'd like to. I'd like to go skiing or walking there.

9A Exercises

I. The words in number 4 are said differently. – *Example:* **1.** You're not very fair! I lent you some money last week. Why can't you lend me some money this week? What's the bus fare from here to the centre of town and back? – **2.** Which route are we taking to London? Ignorance – that's the root of most racism! – **3.** I must go out. I need some fresh air. Who's the heir to the British throne? – **4.** The normal trains aren't very loud but the freight trains are terrible. I got such a fright when you knocked on the window! – **5.** The mail is delivered twice a day. Is flying a male-dominated profession? – **6.** We looked through the album and found some interesting photos. They threw the ball too hard and broke a window.
II. 1. short – **2.** major – **3.** increase – **4.** deregulate – **5.** successor
III. 1. d. – **2.** a. – **3.** e. – **4.** b. – **5.** c.
IV. a. – l. – k. – i. – e. – j. – d. – b. – h. – c. – f. – g.
V. *Examples:* Germany's population is three times greater than Canada's. The population density in Canada is extremely low. More people in Germany live in metropolitan areas than in Canada. More people live in Toronto than in Berlin. About the same amount of people live in Montreal as in Berlin. Calgary's population is not as large as Munich's or Hamburg's.
There are many more ethnic groups in Canada than there are in Germany.
VI. 3 – 75 – 300 – 25 – 59

9B Working with the text

I. 1. … over forty years. – **2.** … all over Canada. – **3.** … sense – and respond to – the needs of their customers. – **4.** … they can serve their customers in many different languages.
II. 1. 106. – **2.** The idea is that the employees are taught to sense what the customers need and respond appropriately. – **3.** It gives them driving directions, driving tips and advice on traffic rules. – **4.** It has employees who speak obscure languages and offers printed material translated into many languages.
III. 1. c. – **2.** a. – **3.** f. – **4.** b. – **5.** d. – **6.** e.
IV. 1. important companies – **2.** slogans – **3.** how to get to a place by car – **4.** a rare language
VI. *Examples:* **1.** It can be dangerous if you have to drive on the other side of the road. – **2.** I think it's important to be served properly – or to put it another way: I don't like bad service. – **3.** If customers are happy with the service they get they keep coming back so happy customers means more business. – **4.** Because people who visit Canada and want to rent a car during their holiday come from many different countries around the world.

9B Exercises

I. 1. future – offer – pattern I – **2.** present – advice – pattern II – **3.** past – promise – pattern III – **4.** present – warning – pattern I – **5.** present – possibility – pattern II – **6.** future – wish – pattern II –
II. 1. It must have stopped raining. – **2.** He must have been running. – **3.** There must have been an accident. – **4.** She can't have heard the phone. – **5.** He must have taken his car. – **6.** Someone must have used my computer!

III. 1. e. – **2.** d. – **3.** a. – **4.** c. – **5.** f. – **6.** b.
IV. This is a service for US citizens renting cars outside the US. If anything goes wrong, people can call the US and get advice in English over the phone.
V. banks – rights – settlers – monopoly – death
determined – made – encouraged – dispatched – offered
over – from – on – about – of
In addition to – However – still
half – capture – control – support – freedom
little – loyalist – French – Constitutional – Lower

9C Working with the text

I. 1. b) – **2.** c)
II. 1. it is 100% natural. – **2.** changes color or flavor.
III. b. – **g.** – **c.** – **d.** – **f.** – **e.** – **a.**
IV. 1. mineral – **2.** pasteurise – **3.** oxygen – **4.** stainless steel
V. 1. … the food you eat. – **2.** … someone appointed by the government to check the quality of food. – **3.** … say how good it is. – **4.** … a factory where a product is put into bottles.
VII. *Examples:* **1.** Yes, I am. I try not to eat too many fatty or sugary foods. – **2.** I shop at my local supermarket. No, I don't choose the things I buy very carefully. However, I do look to see if there are any bargains.

9C Exercises

I. 1. spicy – **2.** sour – **3.** sweet – **4.** tasteless – **5.** salty – **6.** bitter
II. 1. c. – **2.** e. – **3.** d. – **4.** b. – **5.** f. – **6.** a.
III. 1. a) – **2.** b) – **3.** c)
IV. The referendum was defeated in an extremely close vote: 51 per cent to 49 per cent.

10 Ontario

10A Working with the text

I. 1. b) – **2.** c) – **3.** a) – **4.** b) – **5.** c)
II. 1. The House of Commons, the Senate and the Crown. – **2.** He or she represents the British monarch. – **3.** There are five parties in parliament. The Liberal Party, who makes up the government, sits on the right of the Speaker. The Opposition, consisting of four parties, sits on the left of the Speaker. – **4.** First a bill is introduced. Then it is debated. Then it is passed to the Senate. Finally, if everything goes well, it goes to the Governor General. – **5.** It is a written record of everything that is said in parliament.
III. 1. a constituency – **2.** the Speaker – **3.** a bill – **4.** assent – **5.** transcript
IV. 1. part – **2.** at the moment – **3.** nearest – **4.** carry out – **5.** matter

10A Exercises

I. … chambers: … . … MPs … constituency. … majority … election. … opposition.
II. 1. by-election – **2.** running – **3.** elected – **4.** policy – **5.** statesman – **6.** constituency

III. 1. An 'ambassador' is a person who represents his or her government in a foreign country: an 'embassy' is the official building used by the ambassador. – **2.** A 'mayor' is responsible for the day-to-day running of a town: a 'prime minister' is responsible for the day-to-day running of a country. – **3.** A 'chamber' is a large room: a 'cabinet' is a group of government ministers. – **4.** A 'bill' is a plan for a law: a 'law' is a rule which regulates people's behaviour in a country.
IV. 1. d. (*z.B.*) – **2.** e. (*vormittags*) – **3.** b. (*d.h.*) – **4.** c. (*nachmittags*) – **5.** a. (*vgl.*)

10B Working with the text

I. 1. False. It's a daily newspaper. – **2.** True. – **3.** False. It is printed in eight different parts of the country. – **4.** False. It appears only in English. – **5.** False. It is available in Quebec, too.
II. 1. English, French and Oriental languages. – **2.** It is the most multicultural city in the world. – **3.** It has to be printed in different areas which lie in different time zones. – **4.** It can be advertised in English (although Quebec is a French-speaking part of Canada).
III. 1. b) – **2.** c) – **3.** a) – **4.** b)
IV. 1. … is the number of copies that are sold each time it is produced. – **2.** … are people coming into a country in large numbers. – **3.** … are people who speak and read French. – **4.** … prohibit it.
V. *Examples:* **1.** It has a very diverse readership spread across a huge country. – **2.** I read a German national newspaper every day. I read the local news first, then the business section and then the sports pages.

10B Exercises

I. British Columbia
II. 1. … Northern Territories. – **2.** … Central Provinces. – **3.** … Newfoundland. – **4.** … Prairie Provinces … – **5.** … Newfoundland.
IV. 1. A 'librarian' doesn't work for a newspaper. – **2.** A 'crossword' is not a person. – **3.** A 'tabloid' is not a part of a newspaper. – **4.** A 'crossword' is not written by a newspaper's readers.
V. 1. The Chancellor is going to reduce interest rates (in order to encourage people to invest). – **2.** The Prime Minister is planning a trip to Toronto. – **3.** There has been a bomb explosion in the centre of London. – **4.** 14 people died in a fire at an airport.
VI. The newspaper is thanking its readers.
VII.

Region	%
Alberta, Manitoba and Saskatchewan	17
British Columbia	12.5
Newfoundland, Prince Edward Island, Nova Scotia, New Brunswick	8
Quebec and Ontario	62
Yukon Territory, Nunavut Territory, Northwest Territories	0.5

VIII. -3 1/2 = Newfoundland Standard Time – **-4** = Atlantic Standard Time – **-5** = Eastern Standard Time – **-6** = Central Standard Time – **-7** = Mountain Standard Time – **-8** = Pacific Standard Time

10C Working with the text

I. 1. … they were really looking for a route to the East. – **2.** … fur. – **3.** … was able to claim the rights to all the land around the rivers that flowed into Hudson Bay. – **4.** … traded furs. – **5.** … people knew how much they had to pay for them.
II. 1. explorers – **2.** England – **3.** settlers – **4.** Native people – **5.** Hudson's Bay Company

III. 1. a) – **2.** b) – **3.** c)
IV. 1. connection – **2.** ended up – **3.** main – **4.** you needed
VI. 1. Henry Hudson – **2.** Canadian – **3.** blanket – **4.** Hudson's Bay Company

10C Exercises

I. 1. take on – **2.** taking up – **3.** take off – **4.** takes after
II. 1. turned down – **2.** turn out – **3.** turn up – **4.** turn round
IV. Paragraph A: Hudson's Bay Company, formed in 1670, was originally an English corporation. – **Paragraph B:** For almost a century this monopoly was unchallenged. – **Paragraph C:** However, a monopoly that was so profitable could not be held for long.

11 Alberta

11A Working with the text

I. 1. c) – **2.** a) – **3.** b) – **4.** b)
II. 1. It was used for the (steam) trains. – **2.** The Winter Olympics in 1988. – **3.** It has been about three times as fast. – **4.** The town has built wildlife corridors so that animals can move around without being disturbed.
III. 1. to diminish – **2.** to sustain – **3.** to accommodate – **4.** to occur
IV. 1. b) – **2.** c) – **3.** b)
V. *Examples:* **1.** At a Nordic centre you can do sports like cross-country skiing and ski jumping. – **2.** It needs hotels, restaurants, shops and an efficient public transport system.

11A Exercises

I. 1. given up – **2.** giving off – **3.** give up – **4.** gave way
II. 1. call back – **2.** call off – **3.** call in on – **4.** called back
III. 1. c. – **2.** f. – **3.** a. – **4.** b. – **5.** d. – **6.** e.
IV. 1. catty – deliberately unkind: negative – **2.** sheepish – being embarrassed because you have done something wrong: negative – **3.** ratty – bad-tempered: negative – **4.** cocky – proud of oneself: negative
V. This is an advertisement for cross-country skiing.
VI. No, they didn't. Manitoba joined Canada in 1870. British Columbia joined one year later (1871) and Alberta and Saskatchewan joined in 1905. Manitoba is special because it came into being as a province after an argument between the Canadian government and the Métis, an indigenous people.
VII. July 1st is Canada Day, a Canadian national holiday. It marks the anniversary of the unification of Upper and Lower Canada (now Ontario and Quebec), New Brunswick and Nova Scotia as the Dominion of Canada on July 1st, 1867. Originally known as Dominion Day, the name was changed to Canada Day in 1982 when the Canadian constitution was revised. The day is marked throughout Canada by parades, fireworks, and the display of flags.

11B Working with the text

I. 1. True. – **2.** The text doesn't say. – **3.** False. – **4.** False.
II. 1. He was able to sell a lot of T-shirts in a very short space of time and make a lot of money. – **2.** For small or complicated jobs Brooke uses the manual presses. For larger and more straightforward

jobs the automatic presses can be used. – **3.** He's able to print sophisticated designs and do complicated artwork. – **4.** He says that he has done T-shirts for Canadian Pacific who have hotels all over the country.
III. 1. the Olympics – **2.** automatic presses – 3. Canadian Pacific – **4.** a T-shirt
IV. 1. feet (line 6) – **2.** buy (line 8) – **3.** whole (line 22) – **4.** site (line 22) – **5.** through (line 31) – **6.** wear (line 34)
V. *Example:* I think it must be difficult for him to find the right employees, people who are well trained and able to produce a top-quality product.
VI. *Examples:* **1.** My impression is that he still likes his work and that he is continuing to expand his business. – **2.** I think it was clever. People usually remember unusual names.

11B Exercises

I. 1. e. – **2.** a. – **3.** f. – **4.** b. – **5.** c. – **6.** d.
II. 1. dazzling – **2.** dim – **3.** vivid – **4.** shady
III. b)

11C Working with the text

I. 1. It's situated in an area where there are lots of fossils. – **2.** Dinosaurs and fossils. – **3.** The specimen was complete from nose to tail. – **4.** Because it received a royal designation from Queen Elizabeth II. – **5.** The museum does scientific research and organises field digs and explorations. – **6.** 400,000 people visit the museum every year.
II. 1. live in – **2.** Not long ago – **3.** superb/fantastic – **4.** every year

III.

oO	Oo	Ooo	oOo
complete	fossil	dinosaur	addition
extinct	research	history	Alberta
unique	royal	skeleton	museum

IV. 1. the (people who work in the) museum – **2.** people from Alberta – **3.** the specimen – **4.** the royal designation
V. 1. just outside the museum there are – **2.** we like people to go out with us and look for fossils

11C Exercises

I. 1. used to play – **2.** used to go – **3.** used to write – **4.** used to go out – **5.** used to play – **6.** used to smoke
III. 1. Sie hat früher in einem Dorf gewohnt. – **2.** Sie hat sich jetzt daran gewöhnt, in der Stadt zu leben. – **3.** Er hat früher für eine kanadische Firma gearbeitet. – **4.** Er war daran gewöhnt, beruflich (in seinem Job) Englisch zu sprechen.
used to + infinitive = past habit
to be used to + -ing = to do something easily because you do it so often
IV. 1. introducing an explanation – **2.** giving yourself more time – **3.** making a suggestion – **4.** being more precise – **5.** signalling the end of the dialogue – **6.** indicating an afterthought
V. There had been a lot of snow at the weekend. – How dare you say such things about me? – The fireworks were spectacular and memorable. – The position will involve international travel.

12 British Columbia

12A Working with the text

I. 1. b) – **2.** c) – **3.** c) – **4.** a)
II. 1. 'British Columbia is the third-largest film and television production centre in North America … ' (line 1) – **2.** '… we have a selection of those kind of locales … ' (line 15) – **3.** ' … British Columbia is very, very cheap in terms of our international pricing … ' (line 20) – **4.** ' … we are only two and a half hours away by plane from Los Angeles … ' (lines 27-28)
III. 1. They are a script, a producer, a director, a star and money. – **2.** It goes first to its film library and looks at photographs. – **3.** The exchange rate for the Canadian dollar. – **4.** They can be sure of good crews and a good infrastructure. They are close to home and they are in the same time zone.
IV. 1. a book containing the lines the actors speak – **2.** the person who is in charge of the making of a film – **3.** when one car tries to catch another car driving at high speed – **4.** when you get more than you expected when you change your money into a foreign currency
V. *Examples:* **1.** The last film I saw was 'The Beach' with Leonardo DiCaprio. It was OK but I wouldn't go and see it again. My girlfriend would, though! – **2.** I don't watch much TV. I usually watch the news or current affairs programmes. I also like comedy programmes, especially stand-up comedians.

12A Exercises

I. 1. put in – **2.** put up with – **3.** put off – **4.** put in
II. 1. looking for – **2.** look after – **3.** look into – **4.** look up to
III. 1. A 'director' works in the film business: a 'conductor' works in the music business. – **2.** A 'cabin' is a small simple house made of wood: a 'house' is usually made of brick. – **3.** A 'library' is where you borrow books: a 'bookshop' is where you buy books. – **4.** 'Ontario' is a province in Canada. 'Ottawa' is a city in Ontario (and the Canadian capital). – **5.** A 'million' is one and six noughts (1,000,000): a 'billion' is one and nine noughts (1,000,000,000).
VI. The article says that Vancouver came out top with three other cities in a survey on the quality of living in cities around the world.
VII. *Example:* My favourite city is Edinburgh. I like the Scots. They are friendly, have a sense of humour and are proud of their country and their traditions. The city itself is full of history: the Castle, Hollyrood Palace, the Royal Mile and now it's got its own parliament. The other thing about Edinburgh is that there's always so much happening. The highlight of the year must be the Festival in August. I was there two years ago in the summer. It was great. I wish I could go back again.

12B Working with the text

I. 1. True. – **2.** False. It has been in operation since 1986. – **3.** True. – **4.** True.
II. 1. They increased the pollution levels because people used their cars to get into the city. – **2.** First there are emergency cabinets with telephones in the stations and second there are alarms in the trains themselves. – **3.** Yes, they can. There is a red button above the telephones in the station. If you press it, the train will stop. – **4.** It is a silent alarm. It sends a message back to the control room to signal that there is a problem.
III. 1. passenger – **2.** suburb – **3.** to commute – **4.** platform
IV. 1. realised – **2.** Almost/Nearly – **3.** met – **4.** signal/sign
VI. *Examples:* **1.** I think it's marvellous. It's efficient, environmentally friendly and safe. What more can you expect from a public transport system? – **2.** Yes, I am. I'm very concerned about noise pollution. I live near a busy street and there are cars going past all day and night. I can't open the windows. I'd like to live in the country.

12B Exercises

I. 1. The number of cars going into the city has decreased. – **2.** There was a slow increase in pollution levels. – **3.** Below the telephone is a red button. – **4.** In 25 years' time people will be aware of the problems.
II. 1. seeing (having seen) – **2.** hearing – **3.** using – **4.** to maintain – **5.** to lend – **6.** to come – **7.** running – **8.** to consult – **9.** to pay – **10.** to let
III. Yes, the theatre must be very popular in Vancouver. The text says that the Playhouse Theatre Company started out in 1962 with a group of volunteers. In the meantime it has grown into a professional organisation with performances throughout the year.
IV. Immigrants with enough points can become Canadian citizens after three years.
V. Asia is close to Canada's west coast.

12C Working with the text

I. 1. … it is an efficient and environmentally-friendly way of generating power. – **2.** … from the Gemini space programme. – **3.** … in vehicles, buildings, ships, trains and boats. – **4.** … large car manufacturers such as DaimlerChrysler and Ford.
II. 1. the fuel cell – **2.** people at Ballard Power – **3.** Firoz Rasul – **4.** everyone
IV. 1. a series of manned flights to other planets – **2.** a spacious car you use for outdoor activities – **3.** the first model or design of a product before it goes into production – **4.** a development in technology that will significantly change the way we live
V. *Examples:* **1.** I cycle to the supermarket and I take the train to work every day. – **2.** I think so. There are already cars that run on alternative fuel such as rape (*Raps*) or batteries so I am sure that in the next 100 years the conventional car engine will no longer be in use.

12C Exercises

I. 1. Mike first became interested in the environment while helping out on his uncle's farm. – **2.** Before leaving college, he joined Our Earth, an environmental pressure group. – **3.** He started a job in a chemical company soon after completing his studies. – **4.** After being with the firm for two years, Mike decided to do something completely different. – **5.** 'I opened my own fruit and vegetable shop – but not before informing myself about organically-grown food.' – **6.** 'I read a lot and while reading,' he explained, 'I make notes.' – **7.** In the week before opening his shop, Mike was not sure what people's reaction would be. – **8.** 'After they had tasted the difference between my apples and the supermarket's, I knew my customers would buy my produce,' Mike said smiling.
II. 1a. Da Jack in einem kleinen Dorf wohnte, musste ihn seine Freundin jeden Tag zum Bahnhof fahren. – **1b.** In einem kleinen Dorf zu wohnen, ist nicht jedermanns Wunsch. – **2a.** Da er kein eigenes Auto hatte, musste sich Mark das Auto seiner Schwester leihen, wann immer er konnte. – **2b.** Kein eigenes Auto zu besitzen, kommt bei jungen Leuten in Mode.
III. 1. means of transport – **2.** vegetables – **3.** days of the week – **4.** fruit – **5.** seasons – **6.** gases – **7.** soft drinks – **8.** sports – **9.** clothes – **10.** performing arts
IV. … growing … is required. … have been used up, … cannot be renewed. … are now developing … . … receives … . … scientists … using … . … largest … can be found … . … is surrounded … . … reflect … heat … containing … . … giving off … linked … . … produced … to provide … . … particularly … environmentalists … most reliable … cleanest … .

13 Nova Scotia

13A Working with the text

I. 1. True. – **2.** False. The pottery and pewter has been reproduced. – **3.** False. The room is where the men had their meals.
II. 1. Apart from doing the work of a blacksmith he would do other things such as hunting or gardening. – **2.** They were a spit (over a fire) or ovens (on charcoal). – **3.** The idea was to improve the morale amongst the men and to make sure they ate good food.
III. 1. b) – **2.** c) – **3.** b) – **4.** c)
V. 1. The word 'moral' means an awareness of what is right or wrong for a person: 'morale' is how much enthusiasm or determination a group of people has, especially in a difficult or dangerous situation. – **2.** A 'pharmacist' has been trained to prepare medicines: a 'farmer' is a person who manages a farm (with crops or livestock). – **3.** A 'chef' is a person who cooks food in a restaurant: a 'chief' is a person with a high position in an organisation, eg chief of police. – **4.** The word 'pottery' means pots and dishes made of clay: 'pewter' is a grey metal (a mixture of tin and lead). – **5.** A 'meal' is when you eat food, eg breakfast, lunch or dinner: 'meat' is the flesh of animals, eg pork.

13A Exercises

I. 1. They said <u>hello</u> through the window before getting <u>off</u> the bus. – **2.** 'Don't be <u>late</u>,' <u>she</u> said. – **3.** They turned <u>right</u> into a <u>small</u> room. – **4.** <u>Quickly</u> they walked <u>down</u> the hill. – **5.** It was <u>hot</u> so she <u>took off</u> her anorak. – **6.** Who was at the <u>back</u> of the plane? – **7.** 'I <u>can't</u> see <u>anything</u>!' she said. – **8.** <u>Before</u> dinner they <u>unpacked</u> their suitcases.
II. 1. d. – **2.** e. – **3.** f. – **4.** a. – **5.** c. – **6.** b.
III. 1. So what have you <u>been</u> doing in Canada?
I've <u>been</u> staying with my pen pal.
Pen pal?
Yes, she lives in Montreal.
2. And <u>did</u> you have a good time?
Yes, it <u>was</u> lovely.
<u>Was</u> it your first visit?
Yes, it <u>was</u>.
3. <u>Did</u> you travel around a lot?
Yes, we <u>did</u>.
And <u>were</u> you homesick?
Well, I <u>was</u> at the beginning. But I'm not anymore!
IV. 1. d. – **2.** f. – **3.** b. – **4.** e. – **5.** a. – **6.** c.
V. The Micmac are a First Nations tribe who lived in eastern Canada at the time of early European settlement of that region. Today the Micmac live in Nova Scotia, New Brunswick and on Prince Edward Island.

13B Working with the text

I. 1. b) – **2.** a) – **3.** b) – **4.** a)
II. 1. They're important to him because the symbols remind the Micmac of their roots. – **2.** Because he was forced to learn English, which was not his first language. – **3.** He thinks they have lost some of their identity. – **4.** He thinks his work is important in helping the Micmac to understand who they are and where they have come from.

III. 1. the people who have lived before you – **2.** what you can see – **3.** to absorb ideas and information into your mind – **4.** to feel established

IV. 1. designs and symbols (of Micmac culture) – **2.** work – **3.** the Micmac – **4.** searching for one's identity

V.

Oo	oO	Ooo	oOo
also	ago	ancestor	amazing
ancient	design	damaging	extremely
language	today	visible	important

VI. *Examples:* **1.** Yes, I think he is criticising his own people. He probably feels that the Micmac must understand what their people did in the past in order to be able to shape their future. – **2.** I think he means that everybody, not only the Micmac, should try and appreciate their cultural heritage. I agree with him. I think it's important to know about your country's history, art and literature to understand events happening around you at the present.

13B Exercises

I. 1. some – **2.** a, some – **3.** an – **4.** any – **5.** some, any – **6.** some – **7.** any – **8.** some

II. 1. g – **2.** l – **3.** b – **4.** k – **5.** l – **6.** b

III. 1. second – **2.** present – **3.** lunch – **4.** forty

IV. Paragraph 1: b. – f. – g. – **Paragraph 2:** d. – a. – e. – **Paragraph 3:** c.

13C Working with the text

I. 1. … 500 years. – **2.** … it could be stored for a long time and eaten during the winter. – **3.** … were farmers and tradesmen. – **4.** … fish could be cooled and sold fresh or made into other products such as fishsticks.

II. 1. Fishing came first because Lunenburg was inhabited by the indigenous population before European settlers arrived. – **2.** The soil was not good. – **3.** The refrigerator.

III. 1. east coast of Canada – **2.** cod – **3.** European settlers – **4.** fish

VI. *Examples:* **1.** The expression 'New World' refers to North and South America in contrast to what Europeans called the 'Old World'. – **2.** The most important food for the local people.

13C Exercises

I. 1. lived – **2.** have lived – **3.** had – **4.** have had – **5.** have won – **6.** won

II. 1. on – **2.** for – **3.** to – **4.** at – **5.** from – **6.** about – **7.** in – **8.** to

III. 1. The word 'North America' means the USA and Canada: the 'USA' is a part of North America. – **2.** The 'New World' refers to the discovery of America: 'New Brunswick' is a province in Canada. – **3.** 'South America' is the area of the world containing countries like Brazil, Argentina, Chile and Peru: 'Central America' refers to countries like Costa Rica, Nicaragua and Honduras. – **4.** An 'artist' is a painter or illustrator: an 'artiste' is someone who performs on stage, eg a singer or dancer. – **5.** A 'peasant' is a very poor farmer (the word is rarely used today in this meaning): a 'pheasant' is a large brightly-coloured bird with a long tail.

IV. 1. job – **2.** journey – **3.** living – **4.** measurements – **5.** rise – **6.** receipt – **7.** remind – **8.** tell – **9.** sensitive – **10.** stationery

V. d. – **g.** – **f.** – **a.** – **c.** – **b.** – **e.**

VI. It comes from the end.

Wordlist

Note: The letter 'O' refers to the overview sections.

A

abide by 8B	sich halten an
aboriginal O10	Ureinwohner-
abs 7B	Bauchmuskeln
abundance (an ~ of) 11A	eine Überfülle von
access 6B	Zugang
adapt O7	sich einleben
adopt 2C	sich zu Eigen machen, sich aneignen
advocate 7C	eintreten für, befürworten
affect 6A	sich auswirken auf
Airborne (troops/soldiers) 8B	Luftlandetruppen
alternate 6B	alternativ
ancestral O12	Ahnen-, Vorfahren-
anchoring job (to have an ~) O7	als Nachrichtenmoderator(in) arbeiten
anchorman, anchorwoman O7	Nachrichtenmoderator(in)
annual issue 1A	Jahresausgabe
appeal to 7C	appellieren an
artisan O13	Handwerker
as the years evolved … 9A	mit der Zeit …, im Laufe der Zeit …
assent 10A	Zustimmung
assimilation 13B	Anpassung, Integration
associate degree 3B	*Abschluss nach zweijährigem College-Studium*
automotive 12C	selbstfahrend, mit Selbstantrieb
aviation O7	Luftfahrt
awestruck 4A	vor Ehrfurcht ergriffen

B

band (a ~ of) 5A	Schar
band (to be in ~) 2A	im Schulorchester spielen
bar 10B	untersagen, verbieten
basket 3C	Aktienkorb
'bedroom communities' 12B	„Schlafstädte"
best practices (to share ~) 6A	Erfahrungen austauschen
bid 12A	Angebot
bill 10A	(Gesetzes)entwurf
bill 5C	Gesetzesvorlage
blanket 10C	Decke
board meeting 6A	*eine Art Vorstandssitzung oder Beiratssitzung*
Board of Trade O12	Handelskammer

Board of Trade O3	Warentermin-Börse
boast 11C	sich rühmen
bond 3C	Obligation
bone of contention 10B	Zankapfel
break a horse O5	ein Pferd zureiten
break down a script 12A	Drehbuchauszüge erstellen
breed 5A	züchten
brood mare 5A	Zuchtstute
building engineer O3	Bauingenieur
bunch 11B	Haufen
Business Administration 8B	Betriebswirtschaft

C

call upon sb 7C	jmdn. aufrufen, zurufen
cap 9C	etw. mit Deckel versehen
caring O5	sozial denkend, engagiert
carnival 2B	*im Sinne von Straßenfest*
carrier O9	Fluggesellschaft
case protagonists 1B	Hauptfiguren
certified ski instructor 2A	staatlich geprüfter Skilehrer
chair O12	den Vorsitz haben
Chamber of Commerce O2	Handelskammer
charcoal 13A	Holzkohle
Chief Executive Officer (CEO) O12	Vorstandsvorsitzender
circulation O10	Auflage
clerk O10	Schriftführer(in)
cod 13C	Kabeljau
combustion engine 12C	Verbrennungsmotor
come about 10A	zu Stande kommen
command 5C	Führung, Leitung
commodity 3C	Ware
community leadership O6	die Führungsspitze der Gemeindeverwaltung
community relations manager 6B	*Referent mit Zuständigkeit für die Beziehungen zwischen dem Unternehmen und der Gemeinde*
complexity theory 1C	Komplexitätstheorie
congresswoman O4	Kongressabgeordnete
constituency 10A	Wahlkreis
constitutional framework 4B	grundlegende verfassungsmäßige Struktur
Construction Management 8B	Stadtplanung
construction work O3	Bauarbeiten
contract 3C	Terminvertrag
coon (ra~) 8C	Waschbär
cornerstone 9B	Eckpfeiler
counter O9	Schalter
county administrator 6B	Bezirksverwalter
cover 6B	*im Sinne von: eine Lösung finden*

cover page O1	Deckblatt, Titelblatt
critical 4C	entscheidend
critical impact 6B	starke Beeinträchtigung
cure 11B	haltbar machen durch Trocknen
custody 2C	Obhut, Verwahrung
cutting edge 1C	neuester Stand

D

date back to O1	zurückgehen auf
decency 7C	Anstand
deer 8C	Hirsch, Rotwild
defeat by one vote 5C	mit einer Stimme Unterschied ablehnen
Department of the Interior O4	*Ministerium mit Zuständigkeit für Bergwerke, Naturschutzgebiete, „Indian Affairs" u.a.*
deputy principal clerk 10A	stellvertretende(r) Hauptschriftführer(in)
deregulation O6	Wettbewerbsfreiheit
design drugs O1	Medikamente herstellen, entwickeln
designation 11C	Ernennung, Bezeichnung
destination resort 11A	Erholungsziel
development (oil/gas) … 4B	Erschließung (von Erdöl-/Erdgasquellen)
devote 2B	sich widmen
diet 13A	Nahrung, die Art, sich zu ernähren
disease O1	Krankheit
display (to be on ~) O13	ausgestellt sein
diversified O6	verschieden(artig)
downtown core 12B	Stadtkern
Dutch oven 13A	*eine Art großer Kessel*

E

elk 11A	Elch
embark on 1B	etw. anfangen / beginnen
emerge O1	auftauchen
emergency cabinet 12B	Notrufsäule
emissions testing 7B	Emissionstest (von Abgasen)
enact 10A	verfügen, erlassen
encounter a problem O6	auf ein Problem stoßen
enforce sth on sb O9	jmdm. etw. aufzwingen
enhancement O8	Verbesserung
entail 13B	mit sich bringen, verbunden sein
enterprising 5C	engagiert
everyday encounters O7	Alltagssituationen
evidence O11	Beweis

exchange O3	Börse
exchange rate 12A	Wechselkurs
extinct 11C	ausgestorben

F

fare 9A	Flugpreis
feature film 12A	Kino-, Spielfilm
fertilizer O11	Dünger
field digs 11C	Feldausgrabungen
fieldwork O11	Feldforschung
fighting fires O2	Feuer bekämpfen
figure out 1B	herausfinden
fire chief O2	Feuerwehrhauptmann
First Nations people O12	Einheimische, Urbevölkerung
fit into sth O1	in etw. hineinpassen
float O2	Parade-Wagen in einem Umzug
This doesn't float my boat. 6C	Das reißt mich nicht vom Hocker.
flourish 6A	blühen, gedeihen
footing 13B	Stand, Halt
forensic O11	gerichtsmedizinisch
forthcoming 6C	mitteilsam
fossil 11C	fossil, versteinert
freight 9A	Fracht
front-line truck 2B	Feuerwehrwagen
fuel cell O12	Brennstoffzelle
fund 3C	Fonds
funding 2B	finanzielle Unterstützung
future 3C	Termingeschäft

G

gang officer 8A	*Polizeibeamter mit spezieller Zuständigkeit für die Jugendgangs*
garbage O8	Müll, Abfall
GED (program) 2C	*General Educational Development*
give concealed weapons classes O5	Kurse für den Umgang mit nicht sichtbaren Waffen geben
go off 2B	*hier:* losgehen
grade 9C	klassifizieren
grant 2C	Zuschuss
graphic artist 1B	Grafiker(in)
grieve 4A	trauern
gritty 12A	Schotter-

groove O1 — Rille, Furche
groves O8 — Wäldchen, Hain

H

harvest 9C — ernten
home citizen 6A — Einheimischer
hospice O2 — Pflegeheim, Hospiz
human resources O10 — Personalwesen
humble 9A — bescheiden

I

idled (to be ~) 6B — zur Untätigkeit gezwungen sein
implement 10A — durchführen, vollziehen
incorporate into O9 — aufnehmen, integrieren in
inhibit O1 — hemmen
inmate O2 — Häftling, Insasse
interaction 6C — Austausch
interest rate 3C — Zinssatz
involved 5C — engagiert

J

JV (junior varsity) 2A — *zweite Mannschaft*

K

keep track of sth 10A — auf dem Laufenden bleiben
key 4C — Schlüssel-, wichtigste(r,s)
key phrase 9B — Schlüsselsatz, Slogan

L

lack of interest 2A	mangelndes Interesse
law enforcement operation O8	*etwa im Sinne von: eine Operation (ein Einsatz) mit dem Ziel, dem Gesetz Geltung zu verschaffen*
leadership course O1	Kurs für Führungskräfte
limestone base O5	Kalksteinuntergrund
litter 8B	Abfall
livelihood 5C	Lebensunterhalt
livre (*French*) 13A	Pfund (*alte frz. Währung*)
locale 12A	Schauplatz (einer Handlung, eines Films)
location 9B	Standort, Niederlassung
location O12	Drehort (*Film*)
longshoreman O13	Hafenarbeiter

M

magnificent 11C	großartig, prachtvoll
maintenance O3	Wartung
maintenance supervisor 5B	Wartungskontrolleur
mammal 11C	Säugetier
manufacturer O9	Hersteller
map (to be put on the ~) 11A	bekannt werden, einen Namen bekommen
maple O9	Ahorn
mare 5A	Stute
market setting O1	Standort
marten 10C	Marder
MBA (program) O1	*Master of Business Administration*
medical assistant O3	medizinische Hilfskraft
meet production guidelines 6B	den Produktionsvorgaben entsprechen
mesh 11B	Netz-, Gittergewebe
mezzanine O3	niedriges Zwischengeschoss (zw. EG u. 1. Stock)
morale 13A	Moral
mortgage 3C	Hypothek
mortgage rates 3C	Hypothekenzinsen
mounted police O11	berittene Polizei
mourning dove O5	Trauertaube (*amerikanische Verwandte unserer Turteltaube*)
municipality 11A	Stadt, Gemeinde

N

note 3C	Schuldverschreibung
noted (to be ~) 7C	berühmt, bekannt sein

O

oblige 2C	entgegenkommen
obscure 9B	unklar, unverständlich, verworren *hier:* selten, ungewöhnlich
ocean floor 1C	Meeresboden
open outcry O3	(Parketthandel auf) Zuruf
operation (to be in ~) 12B	im Einsatz sein
outlaw 5C	für ungesetzlich erklären
overall 12A	allgemein
overwhelmed 4A	überwältigt

P

palmtop computer O1	*ein Computer, den man in der Hand tragen kann* (*palm* = Handfläche)
paratrooper 8B	Fallschirmjäger
parish 5C	Gemeinde
parishioner O5	Gemeindemitglied
pass sth on 3B	etw. weiter geben
pastor O7	als Pastor/Prediger tätig sein
peace advocate 7C	Anwalt des Friedens
peasant 13C	Bauer
period of Reconstruction 7C	Zeit des Wiederaufbaus nach 1865
pewter 13A	Zinn(geschirr)
pit O3	Box
plant O6	Werk
policing O8	Kontrolle, Überwachung
policy statement O12	Grundsatzerklärung
political entity 4B	politische Einheit
poor 13C	unergiebig
portable 12C	tragbar
potassium 9C	Kalium
pottery 13A	Töpferwaren, Keramik
power 12C	betreiben
power generation device 12C	eine Möglichkeit/ein Mittel, Energie zu erzeugen
prance 12A	tänzeln, herumhüpfen, -tanzen

predecessor 9A Vorgänger
preserve 13B bewahren
preserve 4B Naturschutzgebiet
price discovery 3C Kursbestimmung
primary economy 4B Hauptwirtschaftsfaktor
printing plant 10B Druckerei
process 9C verarbeiten
process engineer O6 Verfahrenstechniker
professional program 7A Studioproduktion
properly O9 richtig, korrekt
prosper O11 wachsen, gedeihen
PT (Physical Training) **test** 7B Fitness-Test
put emphasis on sth O9 etw. betonen
put sb on the air 7A jmdn. (im Fernsehen oder Hörfunk) auftreten lassen, auf Sendung gehen lassen
put (to be ~ on the map) 11A bekannt werden, einen Namen bekommen

R

race a horse 5A ein Pferd bei einem Rennen starten lassen
race track O5 Rennbahn
racoon O8 Waschbär
raise horses O5 Pferde züchten
raise tobacco O5 Tabak anpflanzen
range O13 Reichweite
rapport 8A Beziehung
rational drug design O1 *die Entwicklung von Medikamenten auf der Basis der Biologie einer Krankheit*
recent 1A vor kurzem erschienen
recover O11 sicherstellen
recreational vehicle 12C Wohnmobil, Großraumlimousine
regain 13B zurückgewinnen
regulate O1 regulieren, einstellen (bei Krankheiten)
remote power 12C *im Sinne von: eigene Energieerzeugung für abgelegene Orte*
replicate 13B nachbilden
request 2C Anfrage
rerouting O3 Umleitung
response 9B Reaktion, Erwiderung
retail store 8C Einzelhandelsgeschäft, Laden
revolve around 13B sich drehen um
roam 4B wandern, ziehen
rolling 4B hügelig
run O8 durchführen

S

sacredness 7C	Heiligkeit, Unantastbarkeit
sap 9C	Saft
schedule 2C	Zeitplan
score high 7B	viele Punkte machen
screen 11B	im Siebdruckverfahren bedrucken
script writer 1B	Drehbuchautor(in)
scurvy 13A	Skorbut
segregation O7	Rassentrennung
senior O2	*vergleichbar mit Schüler der Oberstufe*
sense 9B	Gespür
serve businesses 3C	Handel treiben mit anderen Firmen
service member 4A	Militärangehöriger
setback 11A	*hier im Sinne von: Rückzugsmöglichkeiten*
shape (to be in good/bad ~) 7B	in Form/nicht in Form sein
shepherd O5	Hirte
ship 8C	liefern
shoot a film O12	einen Film drehen
shootout 12A	Schießerei
show horses 5A	Pferde bei Veranstaltungen vorführen
sign up 2A	sich einschreiben, sich eintragen
slew 1B	Haufen
slope 11A	Abhang, Hang
softball O2	*eine Form des Baseballspiels*
soil 13C	Erdreich, Boden
solid 8B	fest (im Gegensatz zu „flüssig“)
specimen O11	Exemplar
spill over into 7C	sich ausbreiten auf
spit 13A	Bratspieß
spot (be in a bit of a ~) 11A	in Schwierigkeiten sein, in der Klemme sitzen
spray nozzle O3	Spritzdüse
spread 9C	(Brot-)Aufstrich
squeegee O3	Gummiwischer
stages 12A	Produktionsstätten
staggering 10B	verblüffend
stained glass window O5	Buntglasfenster
stallion 5A	Hengst
staple of economy 5C	wichtigste wirtschaftliche Einnahmequelle
stick with sth 7B	bei etw. bleiben
still photo 12A	Standfoto
stock 3C	Aktie, Wertpapier
straightforward 6C	aufrichtig, ehrlich
supplier 6B	Zulieferer
survey O6	Untersuchung, Umfrage
sustain 11A	erhalten, unterhalten

T

tackle a problem O8 — ein Problem angehen, anpacken
tad (a ~) 8A — ein bisschen
tag 1C — Schildchen, Etikett
take advantage of 1B — Vorteil aus … ziehen
target O1 — Ziel(bereich)
thrive on 5A — prächtig gedeihen durch, mit
tidal generation station O13 — Gezeitenkraftwerk
tides O13 — Gezeiten
tie to O10 — verbinden mit
tools 9B — Mittel
trade 3C — handeln mit
trademark 10B — Warenzeichen
trading desk 3C — Schalter
traffic jam 1C — (Verkehrs-)Stau
train operator O3 — Zugführer
train set 3A — *gemeint ist hier:* der komplette Zug
trap 10C — Fallen stellen
treasury 3C — Schatzanweisung
tribe O4 — Stamm
try out for sth 7A — sich um etw. bemühen, bewerben
turnout 2B — Teilnahme, Beteiligung
type 1A — Schriftart

U

upstate 6A — im Norden des Bundesstaates
utility O6 — Versorgungsbetrieb

V

vagrant O8 — Land-/Stadtstreicher
varsity (to play ~) 2A — *in der ersten Mannschaft spielen*
verbatim 10A — wortwörtlich
versatile 13A — vielseitig
virtual O1 — virtuell
visible 13B — sichtbar
volunteer medical technician O2 — freiwilliger (Hilfs-)Sanitäter

W

warden O2 — Gefängnisdirektor
Whirlwind computer O1 — *Markenname*
wildlife corridors O11 — Lebensräume für wild lebende Tiere
win districts 2A — die Bezirksmeisterschaften gewinnen
wind up 10C — enden, landen
wind up doing sth 10C — am Ende etw. tun
window 6B — (Zeit-)Fenster
wood carvings O5 — Holzschnitzereien
work Monday through Friday O3 — von Montag bis Freitag arbeiten
work-out 2A — Training
wreck 6B — Unfallwagen

Y

young people at risk O8 — gefährdete Jugendliche